Sounds German

Sounds German
*Popular Music in Postwar Germany
at the Crossroads of the National and Transnational*

Edited by
Kirkland A. Fulk

berghahn
NEW YORK · OXFORD
www.berghahnbooks.com

Published in 2021 by
Berghahn Books
www.berghahnbooks.com

© 2021 Berghahn Books

Originally published as a special issue of German Politics & Society, Volume 34, issue 2 (2017)

All rights reserved. Except for the quotation of short passages for the purposes of criticism and review, no part of this book may be reproduced in any form or by any means, electronic or mechanical, including photocopying, recording, or any information storage and retrieval system now known or to be invented, without written permission of the publisher.

Library of Congress Cataloging-in-Publication Data
Library of Congress Control Number: 2020948461

British Library Cataloguing in Publication Data
A catalogue record for this book is available from the British Library

ISBN 978-1-78920-740-8 hardback
ISBN 978-1-78920-475-9 paperback
ISBN 978-1-78920-473-5 ebook

Contents

List of Illustrations   vii

Introduction
    Into the Music Rooms
       Kirkland A. Fulk   1

Chapter 1
    Licht aus–Spot an: How Schlager (ZDF 1969–1984) Beat Disco (ZDF 1971–1982)
       Sunka Simon   13

Chapter 2
    The Birth of Autotune and the Loop of (West) German Identity
       Cyrus Shahan   25

Chapter 3
    Wenn eine Band lange Zeit lebt: Puhdys, Politics, and Popularity
       John Littlejohn   43

Chapter 4
    DIY, *im Eigenverlag*: East German Tamizdat LPs
       Seth Howes   62

Chapter 5
    Poetry of an Alien: Black Tape, Silo Nation, and the Historiography of German Hip-Hop's *Alte Schule*
       Kai-Uwe Werbeck   84

Chapter 6
    Death in June and the Apoliteic Specter of Neofolk in Germany
       Mirko M. Hall   106

Chapter 7
  Knitted Naked Suits and Shedding Skins: The Body Politics of Popfeminist Musical Performances in the Twenty-first Century
   Maria Stehle   126

Chapter 8
  Searching for the Young Soul Rebels: On Writing, New Wave, and the Ends of Cultural Studies
   Richard Langston   144

Index   164

ILLUSTRATIONS

4.1	The Cover Image for *"Live" in Paradise DDR* (Good Noise, 1985).	67
4.2	Front Image of Sleeve for L'Attentat, *Made in GDR* LP (X-Mist, 1987).	69
4.3	Details from Page 2 of the Lyric Insert for *Made in GDR*	71
4.4	Details from Page 7 of the Lyric Insert for *Made in GDR*	72

Introduction

INTO THE MUSIC ROOMS
Kirkland A. Fulk

𝓘 want to begin at the end, the end, that is, of the present volume. In his conclusion to the final chapter, Richard Langston remarks on Diedrich Diederichsen's short music columns published in the Berlin newspaper *Tagesspiegel* between 2000 and 2004. Diederichsen, perhaps Germany's most well-known music and cultural critic, titled these columns "Musikzimmer" [the music room]. Here, as Diederichsen put it in his introduction to the 2005 republished collection of these sixty-two, roughly 600-word music columns, he endeavored to bring together as many disparate things as possible under the designation "music."[1] In any one of these music rooms, readers encounter curious and unexpected combinations and constellations: the (West) German (post-)punk band Fehlfarben is discussed in conjunction with British mod group Small Faces, Bob Dylan, and Leonard Cohen; the Australian-American feminist music group and performance art ensemble Chicks on Speed is brought together with German hip-hop and reggae musician Jan Delay; and the German avant-garde trio BST (which notably includes the well-known German cultural theorist Klaus Theweleit on guitar) finds a place alongside the jazz collective Art Ensemble of Chicago as well as the pioneering Hamburg indie-rock band Blumfeld. I start this introduction to the subsequent essays on postwar German popular music at the end station of this volume, in Diederichsen's music rooms, because in many ways they serve as an analogy for what this volume sets out to do, namely traffic in the intersections, entanglements, and flows between the national and transnational.

Like Diederichsen's music rooms, this volume is neither an all-encompassing nor a typical accounting of German popular music, but rather points to the importance of thinking about the constellations of popular music within and across national boundaries as well as to the ways in which

---

Notes for this section begin on page 11.

popular music facilitates and indeed calls for such thinking. In particular, the contributions to this volume, each in its own way, examines how popular music moves through time and space and across media and musical technologies–be it through television programs and films, musical technologies such as the MOOG synthesizer, vinyl records and samples, or the writing of columns such as Diederichsen's–and how this movement alters and accentuates our understanding of (East, West, reunified, and global) German times and spaces. While most of the popular music discussed here is decidedly German (e.g., the East German rock group the Puhdys and West German Schlager) some of it is most definitely not (e.g., the British neofolk band Death in June and the electro-trash stylings of Peaches). A consideration of how popular music moved within West Germany, between East and West Germany, and continues to flow within and into a reunified Germany doesn't undercut the national particularities of German popular music but rather recognizes that the national cannot be thought apart from the transnational. The title of this volume, *Sounds German*, is, then, meant to be slightly ambiguous and even provocative. As a declarative statement it is almost immediately undercut by the possibility that it poses a question–a question of what it means for something to sound German and how this in turn is always inflected by the transnational movements of sounds and music from elsewhere that take part in the contestations over the definitions and redefinitions of what sounds German. It is in the struggle and interaction between the national and transnational that, I hope, this volume contributes to the continued conceptualizations and discussions of German popular music and popular music broadly speaking.

It goes without saying that a musical undercurrent has long permeated German culture and intellectual life. Theories and practices of folk, art, and classical music–variously understood both in their mutual interrelation and as entirely distinct–have for centuries served to anchor definitions of German national identity and German culture in both (deceptively) nonpolitical ways and politically nationalist ones. This is perhaps best spelled out in Celia Applegate and Pamela Potter's edited volume *Music and German National Identity* (2002). Here, for instance, they detail the "eclectic nature of the intersection of music with German identity" from the eighteenth century through the immediate postwar period and show "that this preoccupation is not exclusively a musical project but far more a complex of ideas and agendas originating from a wide range of players in German cultural and political life."[2] Other volumes such as Nora M. Alter and Lutz Koepnick's *Sound Matters: Essays on the Acoustics of German Culture* (2004) and Florence Feiereisen and Alexandra Merley Hill's *Germany in the Loud Twentieth Century* (2012) have expanded not only the time frame of investigations into Germany's musical cultures and identities, but also our operative vocabularies. Alter and Koepnick's intervention includes music in film and performance while complicating the picture of music's relationship to German national identity by investigating how competing conceptions of Germanness also shaped what and how sounds were made: "Sound mattered to the formation of modern German nationality, but ongoing debates about the contours of national identity also redefined the matter of sound itself."[3] Building on this, Feiereisen and Hill's work asks "what does Germany *sound* like" and investigates music as but one instantiation of sound thereby accounting for different acoustic spaces, for instance architectural and city spaces, and further opening up the arena of German music and sound studies.[4]

When we turn our attention to recent works that focus specifically on postwar German *popular* music, the fault lines of the national and transnational come into sharper relief. On the one hand, for instance, Uwe Schütte's volume *German Pop Music: A Companion* (2017) stresses not only the national and regional dimensions of popular music, but also tethers itself to German-language music, West Germany, and a conception of popular music that excludes commercially successful and supposedly affirmative, rather than subversive, popular music.[5] This conception of popular music is, as Schütte explains, in part pragmatic given the expansive popular music terrain, although the decision to focus on a certain type of popular music and a certain type of popular music from West Germany certainly evinces a valuative judgment vis-a-vis what and where counts as German popular music. On the other hand, Michael Ahlers and Christoph Jacke's volume *Perspectives on German Popular Music* (2017) is notable not only for its breadth and kaleidoscopic outlook that includes popular music from the former East and the popular music that Schütte brackets out, but also for making Germanophone music scholarship available to a larger English-speaking audience.[6] The impetus of the volume, as the editors state, is not to replace the visibility of Anglo-American scholarship on German popular music with a decidedly Germanophone perspective or even to flesh out what could be considered a typically German (study of) popular music, but rather to recognize that "it is really only through transnational/cross-cultural interaction that a clearer, more complex picture of popular cultures can be presented."[7] In many ways, the present volume continues in the spirit of Ahlers and Jacke's work. It is not interested in wading into the debates over the "elitist boundaries between enlightenment and entertainment—as well as popular-elitist ones between trivial and more demanding popular music."[8] As with Ahlers and Jacke, it leans into the "internal struggles" and "ambivalences" of popular music and appreciates the necessarily "fragmented and fragile" nature of any kaleidoscopic view of popular music.⁹ Moreover, the present volume applies the transnational interaction of scholarship to the national and transnational flows of popular music itself and thus adds another lens through which to refract the light of Ahlers and Jacke's popular music kaleidoscope.

Recently, German Studies has become increasingly aware of its transnational contours and experienced something of a transnational turn. In the fortieth anniversary issue of the *German Studies Review* from 2016, Konrad Jarausch details the ways in which the broader transnational and transatlantic interaction of German Studies' scholars "has created greater awareness of the global dimension of German history and culture" and "led to a widening of the scope of topics."¹⁰ In addition, Paul Michael Lützeler and Peter Höyng's 2018 volume *Transatlantic German Studies: Testimonies to the Profession* gathers together personal and professional reflections from both US-born scholars and those who immigrated to the US on the development of German Studies beyond a nationally rooted concept of *Germanistik*.¹¹ Beneath these reconceptualizations of the field of German Studies lies the longer history of the transnational movement of literature film, and music. Responding to the question of the centrality of the national for German Cultural Studies broadly speaking, Kirsten Belgum's contribution to the 2019 issue of *The German Quarterly* reminds us "of the enormous amount of transnational influence that exists in cultural production" and how "transnational borrowing and even outright copying" long evident in writing and publishing practices have played a role in Germany's national projects as well as the "contestations and limits of the national ideology."¹² In the context of German cinema, Sabine Hake points out that the transnational was and is a "constitutive part[] of the national."¹³ The transnational, however, should not be confused with a romantic or utopian notion "of border crossings, cross-cultural exchanges, hybrid identities" and the like that does away with the "containment, exclusion, and canonicity" that often goes hand in glove with the national.¹⁴ For example, Hake writes that during the Cold War on both sides of the Berlin Wall the national often "served as a smokescreen" for "transnational connections … in the form of bloc building and ideological confrontation," such that the supposedly new paradigm of transnationalism in post-Wall Germany is both not new at all and can, consequently and arguably, serve as a smokescreen for the national.¹⁵

The complex flows between the national and the transnational are, then, certainly not the sole purview of popular music's exchanges, transfers, and transmissions. But popular music is particularly adept at capturing these flows and a particularly fruitful site for exploring and further complicating them. As American Studies scholar George Lipsitz puts it:

> Popular music has a peculiar relationship to the poetics and the politics of place. Recorded music travels from place to place, transcending physical and temporal barriers. It alters our understanding of the local and the immediate, making it possible for us to experience close contact with cultures from far away. Yet precisely because music travels, it also augments our appreciation of place.[16]

In short, popular music moves, and it often does so irrespective of the confines and constructs of place or the nation and, at the same time, doubles back on them. The "dynamic dialogue" initiated through popular music's movements, Lipsitz qualifies, "does not necessarily reflect reciprocity and mutuality" and continues to display the internal struggles and contradictions that attend popular music in any given place and especially as it travels.[17] Thus, as anthropologist Mark D. Levin states, the irony of the transnational isn't that it seems to call up what it negates, but rather that it "makes [the nation and the national] more flexible and expands it" even as the flexibility imparted by the transnational also has its limits.[18] To move from these more broad considerations of national and transnational movements toward specific popular music flows, let me briefly detail a couple of examples that aren't directly addressed in the contributions to this volume and yet lay some of the groundwork upon which they're based.

German-German popular music interactions during the Cold War, to pick one notable example, were certainly not just a one-way street leading from the West to the East.[19] Despite the physical separation of Germany with the construction of the Berlin Wall in August 1961, sound waves proved especially difficult to contain behind concrete, rebar, and barbed wire. Indeed, as Florence Feiereisen details, the construction of the Wall was simultaneously the beginning of a sound war, a war of the loudspeakers, that was briefly waged between East and West. During chancellor Konrad Adenauer's visit to the Berlin Wall just days after its completion, "he was greeted by a popular hit" that blasted from the 190 speakers erected on the east side of the Wall.[20] Notably, the song was Gus Backus' 1961 hit, or Schlager, "Da sprach der alte Häuptling der Indianer" [then the old Indian chief spoke] whose refrain stresses the difficulty of taming the wild west. Confronted with and insulted by this song, which was sung by a former American G.I. who had made a name for himself in West Germany and which was hurled from the East back into the representative face of the West, Adenauer turned and walked away.[21] This Cold War musical battle of the loud speakers continued for four years as the West broadcast news and messages into the East from its *Studio am Stacheldraht* [studio at the barbed wire] only to be met in return by music played from the East in an attempt to drown out the West. The West eventually won the sound war when it sonically disrupted East Germany's sixteenth anniversary celebrations leading to both sides dismantling their sound systems.[22] Here, the transnational, trans-border movement of popular music between East and West throws into stark relief the ambivalences of what sounds German—exemplified in the cross-cultural lyrics, provenance, and biographical details of Backus' Schlager—and how these ambivalences defined the contestations over and the sedimentations of the national, and ideological, division of postwar Germany. As John Littlejohn and Seth Howes examine here in their respective analyses of East German rock and punk the musical movements between East and West continued to challenge the Wall's ability to completely solidify a national divide.

West German Krautrock of the late 1960s and 1970s, that most "German" of popular music besides perhaps Schlager, also provides noteworthy insights into the national and transnational movements of music. The "kraut" moniker given to this psychedelic (e.g., Can, Amon Düül, Ash Ra Tempel) and synthesizer-heavy (e.g., Kraftwerk, Tangerine Dream, Neu!) rock by British music journalists often obscures the fact that this *Kosmische Musik* [cosmic music], as it was termed in Germany at the time, in some instances sought to transcend not only national but terrestrial connections altogether while other bands such as Kraftwerk and Neu! weaved the sonic textures of the industrial Ruhr region of western Germany into their compositions.[23] Put differently, between Krautrock and Kosmische Musik, this German rock displayed a struggle with and ambivalent relation to its national origins, its transnational aspirations, and its transnational connections in Anglo-American music such as Pink Floyd, Frank Zappa and the Mothers of Invention, and Captain Beefheart from which it also sought to distance itself.[24]

In turn, however, the transnational flows of Krautrock reversed course and found their way back to Anglo-American popular music and popular culture in often unexpected ways. Tangerine Dream, for instance, went on to score Hollywood soundtracks including two Tom Cruise films—*Risky Business* (1983) and *Legend* (1986).[25] In *Legend*, Tangerine Dream's score replaced the original US one composed by Jerry Goldsmith in the hopes of appealing to a younger *American* audience, while Goldsmith's remained the score for the film's *European* release.[26] Additionally, David Bowie's stint in West Berlin during the mid-1970s "reinfused his profile with Krautrock blood" from Tangerine Dream and Kraftwerk and yielded his Berlin trilogy—*Low* (1977), *Heroes* (1977), and *Lodger* (1979).[27] During the 1987 "Concert for Berlin," Bowie aimed his Krautrock inspired music at the Wall when he requested that the speakers be turned toward the East and away from the West German audience and played his anti-Berlin Wall anthem *cum* star-crossed love story "Heroes."[28] Lastly, Kraftwerk would go on to become one of the cornerstones for Detroit techno—"For Techno, Dusseldorf is the Mississippi Delta," as Kodwo Eshun phrases it—as well as hip-hop in the South Bronx where in 1982 Afrika Bambaataa and the Soul Sonic Force sampled Kraftwerk's "Trans-Europe Express" and "Numbers" for their seminal track "Planet Rock."[29] And just as hip-hop would expand beyond the boroughs of New York into not only West Germany but East Germany as well—where it was officially accepted due to its reflection of disenfranchised minority communities in the US and even promoted through youth organizations and break dance competitions as a form of athletic training—techno found a new home in Dimitri Hegemann's club Tresor, which was founded in 1991 and located near Potsdamer Platz in Berlin.[30] The site of the East-West divide became the space of a German-German and German-American techno alliance, and Hegemann continues to engage in talks to purchase the old Packard Automotive Plant in Detroit for a new techno club that could help revitalize the city.[31]

Without a doubt, these later transnational movements of popular music that were spurred on by Krautrock are still rife with their own internal struggles and contradictions. The cosmic countercultural sounds of Tangerine Dream that sought to transcend terrestrial and with it their immediate environment in West Berlin became a perfect fit for popular Hollywood films and appealed to younger music fans in the US, while the Krautrock blood and German sound that pumped through Bowie's Berlin trilogy formed part of the soundtrack that would rekindle the sound war between West and East Germany.[32] The explosion of US hip-hop beyond the borders, not to mention the cultural and social particularities, of the nation and the national certainly offers "the possibility of sharing different cultures."[33] At the same time, the transposition and transfer of US hip-hop into East, West, and reunified Germany also exposes the uneven exchanges of national, ethnic, racial, and cultural contradictions that come with making something sound German while also holding on to the transnational potentials and possibilities of hip-hop.[34] In a similar vein, techno's transnational flows in a reunited Germany "re-narrated [the true root of techno] as being 'originally German'" and served to articulate "a national narrative of unity and belonging" that erased, or selectively forgot, not only its transnational routes but also its Black influences.[35] The Tresor club was eventually pushed away from

Potsdamer Platz as "neoliberal signs of political power and commercial profit" encroached on its German-German and German-American techno alliance and redefined what this new unity and belonging meant.[36] And while the plan for a new club in Detroit can be seen as re-re-narration of techno's transnational routes, it too comes with its own share of cultural, racial, and economic baggage and uneven power structures. None of this, however, undercuts the national and transnational movements of popular music. Rather, all of the examples traced above highlight the complex interactions, ambivalences, and contradictions of popular music's flows that cut across a simple binary either/or (good/bad, pop/popular, subversive/affirmative, enlightenment/entertainment, national/transnational, and so forth) and the simplicity of what sounds, in fact, German.

German popular music's national and transnational flows are the subject of the following eight chapters. They are organized so as to first zoom in on the national and proceed to zoom out to the transnational without losing sight of the constitutive interrelations between the two. In Chapter 1, Sunka Simon explores the televised contests between and the televisual production of West German Schlager and disco in the 1970s. Here, she homes in on the ways in which these popular musical broadcasts brought the contestations over German national identity, including the struggles between gender ambiguity (e.g., drag) and heteronormativity, into West German living rooms. In the next chapter, Cyrus Shahan mines popular music's emergent technologies (e.g., MOOG synthesizers, MIDI interfaces, and vocoders) in his investigation of post-punk's attempts to harness musical and technological repetition, the loop, in order to critique and escape the malaise of West Germany in the 1980s. Shahan returns to Krautrock's introduction of new technologies and examines how these were repurposed by post-punk bands, and also flashes forward to the global omnipresence of autotune in order to consider how the perfection of musical pitches both undercuts post-punk's desired musical defamiliarizations and differentiations and opens perhaps new musical and political flows. John Littlejohn's and Seth Howes' analyses shift the popular musical focus to the other side of the Iron Curtain. In Chapter 3, Littlejohn sheds light on the cultures and politics of popular music in East Germany by examining the rise and continued influence of the rock band the Puhdys both during and after the Cold War. Despite often being viewed as the quintessential ideological rock 'n' roll sell-outs in the East, the Pudhys' success in both East and West Germany help to facilitate the flow of more East German popular music into the West. In Chapter 4, Howes looks at the unofficial, trans-border crossings of East German punk. Specifically, he probes the DIY production practices, album-cover aesthetics, and musical compositions of five East German punk LPs and the ways in which they participated in a transnational, German-German correspondence and collaboration in the six years leading up to the fall of the Berlin Wall.

Chapter 5 serves as a bridge between the previous explorations of popular music in a divided Germany that takes us into the transnational popular music flows during and after reunification. Kai-Uwe Werbeck's historiographical examination of German (old school) hip-hop pierces its founding myths and decenters its quest to "keep it real" by refracting how post-Wall German hip-hop negotiated a complex constellation of national identity, race, and socio-economic positions. Digging into the crates of German hip-hop, Werbeck explores how hip-hop's samples (of beats, film scores, hybrid identities, and urban geographies) took part in a transnational, transatlantic movement and how this also reveals the enduring blind spots of (made-in-Germany) hip-hop. In Chapter 6, Mirko Hall's analysis of the British neo-folk group Death in June explores how its potential and problematic fascist aesthetics are received in Germany today and, in this way, circles back on post-punk's engagement with Germany's past and present in Shahan's chapter. The intentionally ambivalent positioning of Death in June in regard to *völkisch* myths and occult symbols together with the transnational movement of them helps to shed light on the global rise of right-wing populism, the continued negotiations of Germany's fascist past, as well as our popular-musical listening and reading practices. Chapter 7 expands on the gender(ed) dynamics of popular music addressed in Simon's opening chapter and explodes these into a transnational context. Maria Stehle's reading of two American popular musicians, activists, and performance artists–Peaches and Rose McGowan–explores the popfeminist body politics and aesthetics that not only contest, but also circulate within neoliberalism's cultural, economic, and media flows, and how these can form different communities at the intersection of the national and transnational. In the final chapter, Richard Langston rethinks both German Studies and Cultural Studies by exploring the changing practices of journalistic and scholarly writing about popular music. His analysis of popular music journalism and pop literature teases out the underlying issues of life, death, and the soul that attended popular music writing in 1980's West Germany, and considers how the transnational flows of Cultural Studies between North American academia and German popular music journalism also landed and (re)sounded differently in these distinct national contexts.

Lastly, a couple of final notes. I would like to say that this volume is intended not only to contribute to research on German popular music, but also to teaching German language, history, and culture. I have found the contributions here as well as in Schütte's and Ahlers and Jacke's volumes indispensable resources for both intermediate and advanced German courses. To quote Schütte: "Whilst film courses are now part and parcel of many German degree programmes [sic], popular music is mainly used in language teaching classes. Yet there is eminent potential for teaching German history, society and culture through the medium of popular music."[37] Indeed, beyond and in concert with language learning, the contributions here are valuable for introducing students to German media cultures, West and East German history and politics, German reunification, and postwar Germany's national and transnational connections and contestations. What Lipsitz calls the "dynamic dialogue" of popular music's inherent movements also brings about dynamic and eye-opening dialogues in the classroom. Students are avid consumers of and knowledgeable about the contemporary flows of popular music (even more so than we would at times assume), and their knowledge of the popular musical cultures with which they engage coupled with their own diverse (cross- and inter-)cultural experiences make for fascinating connections and discussions about contemporary Germany and popular music's flows.[38] Additionally, I would like to thank all of the authors who contributed to this volume, the journal *German Politics and Society* for making its first instantiation possible, and Berghahn Books for seeing its further potential and making it available to a wider audience. This volume is very much the product of the type of transnational scholarly exchange that Ahlers and Jacke espouse and grew out of a workshop at the University of Texas at Austin that Sabine Hake and I organized in March 2016 in which Ahlers and some of his contributors took part. Although their works do not appear in this volume, the insights gleaned from our collaborative, transnational discussions were indispensable for the conceptualization of this project. Finally, as I write this largely sequestered due to the current pandemic, I can't help but think about how despite the ability of a new virus to (re)impose borders and freeze movement, music continues to flow. I hope that when perusing this volume, readers will listen to the bands and songs discussed and let the algorithms (of YouTube, Pandora, Spotify, and so on) take them to unexpected places, make surprising connections, and, if possible, lead them to their local record stores.

KIRKLAND (ALEX) FULK is an Assistant Professor in the Department of Germanic Studies at the University of Texas at Austin. He has published on topics such as photography and postcolonialism, neoliberalism and neocolonialism, West German science fiction, and German-American transnational musical exchanges.

Notes

1. See Diederichsen, *Musikzimmer: Avantgarde und Alltag* (Köln: Kiepenheuer & Witsch, 2005), 24.
2. Applegate and Potter, "Germans as the 'People of Music': Genealogy of an Identity," in *Music and German National Identity*, eds. Celia Applegate and Pamela Potter (Chicago: University of Chicago Press, 2002), 1–36, here 34.
3. Alter and Koepnick, "Introduction: Sound Matters," in *Sound Matters: Essays on the Acoustics of German Culture*, eds. Nora M. Alter and Lutz Koepnick (New York: Berghahn, 2004), 1–32, here 19.
4. Feiereisen and Hill, "Tuning in to the Aural Ether: An Introduction to the Study of German Sounds," in *Germany in the Loud Twentieth Century*, eds. Florence Feiereisen and Alexandra Merley Hill (New York: Oxford University Press, 2012), 1–18, here 12.
5. Schütte, "Introduction: Popular Music as the Soundtrack of German Post-War History," in *German Pop Music: A Companion*, ed. Uwe Schütte (Boston: De Gruyter, 2017), 1–24, see here 5–7.
6. Ahlers and Jacke, "A Fragile Kaleidoscope: Institutions, Methodologies and Outlooks on German Popular Music (Studies)," in *Perspectives on German Popular Music*, eds. Michael Ahlers and Christoph Jacke (London: Routledge, 2016), 3–15, here 10.
7. Ibid., 4, see also 12
8. Ibid., 4.
9. Ibid., 10–11, 3.
10. Jarausch, "From National to Transnational German Studies: Some Historical Reflections 1977–2017," *German Studies Review* 39, no 3 (October 2016): 493–503, here 500.
11. See Lützeler and Höyng, "Introduction," *Transatlantic German Studies: Testimonies to the Profession*, eds. Paul Michael Lützeler and Peter Höyng (New York: Camden House, 2018), 1–4.
12. Belgum, "Language Matters, *The German Quarterly* 92, no. 4 (Fall 2019): 435–438, here 436.
13. Hake, "German Cinema as European Cinema," 116
14. Sabine Hake, "German Cinema as European Cinema: Learning from Film History," *Film History* 25, no 1–2 (2013): 110–117, here 112.
15. Ibid., 112.
16. George Lipsitz, *Dangerous Crossroads: Popular Music, Postmodernism and the Poetics of Place* (New York: Verso, 1994), 3.
17. Ibid., 4.
18. Levin, "Flow and Place: Transnationalism in Four Cases," *Anthropologica* 44, no. 1 (2002): 3–12, here 7. The notion of the irony of transnationalism is taken from Levin's reference to Ulf Hannerz's 1996 work *Transnational Connections: Culture, People, Places*. See Levin, "Flow and Place," 6.
19. Cf. Schütte, "Introduction," 5. As Schütte would have it, the "musical transfer across the wall was mostly a one-way affair from West to East."
20. Feiereisen, "They 'Tried' to Divide the Sky: Listening to Cold War Berlin," *Colloquia Germanica* 46, no. 4 (2013): 410–432, here 414.
21. Ibid.
22. Ibid., 417–418.
23. See Jens Gerrit Papenburg, "Kosmische Musik: On Krautrock's Take Off," in *Perspectives on German Popular Music*, eds. Michael Ahlers and Christoph Jacke (London: Routledge, 2016), 55–60;
24. See David Stubbs, "Introduction," in *Krautrock: Cosmic Rock and its Legacy*, ed. Nikolaos Kotsopoulous (London: Black Dog Publishing, 2009), 4–18, here 7.
25. See David Stubbs, "Tangerine Dream," in *Krautrock: Cosmic Rock and its Legacy*, ed. Nikolaos Kotsopoulous (London: Black Dog Publishing, 2009), 139–140, here 140.

26. See https://www.discogs.com/Tangerine-Dream-Legend/master/14563, accessed 13 August 2020.
27. Stubbs, "Introduction," 12; see also https://www.historyextra.com/period/20th-century/bowies-berlin-the-city-that-shaped-a-1970s-masterpiece/, accessed 13 August 2020.
28. See Feiereisen, "They 'Tried' to Divide the Sky," 421–422.
29. Eshun, *More Brilliant than the Sun: Adventures in Sonic Fiction* (London: Quartet Books, 1998), 100. See also Alex Seago, "The 'Kraftwerk-Effekt': Transatlantic Circulation, Global Networks and Contemporary Popular Music," *Atlantic Studies* 1, no. 1 (2004): 85-106; Kirkland Fulk, "'Ohne Musik ist alles Leben ein Irrtum:' Alexander Kluge, Techno, and the Proletarian Counterpublic Sphere," *The Germanic Review* 92 (2017): 245–263; Sabine Haenni, "Urban, Historical, and Musical Loops: László Moholy-Nagy, Alexander Kluge, and the City Symphony Film," *New German Critique* 47, no. 1 (2020): 81–103.
30. For a brief overview of East German hip-hop see www.jugendopposition.de/themen/145417/hiphop-in-der-ddr, accessed 13 August 2020. For more information on Hegemann's Tresor club see Dan Sicko, *Techno Rebels: The Renegades of Electronic Funk* (New York: Billboard, 1999), 173–174.
31. See J.C. Reindl, "German techno club owner eyes abandoned Detroit factory," *Detroit Free Press*, 15 October 2014, available at www.freep.com/story/money/business/michigan/2014/10/14/techno-club-owner-likes-detroit/17278385, accessed 28 November 2016; Max Pearl, "Dimitri Hegemann Dreams of Detroit," 22 August 2017, available at www.residentadvisor.net/features/2954, accessed 14 August 2020; Sarah Hucal, "A Berlin club owner's mission to give back to Detroit, the city that gave Europe techno," 1 June 2018, available at abcnews.go.com/International/berlin-club-owners-mission-give-back-detroit-city/story?id=55583750, accessed 14 August 2020.
32. See Papenburg, "Kosmische Musik," 55; Feiereisen, "They 'Tried' to Divide the Sky," 422–423.
33. Ayla Güler Saied, "Rap Music in Germany," in *Perspectives on German Popular Music*, eds. Michael Ahlers and Christoph Jacke (London: Routledge, 2016), 165–171, here 170.
34. Along with hip-hop, we can also think of the debates and discussions around jazz and blues music in a divided Germany that were characterized by similarly stark national, ideological, racial, and ethnic undertones despite and because of their transnational (im)pluses. On blues, see Ulrich Adelt, *Blues Music in the Sixties: A Story in Black and White* (New Jersey: Rutgers University Press, 2010), especial chapter 4 "Germany Gets the Blues: Race and Nation at the American Folk Blues Festival." On jazz, see the discussions between Joachim-Ernst Behrendt and Theodor Adorno as well as the debates in East Germany's Ministry of Culture and the Association of German Composers both of which are available in English and German on the German History in Documents and Images website: http://ghdi.ghi-dc.org/sub_document.cfm?document_id=4443, http://ghdi.ghi-dc.org/sub_document.cfm?document_id=4444. Helma Kaldewey's recent work treats jazz in East Germany in full detail, *A People's Music: Jazz in East Germany 1945-1990* (Cambridge: Cambridge University Press 2019). For a broader overview of transnational European jazz see, Kristin McGee, *Remixing European Jazz Culture* (New York: Routledge, 2019).
35. Melanie Schiller, "From Soundtrack of the Reunification to the Celebration of Germanness: Paul van Dyk and Peter Heppner's 'Wir sind Wir' as National Trance Anthem," in in *Perspectives on German Popular Music*, eds. Michael Ahlers and Christoph Jacke (London: Routledge, 2016), 217–222, here 218. See also Sabine Haenni, "Urban, Historical, and Musical Loops," 97.
36. Richard Langston, *Visions of Violence: German Avant-Gardes After Fascism* (Evanston: Northwestern University Press: 2008), 231.
37. Schütte, "Introduction," 4.
38. On this point, see also Belgum, "Language Matters," 437.

Chapter 1

LICHT AUS—SPOT AN

How Schlager (ZDF 1969–1984) Beat Disco (ZDF 1971–1982)
Sunka Simon

At first sight, two of the most popular music shows in German television history could not be more different: The *Deutsche Hitparade*, moderated by the staid bespectacled former car salesman Dieter Thomas Heck (alias of Carl Dietrich Heckscher), was filmed at Berliner Union-Film studio and premiered 1969 on the ZDF network,[1] while *Disco* (1971–1982), filmed mostly at Studio Hamburg, featured the young gangly bow-tied Pee Wee Herman look-alike Ilja Richter. In 1972 Heck received the Goldene Kamera (Germany's Emmy) for his moderation of the *Hitparade*, Richter received that honor in 1977 for *Disco*. Ironically, thanks to digital media, especially YouTube, but also to archival digitization efforts on behalf of the networks, legions of collectors and fans have opened a vast archive of recorded content from the broadcast era. Because accessibility to that audio-visual content is still shifting as rules and regulations change and postings deteriorate or are taken down, this article hopes to preserve and analyze a snapshot of the two popular music programs and their contribution to German national identity formation and its struggle between diversity and homogeneity, as well as gender ambiguity and heteronormativity.

During the broadcast era, dominant culture reigned supreme. To understand the causes and effects of this, a short excursion into the organization and history of German television is justified. Between 1950 and 1984, Germany's mediascape consisted of two national public networks–ARD/Das Erste and ZDF/Zweites Deutsches Fernsehen–in the West and one public network in the German Democratic Republic (the DFF or DDR-FS). ARD organized itself as an *Arbeitsgemeinschaft* intent on keeping its members, the state and regional networks (Landesrundfunkanstalten) forming the third program (Die Dritten), relatively independent. ARD was founded in 1950, DFF

Notes for this chapter begin on page 23.

in 1956, and ZDF followed in 1961. Until privatization, before satellite, cable, and digital streaming, the majority of viewers, except for 15 percent of East German citizens living in the so-called Valley of the Clueless (*Tal der Ahnungslosen*), thus had four choices for their information, cultural, and entertainment television needs on any given day during the broadcasting hours—varying from late morning/early afternoon to midnight/1:00 A.M.

As far as televisual flow goes (the horizontal and vertical structure of programming segments across channels and between segments on one channel), one needs to remember that West Germany's networks programmed advertising in blocks between individual segments. Imported programs were usually dubbed on ARD and ZDF, subtitled during the late evening movie lineup on die Dritten. Prime time began with the evening news at 8:00 P.M., followed by a block of current event analysis, movies, music and game shows, and domestically produced original series. The broadcast day ended with the nightly news, and on Sundays with an evening address by a chosen pastor. Due to the popularity of TV and radio programming magazines (*Hör Zu, TV*, etc.) but also the integration of the easy-to-read TV schedule into top selling daily newspapers and political weeklies such as *Stern* and *Spiegel*, 1970s viewers knew what was on each channel and in most cases landed on one program with intention. This arguably encouraged less distracted viewing habits than those of the U.S. audience at the same time. Raymond Williams famously developed the concept of televisual flow while watching American TV in Miami. Out-of-synch after his long trip from England, Williams was struck by the difference in programming and its effects on reception.[2]

What is the relationship between broadcast television, its vertical and horizontal flow, the genre-specific televisual structure of a music show, and dominant culture, especially given the deep rift between the war and postwar generations, the bourgeois *Wohlstandsstaat* on the one side and the antibourgeois, anti-authoritarian movements, on the other? For the 1970s, Susanne Weingarten argues that ZDF's ratings of close to 74 percent during the long Saturday afternoon/evening slot were partially the result of a cultural gap between those in the student movement who did not watch entertainment television, especially not on weekends, and those too young or too old or not interested in joining the political and subcultural fray. Catching the Greek-born Costa Cordalis or Vicky Leandros, among many other international *Schlager* stars, might have also been a draw for Southern European migrant workers familiar with their careers residing in Germany due to West Germany's bilateral recruitment program (e.g., with Greece in 1960). Thus, a Germany divided along generational, linguistic, cultural, political, race, gender, and class lines seemed to unite in front of and in the TV studios, rebuilding a national German imaginary under attack in the streets.³ During this culturally and politically anxious time of change, the more conservative of the two networks, ZDF, sought to counter the evening news' testimony to social change with a steadfast entertainment program: "The internal flow of each broadcast was just as predetermined as the culinary decoration of the cold-cuts served to fellow TV viewers and guests on the sectional sofa-scape."⁴

Indeed, *Hitparade*'s internal sequencing uses and accentuates a stereotypical German obsession with punctuality and effectiveness. It opens with a close-up of the digital clock at 19:30 and Heck's assurance that the audience will find out winners and losers by exactly 20:15 and 20 seconds at *Sendeschluss* (end of the program). Heck would announce the evening's program "*maschinengewehrsalvenschnell*" "in alphabetical order."⁵ As Jane Feuer reminds us in "The Concept of Live Television," the anchor's role

> is to remind the viewer both what time it is (and thus of the 'live' nature of the broadcast) and of what will occur in future segments within a clearly designated future time. The show is obsessed with its own liveness . . . [The anchor] acts as a custodian of flow and regularity, the personification of a force which creates unity out of fragmentation.⁶

Disco also had a standard opening with Richter stating "Einen wunderschönen guten Abend, meine Damen und Herren"–addressing the viewers at home–then, spreading his arms wide, welcoming the studio guests and audience: "Hallo, liebe Freunde," who in turn replied with "Hallo, Ilja!" *Hitparade* is dead-set on assuring viewers that in the hands of an old-school quizmaster, unpredictable live TV is a well-oiled and orderly linearly marching time machine with a preplanned exit strategy, not unlike the parade suggested by its title. *Schlager* dominate the evening, even or especially if sung with an accent.⁷ *Disco,* on the other hand, gives the impression of event television, hanging out with friends in the club–at the "Dizze"–in 1970s parlances. One never knew, what the playlist would be (this was before the screen crawler announcements and integrated previews), who would show up, or what would happen. Kids and adults could watch and learn something, but teens and tweens were "in the house."

Hitparade introduced a reality-based voting component to its slow-paced German-centric top ten music and celebrity culture, long before the *Idol* franchise made this popular. Audience members in the studio and at home were asked to send in postcards with their top song choice of the evening's performances. The winner would get a return performance on the next show adding to the feeling of stability in popular German culture even as tastes and trends, especially in dance and club music, were rapidly shifting. As a matter of fact, voters were so loyal, that a new rule had to be put in place to prevent the *Hitparade* from becoming the Roy Black Show. After the popular crooner (born Gerhard Höllerich, 1943–1991) dominated the charts for weeks and weeks, producers decided to pull the plug after three return visits.

In 1982, *Hitparade* featured the first TED electronic voting system live in what now seems like precious primetime wasted on the close-up of a multicolored graph with six numbers matching the top six songs. The graph demonstrates how obsessed the show is with its own liveness, but it also seeks to exploit the technology of mass demography as a means to assert its interaction with and representation of the historical Real. Hollis Griffin sees the trend towards mass demographics to shore up rankings in real time as a "manifestation of acute anxieties about what television is, means and does in the current moment."[8] I would add that in 1982, these anxieties reflected the dissolution of stable democratic governance, when the tensions between the ruling Social Democrats and their partner, the economic liberal Free Democrats, mounted to result in the dissolution of parliament (Bundestag), and a vote of no confidence in then chancellor Helmut Schmidt. Unlike the confusion over the parliamentary election process that had "Kohl gewählt" on October 1 and then "Kohl gescheitert" on December 17, when he did not gain the majority, leading to the dissolution of parliament to initiate an early general election in March 1983, the TED graph sought to reassure viewers in a scientifically verifiable populist election process in real time.

Until 1987, *Hitparade* had artists sing their full titles in half-playback mode to an instrumental track rather than the abbreviated playback versions or inserted videos of absent bands featured on *Disco*. *Hitparade* allowed English-language pop only in appropriated and sanitized German-language versions throughout the 1970s. Not until the late 1980s did English-language originals first make it onto the show's playlists. By then, Neue Deutsche Welle (New German Wave, NDW) with bands like BAP and Spider Murphy Gang favoring regional dialects, and German Rock (e.g., Klaus Lage, Herbert Grönemeyer) with more substantive sociopolitical texts had not only forged a more self-aware and self-critical path towards the use of German, but also towards an appreciation of rock and popular music made in Germany. With its insistence on German language until the late 1980s, *Hitparade* modeled a niche-market approach prior to deregulation, whereas *Disco* based its strategy on public radio, featuring a mix from the beginning, courting diehard fans of U.S. and British pop and rock but asking them to tolerate the occasional German-language tune. *Hitparade* approached German

Schlager music and its stars with capitalist gravitas; *Disco* did not hesitate to pair internationally acclaimed artists like Fats Domino with one-hit German *Schlager* starlets or comedy sketches performed by Richter and guests.

With its hybrid generic approach and rapid transitions between acts, *Disco* comes closer to the variety *Saturday Night Live* format (1975–). In addition to the live studio guests and audience its format shared with the *Hitparade*, *Disco* became infamous not only for its taped video sketches and guest performances (e.g., with slapstick action film star Bud Spencer), but also for its interactive quiz. Viewers had to recognize a previous performance by a featured band, whose winner appeared spot lit in the studio to Richter's "Licht aus–Womm–Spot an–Ja" announcement. Interestingly enough, the thus-spot-lit guests of honor were more often thirty-plus women and men than the targeted youth audience one would have assumed. *Disco's* hybrid format thus drew a broader range of viewers than *Hitparade's Schlager*-only mode. *Der Spiegel* even argues that it helped "bridge the musical tastes of the different generations."[9]

In the years prior to privatization (generally dated to 1 January 1984),[10] there were several music shows on TV that clearly spoke to a specific fan community. Since 1981, the *Musikantenstadl* (Mitteldeutscher Rundfunk, MDR and Bayrischer Rundfunk, BR) served *Volksmusik* and *Schlager* fans of the older generation. *Beat Club* (ARD, 1965–1972) and *Rockpalast* (Westdeutscher Rundfunk, WDR, 1974-), on the other side of the taste spectrum, targeted international rock fans. Surfing on the broadcast waves of public radio's hodgepodge playlists, listeners were well versed in switching mental gears, not channels, between Santana's "Black Magic Woman" (1971), Howard Carpendale's "Deine Spuren im Sand" (Your Traces in the Sand, 1974), the Rolling Stones' "It's only Rock'n Roll" (1974) and Heintje's "Sag auf Wiedersehen" (Say Goodbye, 1973)–although admittedly the latter was not that easy and often resulted in an ambush at the controls. *Disco* sought to appeal to a wider spectrum of viewers and fans. If one did not like the one song, one could do one's chores, turn down the TV for a bit, and turn it back on for an international hit a few minutes later. The only alternative to avoiding a taste bud-whiplash was not to listen to live or broadcast radio or TV at all.

While *Disco's* more international line-up made it a tad easier for teenagers and young adults to bear the bitter pills of interspersed *Schlager*, *Hitparade*, at first sight clearly marked as a German-language only show, nevertheless featured enough translated appropriations of English-language hits to make it worth a non-*Schlager* fan's while. Jürgen Drews's "Ein Bett im Kornfeld" (Let Your Love Flow) can serve as an example.[11] Written by Larry Williams and recorded by the Bellamy Brothers in 1975, Drews performed this international pop hit in German on *Hitparade* in 1976. The same year, ZDF booked the real deal, as compiled in *Kultnacht* on YouTube.[12] Viewers and listeners thus crossed back and forth between original songs in English and German-language adaptations on television and radio. Yes, young adults at the time tended to prefer the one, but when it came on, they would listen to the other. The music was what mattered. Only Juliane Werding's "Conny Kramer" (set to The Band's "The Night they drove old Dixie down")[13] was granted a temporary pass due to its timely message of young love cut short by a drug overdose. As I have argued above and elsewhere, the onslaught of self-reflexive 1980s New German Wave bands like Nena, BAP, Einstürzende Neubauten, Geier Sturzflug, Extrabreit, and Trio paved the way for German-language music to make a comeback and aided the *Schlager* in reinventing itself.[14]

Otto, the German comedian reigning over the 1970s and 1980s, brought NDW's successful parodic strategy to a point with his Hänsel and Gretel variations, in which he mixed folksong and several NDW hits' lyrics and sang them compilation-style to the NDW melodies. The result adapts the fairy tale of two wandering, abandoned children for the post-Hippie generation. The original Grimms' tale features a girl, who outsmarts the witch with her intelligence and sass, saving her brother. The early 1980s produced young feminists and female punks, coming of age in anti-authoritarian and authoritarian households at a time, in which Alice Schwartzer's feminist flagship journal *Emma* debated pro and contra pornography. Otto's adaptation to Spider Murphy Gang's "Skandal im Sperrbezirk" (Scandal in the prostitution-free zone) can contextually match the gingerbread house to the *Freudenhaus* (brothel) in the band's lyrics, transforming Rosi, Munich's top whore in the song, into Gretel, and the witch into her pimp. Instead of the street prostitutes that get sore feet at the edge of town, where prostitution is legal, Rosi gets all the business. In Otto's version, the *Jugendschutz* (special victims unit) is the one getting sore feet trying to catch the witch/pimp in action. Add to this Extrabreit's "Hurrah, die Schule brennt" (Hurra, the school is burning), which tells the saga of the punky "little girls of the suburbs" with their "neon nose rings, blue lips and green hair," whose destructive paths set off all fire alarms in the city, and Otto can end the fairy tale adaptation appropriately with "Hurra, die Hexe brennt" (Hurra, the witch is burning). His socially critical adaptation approach, reading the political present through German folklore, has proved so popular with listeners and viewers that he has done a series of these since the early 1980s.[15]

Otto's comical hybridization of old and new genres and lyrics, of folklore, punk, rock and pop comes closer to Richter's MCing of *Disco* than

Heck's lording over his parade of *Schlager*. Otto's continuing popularity makes one wonder, why *Disco* is not still around today. At the dawn of privatization, *Disco* called it quits, relinquishing its audience into the folds of MTV and their separate niches on TV and the radio. *Hitparade* lasted until 2000. Ironically, despite the vitriol heaved at *Schlager* by alternative music fans and left-leaning citizens over the years "the most astonishing aspect of German *Schlager* is really that it never had to fight for its life … TV *Schlager* shows continue to thrive on the lowest common denominator level–it's just that switching the channel is easier with a remote today."[16] The public broadcast era structure of *Disco* was no longer sustainable after deregulation, whereas *Hitparade's* niche-approach, integrating NDW in the early 80s and English language titles later on, but never straying too far from its one genre format survived and continued to flourish as a steady mainstay in the sea change of new channels and emerging as well as converging media.

I would argue, that *Disco's* format actually underscored and supported the German-centric focus of *Hitparade* in ZDF's larger scale program mission to both exploit trend changes in popular music and make sure to adapt them for and assimilate them into the German-language sociopolitical and cultural landscape of the 1970s and early 1980s. In the next section, I analyze one example from each show that speaks to the intersectionality between the public broadcast era, the popular music scene in the German 1970s and early 1980s, and the specific televisual aesthetics of *Hitparade* and *Disco*.

The 100th Episode of *Hitparade* (1977)

For the 100th episode of *Hitparade* in 1977[17] the top winners since its first show in 1969 were asked back to perform their new records, a promotional show for the likes of Chris Roberts and Cindy und Bert, a chance at a comeback for Peggy Marshall and a trip down memory lane for studio and TV audiences. Heck wields the number of their hits and placing on the show like baseball statistics at the same time as he is exhibiting his close ties with most stars, asking Peggy about her son, hugging Chris Roberts and telling him "I'll see you later." He does not shy away from breaking the 180-degree axis, demonstrating a damaged camera and directly addressing the cameraman as he self-reflexively and proudly makes audiences aware that "we never had a technical break-down" over the eight-year run of the show. This little aside serves to assert Heck's position in the captain's chair of the show's control deck. It assures the audience in the studio and more so at home that even with technical glitches, the show will go on—the starship and its enterprise will continue to sail into the future (*Raumschiff Enterprise* began airing in Germany in 1972). "Due to your continued support, the studio heads have decided that we will have a 101st *Hitparade*, and while it is unusual in TV to guarantee the future, we are planning for our 1978 show." Heck thus masterfully negotiates the multiplicity of viewers' entry points to *Schlager* music and TV as a medium by professionalizing and scientifically encoding popular culture preferences as fan knowledge.

The studio design with audience members sitting on simple metal bleachers (some of them not too comfortably shifting in their seats) underscores the parallel to a live sports event. While Heck's familiarity with the star's personal lives humanizes them and expands existing fan lore, the numbers add to our sense of his authority and control, as well as masculinizing his presence vis-à-vis the sexually more ambiguous 1970s male celebrity styles. The way he masterfully wields the expository mode of direct address draws the non-diegetic viewer into the studio. Even the stars seem daunted by Heck's MC talents, especially Tony Holliday who almost begins to cry upon being presented with a special pin for his frequent wins. By stating, "I am sure, Marianne Rosenberg would have liked one of these," Heck is simultaneously building a team and a competition, creating a subnarrative of suspense, even in a show where winners are already predetermined. The singers deliver wooden performances, are only briefly animated as puppetmaster Heck addresses them, most do not get to say a word and disappear into the audience again. He speaks, they sing—period. As the unsympathetic viewer I was then and the temporally distanced viewer that I am today, I cannot help but notice the centralized patriarchal authority he wields over the proceedings, how he lets no one, not even the singers, engage with the audience on their own terms, how everything is scripted to the T, every minute and second accounted for, a conservative inflexibility that even his forays into the audience's space cannot loosen up. Combined with the mostly middle-aged all-white audience, the counterpoint to the montage-aesthetics of *Disco*'s twentieth broadcast special could not be starker.

The Twentieth Episode of *Disco* (1972)

The title sequence depicts a hand and close-up head-shots of longer haired youths with "Disco" stenciled on sunglasses and tattooed on foreheads and cheeks, followed by Ilja peeking through the O in Disco, seemingly surprised to hear the sounds of Love Generations' "Love for Everybody." For preteens having watched the test-run of unsynchronized *Sesame Street* episodes since August 1972, the hip montage aesthetics of painted, animated and live action sequences and the Hippie score must have seemed familiar and today would be considered clever brand extension to a younger audience demographic. Instead of asserting his presence in the studio, Richter cartoonishly edits himself into the logo of the show, pokes his face over the neighbor's fence, so to speak, to check on the happenings there, functions as a mostly unobtrusive continuity device between the individual segments of the show. This stays true for his skits, which pave the way—metaphorically, literally and musically—for the next performance. The first skit has Richter singing the list of stars the viewers ranked as their top choices, reminiscent of the opening number at the *Oscars*. Immediately afterwards, Ilja dispenses advise to Bärbel, who took the wrong train: "Just tell the driver he's going in the wrong direction." The cheeky response jives well with the set-up in the studio and could be read as a metaphor for the counterpolitical rhetoric, yet very communal flow of Disco—a Gospel train leading to a spontaneous-looking Polonaise integrating audience and stars at the end of the show.

The mostly teen and tween audience members sit on the six steps around a slowly elevated musical-styled podium, on top of which, framed in red by two older *Fernsehgeräte*, Richter holds forth during his skits and announcements. On one of these TV box screens appears in a classic musical spotlight his drag queen alter ego Frau Schlüter, complete with a glittery red dress and blond wig. She sings about meeting a man on the train, whose lack of knowledge about Roman art and architecture entices her into playing a trick on him. This number features cabaret/vaudeville style piano accompaniment and continues the irreverence from the advice column, making fun of high art ignorance, but meta-discursively also raising questions about the culture war between popular and *Leitkultur* (dominant culture). Doing so in drag illuminates and critiques the feminization of modern popular culture Andreas Huyssen attests to in *After the Great Divide*.[18] This self-reflexivity, unafraid to cross—here also meant to insult—fixed culture, class, and gender binaries is striking for a ZDF program in 1972. On the one hand, Heck insists on the success of *Hitparade* because of his and his crew's unfailing ability to control live TV flow, on the other, Richter pokes fun at the temporal and musical genre-related unpredictability of the *Disco* theme: "Schubert never wrote that, and that I never meet Franz Schubert here, the whole ZDF hopes fervently." Indeed, the show rapidly moves from Joe Dolan and Middle of the Road to Ekseption's "Peace Planet," a fast-paced electronic rock adaptation of a dance by Johann Sebastian Bach, as an inter-title informs us.

Because Schubert is not that far behind, after all, Olivia Newton John's "Banks of the Ohio" helps to rail in the runaway train. When Samantha Jones sings to Richter's image on the TV screen, while the diegetic and extra-diegetic audience members see her on the studio stage, the border between what is live and what is recorded for playback has been corrupted, as has any illusion of generic, musical, or taste boundaries, not to mention any idea of a central authority.

The diverse Les Humphries singers emerge individually spot-lit around the studio and come together in the gospel "Ole Man Moses." Their race and gender-based diversity and dynamically decentered interactive choreography, while still contained by Les's white leadership, visually and acoustically transforms the seated white German audience into an impromptu mixed race congregation at the same time as modeling what the German equivalent of an immigration country like the UK or the U.S. might look like. A few minutes later, however, Tony Marshall with "Schöne Maid" leads the Les Humphries Singers and audience members in a traditional Polonaise. Marshall's *Schlager*–a rowdy march and drinking song–stands in stark contrast to both the "Love Everybody" anthem from the beginning of the show and the Les Humphries gospel. The Polonaise changes the dynamics by forging a physical–not just visual and acoustic–unity out of the singers and the audience, a grouping with one clear leader and followers. The channeling of linguistic, musical, choreographic, and cultural diversity into a single-file, harsh communal German chorus of "Hoya-hoya-ho" becomes an allegory of the cultural and political labor the two music shows accomplish against and in conjunction with one another. The abrupt absorption of diversity into a mass leader-based reordering of the sociopolitical body would seem too conspicuous to be accidental were it not for Richter's final gag.

To crown the evening, Richter appears as *Schlager* icon Heino, complete with blond wig and dark sunglasses, in front of a snowy mountain backdrop. With this skit, he constructs a bookend to his Frau Schlüter drag, and invites, even encourages queer appropriations of German *Schlager* and their stars. Due to the segment's vicinity to the Humphries singers and their African-American gospel and to the coercive Polonaise, the Alpine backdrop questions the validity of a national German imaginary of *Heimat* based on the racial equivalent to "Edelweiss." With his Heino act, Richter commits his own act of appropriation, but instead of *Hitparade's* policy of dominant and therefore invisible cultural assimilation, he deliberately and self-referentially exaggerates the performativity of *Schlager* and their stars, camping them up in the process.

In conclusion, it is perhaps no surprise then, that the show's broadcast era montage—and camp aesthetics—combined with its over-the-top self-reflexive media politics did not outwit or outlast the ZDF regime during the seemingly endless Kohl era.[19] *Hitparade's* efficiency-oriented reliability and its appropriation-based German-language culture politics contrasted all too sharply with *Disco's* early attempt at a formal and representational hybridity. But it is also thanks to *Disco's* campy transgressions that *Schlager* extended its fan base to develop and sustain a significant LGBTQ connection, one that fed the attraction for *Schlager* Parades all over Germany beyond the demise of the Love Parade.

SUNKA SIMON has a PhD in German from Johns Hopkins University and is currently Professor of German and Film and Media Studies at Swarthmore College. Simon teaches popular music, film, television, and new media. Since 2014, she is Associate Provost for Faculty Development and Diversity. Simon is the author of *Mail-Orders: The Fiction of Letters in Postmodern Culture* (Albany, 2002) and co-author of *Globally Networked Teaching in the Humanities* (Abingdon, 2015).

Notes

1. *Die deutsche Hitparade* continued with other moderators after Heck's departure in 1984 and aired its final episode on 16 December 2000.
2. Raymond Williams, *Television* (London, 1974).
3. Susanne Weingarten, "Immer wieder samstags...," in *Flimmerkiste,* ed. Nina Schindler (Hildesheim, 1999), 239.
4. Ibid., 237. All translations by author.
5. Nina Schindler, "Weiter geht es ohne Gnade und dann kommt die Hitparade...," in Schindler (see note 3), 289.
6. Jane Feuer, "The Concept of Live Television," in *Regarding Television,* ed. E. Ann Kaplan (Frederick, 1983), 17.
7. On the complicated aspect of Germans and foreign nationals singing *Schlager* with an accent, see Sunka Simon, "Der vord're Orient: Colonialist Imagery in Popular Postwar German *Schlager,*" *Journal of Popular Culture,* 34, no. 3 (2000): 87-108 and Richard Langston, "Roll over Beethoven" in *Sound Matters,* ed. Nora M. Alter and Lutz Kopenick (New York, 2004), 183-196.
8. Hollis Griffin, "Manufacturing 'Massness'" in *A Companion to Reality Television,* ed. Laurie Ouellette (Oxford, 2014), 166.
9. Wiebke Brauer, "Als Disco nach Deutschland kam," *Der Spiegel,* 20 October 2008; available at http://www.spiegel.de/einestages/legendaere-tv-show-a-947972.html, accessed 26 April 2017.
10. http://www.bpb.de/apuz/32160/die-zweite-saeule-des-dualen-systems-privater-rundfunk?p=all, accessed 1 March 2016.

11. Jürgen Drews on *Hitparade*; available at https://youtu.be/RwHcohP7y3I, accessed 12 October 2016.
12. *Kultnacht im ZDF*; available at https://youtu.be/Dft63gHqqKo, accessed 1 March 2016.
13. The Band's "The Night they drove old Dixie down" from the 1978 film *The Last Waltz*, available at https://www.youtube.com/watch?v=jREUrbGGrgM, accessed 12 October 2016.
14. Sunka Simon, "Irresistible Innocence: Reappropriations of Weimar and Nazi-Era *Schlager*" in *Reworking the German Past: Adaptations in Film, the Arts, and Popular Culture*, ed. Susan Figge and Jenifer Ward (Columbia, 2010), 130-153.
15. Otto's versions are available at https://youtu.be/6k8_Mw2hKBE (2:15); compare to Extrabreit's original from 1982; available at https://youtu.be/myyd5HAzxqg, accessed 1 March 2016.
16. Schindler (see note 5), 292.
17. The 100th Episode of *Hitparade* (ZDF 1977); available at https://youtu.be/Os_MhDJls8I, accessed 12 October 2016.
18. Andreas Huyssen, *After the Great Divide: Modernism, Mass Culture, Postmodernism* (Bloomington, 1987).
19. The Twentieth Episode of Disco (ZDF 1972); available at https://vimeo.com/radiolux/disco-72-pick-ups, accessed 1 March 2016.

Chapter 2

THE BIRTH OF AUTOTUNE AND THE LOOP OF (WEST) GERMAN IDENTITY

Cyrus Shahan

𝒜udible in the technological aesthetics of West German post punk is a 1980s strategy for escaping the political, cultural, and aesthetic contradictions of a nation trapped by the compulsion to, reconstruction of, and march toward a democratic state.[1] Against the confinement of that democratic state's attendant freedoms, post punk's technological turn tested the Federal Republic's experiential limits of liberation and confinement. Although post punk's analog distortions, feedback, and loops sprang from products of historical avant-gardes—from Futurism's visual fusion of sound and speed, over the human insurrection against mechanistic dystopia in Fritz Lang's *Metropolis*, and into the apocalyptic specter of its present—they were not the old disguised as the new. Rather, post punk's electronic distortions signal a "militancy of noise"[2] dependent upon aesthetic repetition. That repetition, in theory, contained potential escapes from the horizons of experience made seemingly absolute by technology's capacity to stabilize coercive unity. The fate of post punk's repetition, the extent to which it resurrected insurrections past or released products in which metamorphosis and transposition harnessed an everyday wealth of hidden possibilities, is the focus of this article.

A year after Kraftwerk included German-language lyrics on their international bestselling album *Autobahn*, Rolf Dieter Brinkmann wondered in *Westwärts 1 & 2* "Maybe German will soon be a dead language. It is so bad to sing." Two years later, West German punk bands such as S.Y.P.H., Die tödliche Doris, and Pyrolator began to reproduce—for some obliquely—the sociocultural and linguistic tension between the buttoned-up, technologized aesthetics that Kraftwerk used to imagine a German identity liberated from National Socialism alongside the dystopic, violent aesthetics in Brinkmann's attempt to bring forth Germany's ultimate demise. The return to Kraftwerk's

---

Notes for this chapter begin on page 40.

technological means of representation and their simultaneous trafficking in Brinkmann's avant-garde practices of collage and *détournement* (rerouting, hijacking) illustrate, in part, the process of adaptation and continuation that underwrites punk's efforts to undo the regressive and violent politics of its present. Brinkmann's actual listening preferences aside, his fascination with and return to folk music, particularly the folk music of the United States of America, and his revulsion at the barbarity of his national culture, gesture to a disinterest in the Germanness of the band that brought Krautrock to the world. He certainly never listened to German punk rock, for he was dead before its birth circa 1977, though punk's aesthetic practices operated with a related vision of collage, aggression, and anti-Germanness, and the writer/ artist was an aesthetic-political wellspring for certain factions of German punk. While the empirical content of Kraftwerk, Brinkmann, and punk highlights a quotient of repetition and cooption in the aesthetic and subcultural tête-à-tête with the recursive dynamic of West German democracy, technology in post punk stressed the presumed limits put on representation and experience by violent politics. Technology and its loops, distortions, and samples made audible a transformation of the process of production and anticipated reception. These sounds troubled the representation of, anxieties about, and potentials for intervention into the public sphere.

The first part of this article frames through the band S.Y.P.H. how repetition in media—its representation of unity and violent intervention—could be more than a void of associative possibilities.[3] The remaining two sections focus on the minutely theorized praxis and products of Die tödliche Doris and the obscure Brontologic in the hands of musician and producer Pyrolator (Kurt Dahlke). With each case study, I unfold the sonic architecture of post punk as an electronic process of differentiation that avoided becoming a Teutonic "obsessive repetition" (Gilles Deleuze) of postwar aesthetic practices engaging German identity.[4] Opposition and support, repulsion and attraction, and the effects of differentiation in the social sphere, certainly play a role. But their representation and reception become through the circuit of a differentiator—a Minimoog, for example—more subtle and significant. Because the differentiator's output is bound to the rate of change on the input and its oscillators redefined the fundamental representation of the referent, conceptual difference between new and repetition, between what might attract or repulse, is inconsequential for post punk's technological process. Instead of taking a side fated to merge with its opposition, music by Die tödliche Doris and Pyrolator made the amount of change affected by a differentiator on source material central and continuous. Both bands drew from the well-worn rhetoric of violence, capitalism, and democracy in the Federal Republic; language that by the

1980s was hardly new, yet nevertheless still hedged citizens into support of or resistance to the state. Using electronic devices to transform the qualities of the ideological source material, the music made by these bands took up a remainder position, neither for nor against. Though that remainder position was minute, Alexander Kluge and Oskar Negt have argued through the example of electric bonds in physics how especially weak- or remainder-valences expend centrally organizing labor in the public sphere. Their work on the differentiation of strong and weak forces and the ability of weak forces to effect social prosperity through fleeting combination provides a way to understand post punk's electronic differentiations. They define the interest in differentiation production as "an interest to orient oneself realistically toward the production process–that is, determining what a laborer is actually capable of doing." Post punk's position of neither for nor against signals what Kluge and Negt read to other ends as an "interest in differentiation [that] translates into answers. The results are heterogeneous demarcations ... But one differentiation is not incorrect if the other is correct; they coexist next to one another, signifying different perspectives."[5] The sounds of post punk's technological turn emerged from a process of electronic differentiation, seeking what I read below as potential sonic escapes from the canonical legacy of German experience to avoid the hermetic fate of associative social forces past.[6]

Repetition and Violence

Through samples of media production and a narrative of experiential limits set by media reception, S.Y.P.H.'s four-minute-and-ten-second song "klammheimlich" lays bare punk's assessment of its present. Within the subculture, "klammheimlich" signals its intention to create a salient distinction between itself and its predecessors–hippies, students, and for many Düsseldorf-area punks, Kraftwerk itself–and to thereby be classically rock 'n roll. Though it traffics exclusively in the superficial experience of the old and its emergent sound technologies are new, "klammheimlich's" contradictions refused the compulsion to employ dominant forces of sociopolitical action or to the new as the only possibility for prosperity.

In that choice of neither, the song samples nightly newscasts to narrate the Baader-Meinhof Gang's counterviolence. The precisely truncated lyrics, "*heldentum / eigentum / eigenheim / stammheim,*" keywords to the "German Autumn," overshadow the track at irregular moments. Paired with sequencer and synthesizer distortions cresting and dying off, this song indicts the experience of daily life as nothingness. Experience had been reduced to consumerism and private ownership of goods (*eigenheim* / *eigentum*), by the trap of political and critical reason (*stammheim*), and by fairy tale heroism. Instead of reviving ideological repetition, however, S.Y.P.H. differentiated the repetition in media broadcasts and terrorist mantras to signal a potential rescue from that teleological fate. Through instable amplification and syntactical black holes, the band's electronic processes effected change in the lyric and sampled source material. Syntactically bracketed by the regressive dynamic of possibilities in the social sphere, the prefix/adjective "*eigen*" (own) is destroyed by the contemporary instance of political experience (*stammheim*) and the strong forces of the German cultural canon (*heldentum*).[7] Against the limits of West German sociopolitical experience set by a compulsory choice of "*stammheim*," the terrorists' home, or "*eigenheim*," one's own home, "klammheimlich" inverted that which was meant to be distinct (*eigen*) and its capacity to orient German citizens and institutionally stabilize democratic binaries. Instead the song creates verbal arcs thrust into motion by distortion and disorienting use of nightly news broadcasts. As such, the song troubled subject and object in the process of production to signal a process that harnesses potential to give form through what Kluge and Negt call the "LOQUACIOUSNESS OF MATTER." Though trapped by their materiality, the song's "illegitimate agglomerations and their immediate disaggregation" nevertheless signaled the possibilities resonating and moving through external fields.[8] The potential escape imbedded in those fields was in "klammheimlich's" use of the old to emphasize its under-theorizing (*Heldentum*), how it replaced the desire for the always yet-to-be (*Eigentum*) with amplification of its clandestine potential in the already-present. The four-word sequence highlights how theirs was no logical telos, but rather experiential motion that infolded. The sampled and spoken narratives made audible the Enlightenment's dialectical trap of state imprisonment or private freedom, of action for the self or for the public, of the legacy of Immanuel Kant's confinement of private use of critical reason and liberation of its public use.

As a punk aesthetic appraisal of the misunderstood horizon of eternal return lurking at the core of Enlightenment philosophy, the song willfully demonstrates repetition. On the one side, it makes unmistakable the absolute lack of difference between newscasts narrating the German Autumn when it mashes so many together, a fact reinforced through the cyclical synthesizer noise. At the same time, it marks its own repetition, namely the attempt to create from the trap of social insurrection or state-sponsored terrorism a different capacity for transforming the social field. Because of the compulsion to be recognizable as social agents, to pit one representation against another, and verifying, as such, one critique via the other, "klammheimlich" partners the Federal Republic's obsessive repetition with its own.[9] A call for recognizing possibilities, the song's demonstration of repetition paired with its associative-discontinuous motion are, as such, its esoteric line of flight. The briefly polarizing product aimed to escape the hierarchical character of dualisms such as terrorist/citizen, watcher/doer, public/private, or freedom/imprisonment. S.Y.P.H.'s song and first issue of the fanzine *Die Düsseldorfer Leere* from which the lyrics come, illustrate sonically and visually how the band and fanzine author Ralf Dörper harness an absolute negativity (what could be identified as the affective counterpoint to Deleuze's positive difference-in-itself). The band and author confirm the possible production of German identity not trafficking through the violent legacy of National Socialism: the use of analog tools does not affirm some kind of miserable, ill-fated conception of Germanness, but rather broadcasts an undefined potential that production, recording, and consumption holds for subjects who consume the ideological. An engagement, as such, with connective, disjunctive, and conjunctive memory and their role in giving form to social forces, "klammheimlich" and Dörper's fanzine link interpolated possible relationalities between nonregressive relationships and experiences.

The fanzine cover's intersection of consumption, use of reason, and "illegitimate agglomerations"[10] highlighted possibilities beyond ideological horizons. Against oppositions of desire and a negative beyond that inhibited their own fullness, Dörper asserted that "[t]hrough the purchase of this consumer good you will become: ... an enemy of the classes / an enemy of the system / a Vietcong / a Nazi / an urban guerilla / Clark Kent / Peter Parker / a homosexual."[11] When read in tandem with the four words of "klammheimlich"–that run across the bottom margin of issue #1's last page like a ticker on a news broadcast–the trap of choices and the inescapable vortex of identity politics are transformed. The options that were believed to govern and limit experience in 1979 instead illustrate the potential to constitute an index of actual, concrete, and contingent possibilities. The differential force of the song and fanzine texts lies in how they defied practices that explicitly and constrictingly limited consumers and producers into fixed positions. The band's never-defined ends signal an effort to reconcile the dominant affect of West Germany post World War II–anxiety–with hopeful evidence of the immanence of potential. "Klammheimlich" explicitly distanced itself from the registers of experience that the song unmasks as echoing nothing but a void–a *Leere*–beyond the given possibilities of experience and identity. Via sonic and visual amplitude of repetition, the song and fanzine engaged abstraction as a "mode of production sufficient to regulate the larger historical relation formed between the two original terms," in this case, German identity and violence.[12] Though I suggest S.Y.P.H.'s song and Dörper's fanzine are thus not representative of "obsessive repetition," it is hard to argue that either the band or the author thought their efforts made a difference: the band famously poured concrete over the world in an attempt to halt the forward march of its failures.[13] In that wake, Die tödliche Doris and Pyrolator amped up the frequency on technology in their music in what I read below as a psychophysical practice. Their songs are evidence of a perceptual process of experience; to make audible that process, both bands systematically varied the properties of their stimulus along one or more physical dimensions—with fabricated or recorded sounds wired into differentiators—to investigate the relationship between physical stimulus and the sensations and perceptions they affect.

Live Playback

Even the most cursory reading of Die tödliche Doris's song titles highlights the repetition of two themes that belie the "miracle" rhetoric of the emergent West German democracy: death and mundane daily life. That loop is a form of repetition invested in abstraction; Doris's sounds, read through Makenzie Wark's definition of hacking:

> construct a plane upon which otherwise different and unrelated matters may be brought into many possible relations. To abstract is to express the virtuality of nature, to make known some instance of its possibilities, to actualize a relation out of infinite relationality, to manifest the manifold.[14]

Doris's hack embraced death, suicide, commercial repetition, and banality to broadcast the "immaterial virtuality of the material, its qualities of information."[15] Put otherwise, the structure of the band and the sensations of its products wielded Martin Kippenberger's depressing realism,[16] Vivian Westwood's bondage clothing, and the body as corporal and metaphorical—thereby showing the falsity of the given and the tenacious potential remaining.

Doris theorized—at length—that the heterogeneous combinations and differentiations in their sonic products sounded out the possible; and co-founder Wolfgang Müller frames Doris as an antagonist and agent to that end. The band put into action the dissolution of performer and audience, in its own theory, by situating itself as "an amorphous, amoeba-like being that constantly expands the boundaries of its body, constantly transforming its form. Thereby alternative border-tensions between an inner form and the exterior originate."[17] Dubbed a "7-headed informer," Doris and its theorized project problematized forms of transcendental empiricism by affirming the potentiality that conditioned their present. Perhaps the most overly theorized band of West German post punk, Die tödliche Doris, formed in 1980 by Wolfgang Müller and fellow art student Nikolaus Untermöhlen, was indeed amoeba-like in its steady transformation by its over forty-six fleeting members.[18] Inextricable from the concert "Ingenious Dilletantes" and its willful misspelling, Müller saw "misplaying and miswriting as the possibilities to new forms of expression," forms evident in the dialectical tension and subversion on their album titles. "Choruses and Solos" begs questions of collective action or individual heroism, the purposeful void of the only seemingly eponymous first LP " " is not outside of the realm of experience but rather the differential operation underlying all experience, and their fifth released LP titled "sechs" used invisible logic to make audible loquacious matter.

But neither the will to a new form of aesthetic expression nor Doris's investment in the productive value of shock was radical. What distinguishes the band, in part, from other punk bands while aligning it with happenings from the 1960s is how Doris's expressed interest in shock—in public death—was made real through its opposite affect, the mundane. In "7 Deadly Accidents," for example, each accident is narrated without the breathy sensationalism of news broadcasts and without the authoritarian male broadcaster to anchor viewers. The band thus fuses the two motifs running to the core of its oeuvre when it inflects the nightly news cycle with boredom. What separates Doris from the obsessive repetition of post punk's miming aesthetic provocateurs of a decade earlier is the band's investment in the opportunity for abstraction. Doris's loops treated the material as immaterial while performing the preservation of sound as a document of possibilities rather than certainties. They thereby transformed the angst of death into mundane moments, anachronistically and distortedly deployed in their present. Live performance of recorded sound aimed to create associative tensions in form—part of a sonic field of possibilities that transforms the relationship between production and use. Those amoebic ideals of the "7-headed informer" and live playback signal a Deleuzian line of flight, and one hears echoes of Doris's "7-headed informer" when Deleuze and Guattari write of an "acentered, nonhierarchical, nonsignifying system without ... central automation ... whose development avoids any orientation toward a culmination point or external end."[19] The dedication to amorphous structure informed Doris's relationship to technology. Though Doris may seem out of place in an article on the technological in post punk, technology and its capacities in users' hands was obviously a major concern of the band. It is Doris's engagement with the concept and effects of electronics in representation, specifically the loop that makes them so central to electronic differentiation in post punk.[20]

In their hands, the loop was what Müller has called a "*Tonkonserve.*" But rather than a contained experience, Doris's were unstable objects through which the band amplified difference into the role of media as index for identity. Recordings of all manner of narratives, noises, and samples, the Tonkonserve underlines the band's intervention into ideological repetition by way of undermining the practice of preserving the immaterial as if material, the transubstantiation of ideological rhetoric into a life-preserving product, and the actualization of a single relation from infinite relationalities. Oddly, the humble tea kettle, deployed in what at first sight are Luddite-like performances, demonstrates this rather esoteric framing of Doris's music. A mundane vector for associative qualities of information, the tea kettles were technological elements of their shows: the band timed the kettle's whistle to very precise moments in the playback of their recorded sound, a process that involved scientific experimentation with heat and volume of water over time, to the effect that they used cookware as performative technology "to make known some instance of its possibilities."[21] While one can dismiss the technology of this element of Doris's shows, it amplified on stage the intersection of banal (tea kettles), sensational (death), and oppositional (screaming) while performing and transforming the recorded possibilities remaining in the constricting form of a "preserved" sound. Rather than an affirmation of ill-fated Germanness, the qualities of information Doris changed sounded out a form of repetition bound to the process of electronic differentiation. When Doris transformed the concept "*Tonkonserve*" from something preserving signification to something enabling differentiation, the preservation that Doris channeled was both theoretical and phenomenological. For the latter, their sampled sounds and renarrated news broadcasts were indeed the performance of the past on stage; they were, superficially, musical circulations of the politics of their present. But, insofar as they enacted circularity, they simultaneously critiqued the closed circuit system of experience witnessed in "klammheimlich." Doris's loops thereby preserved, and made audible with the tea kettle's scream, the violent bracketing done to experience. They thereby problematized the internally loaded preservability of and escape potential in their mundane source material.

Similarly, when the band looped in lyric form the nightly news, they did not seek to destabilize the rhetoric of public violence for private safety. Instead, they insinuated themselves into the process of codifying discourse and its hegemonic organization, whereby the tea kettles in part provided kinetic energy able to interrupt passive consumption and form new associations. Thus, the loop in Doris's hands was about the event as continuous and alterable; the band's processing and production screamed for awareness of the potential in the given. An example loop appears on two separate albums: on "Auf dem Lande / Tatasche," (in the countryside/fact) the intro track of "Unser Debut" (our debut) is the same as track 5a of "sechs." Rather than a narrative trick meant to hide its sonic shortcut at sound prolongation, the mechanics of the looped sample on both tracks is antagonistic—it is excessively mechanical and incongruous with the rest of the songs.[22] The redoubled sample was, as such, ultimately about transferring that antagonism to the answers in the content of the track itself. The phenomenological, psychological, and philosophical differences that Doris's technologized aestheticization of the past and present effects is not the same witnessed with Kraftwerk. Whereas a band like Kraftwerk used technology to create a new, hybrid identity that trafficked in the past, Doris used it to create unmistakable ruptures and gaps, empty spaces in sound that the listener was left to fill and bridge. In this way, Doris can be understood as a post-punk revelation of Germany's entrenchment in the (romantic) enactment of the same with an expectation of a different result.[23] The band's riposte was a sharpening of possible uses for present purposes rather than bringing the past back to its "original" truth or seeking potential solutions in a not-present. They did so by discovering the gaps accessible via existent technologies and projecting potential change (the sound of a tea kettle or a jarring sample) through these gaps.[24] But this still does little more than cast Doris as a band that in innovative ways continued in familiar avenues the oppositional politics of so many. For while their work verges on the subversiveness of "computational subjectivity" able to bring many possibilities into dynamic interaction with one another, they did not really engage their audience in a way that tested the possibilities in their listening practices. Doris were in the end performers in control. That would all end with the release of the "Invisible LP."

The story and phenomena of Doris's "Invisible LP" are certainly entertaining, but more than that, both make audible and signal the apex of Doris's attempts at abstraction. Chronologically, the album was to be the fifth LP released by the band, although it would necessarily come to fruition *after* the release of its sixth album, informatively and confusingly titled "six." Conceived with media reception in mind, the fourth album released by Doris was panned as the band's attempt to capture the financial gains to be made from a "commercial sounding" album. Music journalists in their reviews of "Unser Debut," lamented the fall from avant-garde sounds that the album, in their ears, trumpeted loudly and clearly.[25] Two years later, the release of "sechs" was heralded by the same journalism outlets as the longed-for return to Doris's theory-influenced music familiar from the band's origins. But music journalists had unwittingly played directly into the band's hands, revealing themselves as an ideological farce with ossified listening and consumption habits. A testament to their linear listening and consumption, and by extension to their ignorance of the field of possibilities untapped in the everyday, none of the reviewers asked why the band's fifth published album would be called "six." Enter the "Invisible LP." A truly collaborative product between the band and its listeners, the LP can only be heard if a listener plays both "Unser Debut" and "sechs" simultaneously. The A-side of each album must be started at the same time on different record players to produce a result wherein the pop of "Unser Debut" and the noise of "sechs" create tracks that are quintessentially "generating constructions" and invested in a mode of listening to music that is "against the sinking-into of music and the belief in music because that creates a musical consciousness."[26] By giving the audience a chance to engage in practical ways the "*Lärm*" (noise) of "sechs" and to escape the imperative to be "in the service of the instruments," the "Invisible LP" sets up Doris not as the differentiator, but as a band that, to take Müller's words, "*verleiht*" (distributes) this power.[27]

Though the band certainly channels the practices of a host of postwar subcultures and aesthetic and political oppositional actors, their project of engaging their present with its "wraith-like image of a past and the image of a future past," was at the very least one of the best attempts at the liberating potential of abstraction. Their invisible LP obliquely engaged mainstream media, but only when it used the kind of music journalism that curated punk and post-punk music as a vector. As such, the kind of scene that Kippenberger, amongst others, derided while sustaining, was a phenomenological instance of S.Y.P.H.'s and Dörper's keywords. Doris's avowedly decentered mode of production was an earnest, if obtuse, attempt to inhibit any kind of what Wark calls a "vectoralist class"—the emergent ruling class of one's time.[28] The "Invisible LP" was in certain ways a step beyond the more technologized practices of genealogically related Krautrock bands or Kraftwerk. It expanded the possibility of experience through technology when the LP amplified the number of tracks in a song by requiring both LPs to be played simultaneously. The album's conditions of possibility demanded precise engagement with "loquacious material," a requirement that informed the individual of their realistic capacity vis-à-vis the production process but did not enforce it. The band's antagonism toward music journalism engendered in the interest of differentiation the existence of multiple framings of Doris's sonic triptych.[29] Doris took advantage of analog manipulations of aural representation of identity, from sequencers, to cassette loops, to tea kettles, in the band's efforts to test the possibility of escaping the structuring soundscapes of the Federal Republic. In an age of reforming German identity via a canon rescued–by state fiat–from National Socialism, Doris's "dematerialized product" engaged in the postwar reimagining of German identity free from–or perhaps able to escape the event horizon of–German identity in the age of National Socialism.[30]

The Logic of Sound

While Die tödliche Doris's use of technology was subtle in its differentiation of ideological source material, the Brontologic used by Pyrolator was overt. And though his core devices and their functions are familiar–Minomoog, Polymoog, Korg MS-20, and MIDI (Musical Instrument Digital Interface)– Pyrolator made music that went beyond the mere connection of multiple devices and the sequencing of sounds through them. The dizzying phenomenology of the Brontologic in the hands of Pyrolator certainly livens and circulates in a version of DIY, though one beyond the assembly of fanzines, self-altered clothing, or recording songs in basements. A laughingly complex sequencer originally designed by former jeans salesman Werner Lambertz circa 1979, the Brontologic was meant to "automatically produce good music, without any faults that musicians would create."[31] But listening to his musical productions makes clear that faultless music (in the classical sense) was not the end to which Pyrolator sought to involve his self-built Brontologic. In practice and in reception, the Brontologic signals a clear apex of differential repetition in post punk.

A controller for his Korg MS-20, Yamaha DX-7, and Emulator 1, Pyrolator's Brontologic on "Home Taping is Killing Music," engages the retrograde progress of German democracy as a problem with the materiality of democratic freedom.[32] In that hapless system of repetition and simulation wherein democracy circulates, progress from the conflict of state and nonstate actors is nothing of the sort, merely the association of strong social forces "that [made] the aggregate explode."[33] Against that destructive ideology of democratic multiplicity, the Brontologic escapes the mere juxtaposition of concepts in space to highlight German progress and experience as difference in degree rather than difference in kind. A collaborative effort between Pyrolator and A. K. Klosowski, "Home Taping is Killing Music" emerged after Klosowski approached Pyrolator about producing a record from a chain of strung-together Walkmans and self-made noisemakers. Pyrolator quickly found himself collaborating with Klosowski rather than producing.[34] Certainly quirky, the Brontologic was more than an unwieldy instrument—it was approximately 2.5 meters square—and its complexity was more than the replication of loops and sequences. Its operations too complex to detail here, most important within the confines of this article is how the Brontologic allowed Pyrolator to shift the beginning and end points with/in distinct sequencer patterns, as well as to shift the direction for each loop. The result was music moving in quantum fields of probability, ignoring the imperative of forward marching sheet music and its classical use of time to instead release sounds subversively fractal in their complexity. Listening to "Home Taping is Killing Music" is not, however, as esoteric as the Brontologic would hint. The tracks are rhythmic in more or less consumable ways, they do not alternate between loud and soft pitches with any kind of particularly alienating frequency, and for those listeners already initiated in the music made by Pyrolator's band Der Plan, there are distinct references.

Nevertheless, in comparison to Kraftwerk and the electronic machinations of Krautrock bands, the songs differentiate themselves through song length and what is really a mess of sounds. Whereas Kraftwerk tracks are predominately between five and eight minutes—a length matched by bands such as Faust, Tangerine Dream, and Neu!—the tracks on "Home Taping" are mostly in the 3:40 range. Certainly longer than punk rock songs and much closer to the contemporary radio edit length of pop songs, Pyrolator and Klosowski operated in a similar sprit as Die tödliche Doris with its production of "Unser Debut" as a foray into "popular music." Though again, it is hard to imagine "Home Taping" surpassing the top West German hits of 1984 by bands such as Frankie Goes to Hollywood, Cyndi Lauper, Wham!, and Stevie Wonder. While songs such as the second track on the album "Tschak" are playful lounge music, those upbeat and consumable sounds are far afield from "I just called to say I love you."[35] Nevertheless, the album is not about alienating listeners; instead it seems to retrain the listener, tuning their auditory reception in ways that make audible the intricacies and subversiveness of loops. The key function of the Brontologic, in Pyrolator's estimation, is its ability to play loops forwards and backwards simultaneously. A quality rapidly audible when listening to the album, its diachronic unfolding of soundscapes plays out in stark contrast to the LP's first track "Overture." That moniker orients a listener to the classical oeuvre of German composers past, and thereby lures them into a familiar canon of listening, thinking, and experiencing music. The ominous sound of the thirty-six second track, whose crashing cymbals promise a kind of eighties orchestral *Götterdämmerung*, are, however, a ruse.[36] And though track two–"Österreich"–would seem to locate the listener in a kindred seat of classical music, its sounds sample the goofy, carnivalesque sounds on Der Plan's album "Japlan," not Mozart.

It is unsurprising to find punk and post-punk music that wields musical and aesthetic history, since many of its practitioners were schooled in these very subjects. Die tödliche Doris put theory into action in a sonic challenge to facile understandings and uses of technology; Pyrolator and Klosowski can be understood as a dramatically more cabled version of the "illegitimate agglomerations"[37] signaled by Doris's amoeba-like "7-headed informer." Indeed, the optic of Pyrolator's Brontologic and Klosowski's linked Walkmans reflect Doris's (and Deleuze's) polymorphous concept made physical; together the electronics signal the possibility par excellence of systematically varying the properties of stimulus along multiple dimensions. Making the quantum field of psychophysics audible, the loops' simultaneous backwards and forwards motion seeks out more elementary differentiations; "Home Taping" amplified the systematic variation of its source material to a frequency that escaped obsessive repetition. The songs made audible the potential of metamorphosis and transposition of the mundane without the anchor of an original, liberatory truth to be located in its tracks. Though an attempt to reanimate a defiant modernism lurks in the sonic practices of sound mattering, the "fractal-like sequencer patterns" of sound are qualitatively beyond modernist manipulations of music.[38] While that may sound like material best suited for an audiofile, the sounds of "Home Taping" are listener friendly. Though, if using Kraftwerk's contemporaneous electronica as a referent, then the playfulness of track 3, "Tschak," is beyond popular music, but rhythmic in very understandable ways. Despite that consumability, there are audible reasons why "Home Taping" did not make the hit charts in 1984. Side A's penultimate song "Heimat" crystallizes the differentiating logic in the complex production of the album, a complexity that simultaneously, and obviously, sets its sights on the regressive logic of a transforming Germany. With a length of 2:41, it is the shortest song on the album, but for that it presents the capabilities of the Brontologic best of all.

The impressive number of loops and tracks that constitute "Heimat" are fused with samples of indecipherable spoken words. Adding texture to the track, stretches of the song cycle between muffled sounds seemingly playing through a wet rag and strikingly clear synthesizer noise, to the effect that the frenetic and racing sounds become almost physical in the air. This unsettling of hearing in "Heimat" takes advantage of frequency and amplification, and aims squarely at the song's titular concept. Unmoored as an anchor for the state or a yoke for its opposition, Heimat becomes in Pyrolator and Klosowski's hands cacophonic. Because it had proven itself repeatedly to be a concept stuck in an antagonistic quagmire, "Heimat" broadcasts *Heimat* (the German motherland) as at times incomprehensible and at other times crystal clear, yet in both cases disorienting. When the sounds are clear and discernable while running amok, "Heimat" becomes a valence that manifests the appearance of clarity in the service of actual disorientation. In those moments, the song mimes the numbing rhetoric of a new Germany in the public sphere. When the most audible moments in "Heimat" sound as if an input button is stuck down—clarity overloads the processors that now only produce destructive repetition—the song indicts *Heimat* as a concept that only seemingly changes external fields. When the sounds are muffled and garbled, "Heimat" indicts *any* nationalist rhetoric as trafficking in a (willfully) misunderstood and obfuscated concept. That obsessive repetition of clear moments, of muddled moments, and of signals run amok is "Home Taping's" sonic representation of German reality: the frenetic repetition of the single originary concept. In the case of S.Y.P.H.'s "klammheimlich" keywords of the German Autumn were *détourned* to highlight the leadenness of the 1970s and 1980s; "Heimat" goes further back in German sociocultural history to indict the etching out of boundaries and identities witnessed in Fallersleben's verses and the Grimm's fairytales. With "Heimat," Pyrolator and Klosowski undo the naturalness, the Germanness of structuring experience through the concept of *Heimat*. The Brontologic takes the overused concept, its reduction of social experience to two axes, and its centralizing elementary qualities to produced multiple sequences all running at different rates and cycles.[39] It is in that very richness of sound in "Heimat" that the album uses to signal the possibilities untapped and the destruction unleashed by and in Heimat.

Conclusion: Repetition in the Machine

Post punk's electronic differentiations are aural ripostes to the eidetic reduction and bracketing that plagued experience in the Federal Republic. They were escapes from what Müller called "the intensive immersion into the material, from automatic suggestions in the form of *repetition of material* that ultimately forms a 'musical consciousness' with which they come full circle: the serious musician, victim of his own inbreeding, is born."[40] This sentiment is precisely the same spirit of Pyrolator's valuation of the Brontologic's capacity to make "music without faults." That music was not about musical errors, but rather music that did not contain the error of repeating ideological source material. Against that serious musician and their "obsessive repetition," Doris amplified awareness of abstraction and difference through the idea of "permanent absence." Fundamental for the constitution of the band, absence—of normative affect, of progress, of the material itself—was also at the core of its products. And while the dialectical sounds and synthetic phenomenology that materialize the immaterial "Invisible LP" could be read as the inverse to the quantum qualities of Pyrolator's Brontologic, that would dismiss the abstraction meted out on the original sounds. Differentiated source material turned over to an unknown layman for further differentiation, the amoeba of Doris's "7-headed informer" metamorphosed with the "Invisible LP" through another dilletant (sic). Distributing potential rather than certainty, the band shows how despite its ridiculous amount of self-theorizing, Doris did not proselytize the relevance of theory for music. Rather, they made music as theory and thereby vacated the ideological distinction between the philosophy of noise, the aesthetics of classical music, and the tyranny of the genius-cum-authoritarian that ran to the core of bracketed experience in "klammheimlich."[41]

Though often a boogeyman for punks, the band Kraftwerk and their contemporaneous use of an early variant of the vocoder are an accurate foil to illustrate how post punk's technological differentiations represents a distinct shift in the perceptions of and absoluteness of experience. The vocoder examines speech by measuring how its spectral characteristics change over time and splits the original into a number of bands. Distinct from the processes to which post punk submitted their source material, a vocoder functions automatically and as such signifies an emergent technology with the capacity to sonically level and bracket (aural) experience. That musical practice is part metaphor, part reality for the affective and experiential leveling in the Federal Republic because vocoders signal the ability to produce music—that is to say, to engage the materiality of perception—better than their actual engagement therewith would normally allow, that is, without automated technological assistance. As such, deploying a vocoder makes everyone's engagement with soundscapes flawless in the opposite sense of Pyrolator's. Without ever having to truly reckon with soundscapes of the present past, that iteration of technology levels associative experience because it levels psychophysical possibilities. And while Die tödliche Doris and Pyrolator may qualitatively sound like a tradition of anti-institutional aesthetic practices, quantitatively their misuse of analog sounds does not just rehash avant-garde practices; their difference in kind must not be heard as difference in degree. Rather, through sonic antagonism in the interest in remainder positions, the bands' music signals the potential to escape the loop of West German identity and countercultural production by discovering holes in existent technologies and projecting potential change through these holes. Against the naïve reenactment of known possibilities in obsessive repetition, their amorphous sonic architecture aimed at the production of a technological sound able to rip itself from the centripetal forces of West German obsessive repetition. While the songs in this article are read as evidence thereof, the ultimate failures of these bands to alter the mainstream listening and production processes, the affective intersection of experience and fantasy, can be heard in the global dominance of the vocoder's technologically advanced present: autotune. The global dominance of that advanced audio processor and its automatic pitch shifting poses, in light of the potential in precision engagement with sonic technology, an existential threat to the "aesthetic[s] of defamiliarization" and differentiation; that is, to the subversive possibilities of musiking.[42] But the obstinacy of materiality in the hands of contemporary DJs—records—and the dynamic sonic space of a dance floor certainly demark a potential to work against that threat. The subjects in those environments retain the capacity to harness potential from information's sonic flows as they process aesthetics for a politics of the self.

CYRUS SHAHAN, academia emeritus, is an independent scholar. He is the author of *Punk Rock and German Crisis: Adaptation and Resistance after 1977* (New York, 2013), co-editor of *Beyond No Future: Cultures of German Punk* (New York, 2016), and author of articles on the intersections of terrorism and technology, violence and aesthetics, music and gender, and Alexander Kluge and Peter Sloterdijk.

Notes

1. Throughout this article, the concept "post punk" is used not to distinguish genres, but rather to signal a temporal difference between the original moment of punk in West Germany—1977—and the subculture after 1978. Unless otherwise noted, all translations throughout this article are my own. I thank Sabine Hake, Alex Fulk, and the University of Texas Department of Germanic Studies for inviting me to present this research. I also thank my colleagues Mirko M. Hall and Seth Howes for their input and conversations on earlier versions of this article.
2. See Thomas Meinecke, cover notes, Pyrolator and A. K. Klosowski, *Home Taping is Killing Music*, Ata Tak, 1982, LP.
3. For more on the media and its representations of punk's present, see: Wolfgang Müller, *Subkultur Westberlin 1979-1989* (Hamburg, 2014).

4. See Gilles Deleuze, *Difference and Repetition*, trans. Paul Patton (London, 2004). See also Gilles Deleuze and Felix Guattari, *A Thousand Plateaus: Capitalism and Schizophrenia*, trans. Brian Massumi (Minneapolis, 1987), 310-350, and Simon O'Sullivan and Stephen Zepke, *Deleuze, Guattari and the Production of the New* (London, 2008).
5. Alexander Kluge and Oskar Negt, *History and Obstinacy*, trans. Richard Langston, Cyrus Shahan et. al. (New York, 2014), 144-145. In a musical-historical frame, Kluge and Negt provide both an appraisal of the compulsion to the new in rock music, and in a sociopolitical context of the Cold War, of the logic of escalation and the assurance of mutual annihilation. On a level more directly in line with my narrative, they provide a means of escaping the compulsion to genre definitions, a random moniker given authority due to the preference of record labels and their marketing programs.
6. Kluge and Negt (see note 5), 140.
7. For more on the influence of the Brothers Grimm, the idea of forests, Germanness, and the politics of reclaiming from National Socialism's these tropes, see, for example, Kluge and Negt (see note 5); Jack Zipes, "The Struggle for the Grimm's Throne: The Legacy of the Grimms' Tales in the FRG and GDR since 1945" in *The Reception of Grimm's Fairy Tales: Responses, Reactions, Revisions*, ed. Donald Haase (Detroit, 1993); Margarete Johanna Landwehr, "Märchen as Trauma Narrative: Helma Sanders-Brahms's Film *Germany, Pale Mother*" in *Folklore/Cinema: Popular Film as Vernacular Culture*, ed. Sharon R. Sherman and Mikel J. Koven (Logan, 2007), or more recently the film *Deutschland. Ein Sommermärchen*, directed by Sönke Wortmann, Little Shark Entertainment GmbH and Westdeutscher Rundfunk (WDR), 2006, DVD; or *Die Patriotin*, directed by Alexander Kluge, Karos-Film, 1979, DVD.
8. Alexander Kluge and Oskar Negt, *History and Obstinacy* (unpublished draft, 5 October 2011) Word Document file.
9. McKenzie Wark, *A Hacker Manifesto* (Cambridge, 2004), §214.
10. Kluge and Negt (see note 8).
11. Ralf Dörper, *Die Düsseldorfer Leere* #1 (1979).
12. C. D. Blanton, "Theory by Analogy," *PMLA* 130, no. 3 (2015): 750-758, here 756.
13. See S.Y.P.H.'s song "Zurück zum Beton" *S.Y.P.H.*, Pure Freude, 1980, LP.
14. Wark (see note 9), 008.
15. Ibid., 015.
16. Müller mocked Kippenberger's painting "With the best will in the world I can't find a Swastika [Hackenkreuz]" in a 1980 photograph taken by Elfi Fröhlich that Müller titled "With the best will I can't find a 'hair cross' [Haarkreuz]." Image available on Müller's website section "Musik;" available at http://www.wolfgangmuellerrr.de/Musik, accessed 11 October 2016.
17. Müller's website, "Musik."
18. The band Der 1. Futurologische Congress (named after a novel by the Polish science fiction author Stanislav Lem) was conceived as an open project by its three core members; 1. FC eventually had six members and at times performed with seventeen musicians.
19. Deleuze and Guattari (see note 4), 21-22. It is unsurprising that Müller would use language strikingly similar to Deleuze and Guatarri, since the Berlin-based Merve publishing house published German-language versions of the two philosophers' work as well as Müller's edited collection, *Geniale Dilletanten* (Berlin, 1982).
20. In his subterfuge of the canonical *Musik in Geschichte und Gegenwart*, punk Frieder Butzmann (wryly) supports Doris being out of place in an article on electronics and German music. Butzmann defines Die tödliche Doris as a "band with little electronics," the opposite of a group such as Tangerine Dream. Of course, the opposite of a band such as Tangerine Dream was precisely what Doris was aiming for. The "little" electronics, as such, is more an assessment to the ceding of authority to devices than presence thereof. Freider Butzmann, *Musik im Grossen und Ganzen* (Berlin, 2008), 83.
21. Wark (see note 9), 008.

22. The sound is so jarringly out of synch with the rest of the song, it seems as if an intertextual play is afoot, one harkening back to the automaton Olimpia of E.T.A. Hoffmann's "The Sandman," whose faux life-like characteristics fooled the romantically delusional Nathaniel. Here the romantically delusional would be, on the one side, those sowing the seeds of Germanness in classical, fairytale-like ways. On the other side would be those artists too wedded to a single form of representation.
23. My use of the short-handed definition of insanity is not metaphorical, but rather is indicative of punk's assessment of its present as such (an assessment shared by the host of postwar subcultures).
24. Yves Citton, "Learning to Read in the Digital Age: From Reading Texts to Hacking Codes," *PMLA* 130, no. 3 (2015): 743-749, here 745.
25. Wolfgang Müller, "Kann maN etWas mACHen, was nicht Musik ist?" in *Spannung. Leistung. Widerstand. Magnetbanduntergrund DDR 1979-1990*, ed. Alexander Pehlemann and Ronald Galenza (Berlin, 2006) 150-155.
26. Müller (see note 19), 14 n5.
27. Ibid., 32, 47-49, and 66, respectively
28. Wark (see note 9), 020.
29. On one level, the "Invisible LP" replicated the band's own use of tea kettles when it demanded listeners use multiple record players. That demand implicated human as-and-in technology and technology in-and-as human. But this fusion is not Kraftwerk's famous machine-man, a project much more about reclaiming technology from the legacies of National Socialism.
30. Müller website "Musik" (see note 16).
31. "The Brontologic" *Matrixsynth: Everything Synth*, 13 February 2006; available at http://www.matrixsynth.com/2006/02/brontologic.html, accessed 11 October 2016.
32. The album shares its name with the 1980s antipirating campaign "Home Taping is Killing Music."
33. Kluge and Negt (see note 5), 143.
34. For much of this description I draw from the description of the Brontologic available at http://www.matrixsynth.com/2006/02/brontologic.html, accessed 13 April 2017; and Pyrolator's own comments and informative videos linked to this website. I am also indebted to N. Katherine Hayles's *Writing Machines* (Cambridge, 2002).
35. As the Internet would have it, "What Made You So No Good" from "Home Taping" was featured on the WFMU show "Busy Doing Nothing With Charlie" on 2 February 2015, almost a year prior to the drafting of this article; available at https://wfmu.org/playlists/shows/59288, accessed 14 January 2016.
36. "Autobahn" signals Kraftwerk's transition to making a *Gesamtkunstwerk* (total work of art), this is not the case for "Home Taping." For more on Kraftwerk and the total work of art see Ulrich Adelt, "Machines with a Heart: German Identity in the Music of Can and Kraftwerk," *Popular Music and Society* 35, no. 3 (2012): 359-374, here 368. Alternately, see John T. Littlejohn "Kraftwerk: Language, Lucre, and Loss of Identity," *Popular Music and Society* 32, no. 5 (2009): 635-653.
37. Kluge and Negt (see note 8).
38. "The Brontologic" (see note 34).
39. See Kluge and Negt (see note 8).
40. Müller (see note 19), 14 n5, my emphasis.
41. Beyond the scope of this article is an inquiry to the intersection between Doris's demands for its listeners to play two records simultaneously and the work of DJs. Additionally, Doris's demand locates their project and their fans as subject to a core critique of so many youth subcultures, namely the socioeconomic privilege required to enact Doris's "Invisible LP" (free time and purchasing power for records and multiple LP players).
42. Mirko M. Hall, *Musical Revolutions in German Culture: Musiking Against the Grain, 1800-1980* (New York, 2014), 5.

Chapter 3

WENN EINE BAND LANGE ZEIT LEBT

Puhdys, Politics, and Popularity
John Littlejohn

Any history of East German rock music that overlooked the Puhdys would necessarily be incomplete. The Puhdys, founded in 1969, became the best-known and most popular rock band of the German Democratic Republic (GDR), selling more than twice as many albums as their nearest competitor, and producing the top song in the country's annual hit parade six times between 1976 and 1984. The band continued to record and perform long after reunification, in fact, finishing their last tour with a concert on 2 January 2016.

A lot of people hate the Puhdys. Some rock fans, journalists, and critics have berated the group as pawns of the state or *Anpasser* who only achieved their place atop the East German music business by staying well within the lines prescribed for Ost-Rock by state officials. The East German's government decision to award the Puhdys the National Prize Second Class for Art and Literature gave the naysayers further reason to hate or dismiss the band. This sign of state approval took away significant public credibility and alienated the Puhdys from large parts of the East German rock community.[1]

All rock musicians in the GDR found themselves pulled on one side by the authorities and on the other by their audience. In this contentious atmosphere, the Puhdys managed to survive and indeed to thrive. It would prove enlightening to examine the ways the band rose to the forefront of the East German rock scene and laid the groundwork for their enduring success. An analysis of the band's early work, collected on the band's first, eponymous album[2] provides an optimal case study. Such an analysis reveals why the Puhdys rose to the top and stayed there: more than a modicum of luck–but also a great deal of talent and political savvy.

Notes for this chapter begin on page 59.

To understand the rise of the Puhdys, one must first understand the cultural and political environment facing rock musicians in the GDR. From the earliest days of rock music in East Germany until the fall of the Wall, the government could not or would not embrace the music or the youth movement around it. Patricia Anne Simpson notes that "the history of official reception [of rock music] alternates between efforts at resistance and cooptation."[3] In essence, between the government's attempts to eradicate rock music existed waves of grudging acceptance, during which the government attempted to manipulate the music to its own ends.

The initial rock and roll craze hit East Germany in the 1950s around the same time as West Germany. Almost immediately, the authorities demonstrated their desire for the control–if not elimination–of rock music. Again, Simpson notes: "As early as 1958, Walter Ulbricht called for an end to the influx of '…currently mass produced (musical) products of dubious origin.' He wanted instead music that would contribute to the construction of the socialist personality."[4] Rock and roll came from the West, and was therefore "decadent" by its very nature, and "worse still, it was seen as an instrument of the enemy, deliberately targeted at the Republic's youth in an effort to make them hostile to the principles of Socialism."[5] It was also in 1958 that the government implemented the quota for music on the airwaves and in live performances. The quota allowed a maximum of 40 percent of music played to come from the West, whereas at least 60 percent of music had to come from the GDR or other East Bloc countries. It was at the end of this decade that the East German authorities came up with the "Lipsi," an awkward and artificial alternative to rock and roll, one that thoroughly earned the derision it received from GDR youth.

In the 1960s, thousands of rock groups formed all around East Germany, including an early version of the Puhdys, and it was at this time that the government policy toward rock music truly began its vacillations. In September 1963, the Politburo issued "Youth Trust and Responsibility" (Der Jugend Vertrauen und Verantwortung), a communiqué that "launched an amazing liberalization–and at the same time justified the Party's claim of competency in all matters dealing with the development of popular music."[6] This liberalization occurred during the great wave of beat music[7] spearheaded by the Beatles. AMIGA–the popular music branch of the state record company VEB Deutsche Schallplatten–even licensed and released a Beatles album during this period. This era of relative openness towards rock music did not last long. 1965 saw a series of official moves that restricted rock and reestablished the government's anti-rock agenda. In the fall of that year, for instance, all "guitar groups" were banned in Leipzig, a leading city for rock music in East

Germany at the time.[8] The infamous Eleventh Plenum of the Central Committee, which took place in December, marked the end of this brief period of cultural liberalization.[9] The Central Committee decided here "that rock music was not and could not be in accordance with the goals of a socialist society,"[10] while Erich Honecker–then Security Secretary of the Socialist Unity Party's (SED) Central Committee–repeats the old accusation that the opponents of communism are using this music to negatively influence the youth of East Germany.[11] As Peter Wicke notes: "The fact that Honecker, who was in charge of security, gave the report of the Politburo at this meeting which was devoted to culture and ideology, was of vast symbolic significance. From then on, it was the security forces who determined what was aesthetically acceptable."[12] This antagonistic attitude to rock music from official channels remained for the rest of the decade, although restrictions began to slowly relax beginning in 1967.[13]

The end of the 1960s and particularly the beginning of the 1970s brought major changes for rock music and many other segments of artistic and intellectual life in East Germany. One major cause of these changes was, ironically, Honecker's rise to head of state upon the resignation of Walter Ulbricht in May 1971. In December of that year, Honecker famously declared that "When one starts out from a solid socialist position, in my opinion there can be no taboos in the realm of art and literature."[14] In the first years of Honecker's regime, the authorities did indeed become relatively permissive, even allowing publication of controversial works such as Ulrich Plenzdorf's *Die neuen Leiden des jungen W.* (*The New Sorrows of Young W*). Ian Wallace sums up this period tidily: "The years between 1971 and 1976 can be regarded as the honeymoon period in Honecker's cultural policy, years of hope in which it seemed possible that an atmosphere of trust between the Party and the different branches of the arts might gradually be built up."[15]

Honecker's stated policy of "no taboos" undoubtedly contributed to the emergence of rock and roll in East German, but this policy was far from the only factor leading to the official reception of rock music in the early 1970s. By this time, the state had "clearly lost" the battle it had been waging against rock for well over a decade.[16] Radio contributed greatly to this defeat. The vast majority of East German citizens could receive West German radio and television,[17] so they were exposed to Western rock music through innumerable direct and indirect means. Not only did they have to try to pull the youth audience away from Western radio, they had to do so while adhering to the 60/40 quota. The situation became even more dire after 1973, when Honecker declared the East German citizens were allowed to tune in to West German radio and television,[18] which, of course, many had been doing for years anyway. GDR radio desperately needed more material from homegrown artists. In late 1969, because of pressures both external and internal, the Central Committee's Department of Agitation began to actively encourage GDR radio to produce more of its own dance music for the youth of the country, a move that amounted to a tacit recognition of rock music.[19] With this directive, East German radio increasingly focused on the youth audience in the early 1970s.

Instead of fighting rock music, the GDR now began to support it. For this support, however, the authorities expected (if not demanded) rock music to serve a pedagogical function: to expand commitment to the government's brand of socialism and, indeed, to mold listeners into active socialists.[20] In April 1972, the GDR ministry of culture held a dance music conference (*Tanzmusikkonferenz*), which had the dual purpose of recognizing rock in an official fashion and to proscribe the ways that the music would function in East Germany.[21] The conference, and Honecker's new openness with the arts, set the stage for the GDR to proudly present its native rock acts at the Tenth World Festival of Youth and Students (*Weltfestspiele*), which took place in East Berlin in the summer of 1973. For the *Weltfestspiele*, East Berlin played host to over 25,000 visitors from 140 foreign countries, along with over a half-million GDR citizens.[22]

Just months before the *Weltfestspiele*, and a full year after the *Tanzmusikkonferenz*, the government made a rather tardy maneuver. As Timothy Ryback cheekily notes:

> In April 1973, East Germany, in good socialist fashion, braced itself for the official rehabilitation of *Beatmusik* by creating a bureaucratic mechanism. The Committee for Entertainment Music, under the aegis of the Ministry of Culture and manned by ideologically "sound" individuals, was intended to police the development of official rock music.[23]

Of course, the GDR already had several ways to control its musicians. For starters, the state controlled the only record company. All bands furthermore needed a *Spielerlaubnis* (permission to play) from the government to play music, and musicians were compelled to go to state-run music schools in order to attain professional status. Just as the government regulation of rock music did not achieve anything resembling stability over time, neither did it remain consistent across governing bodies:

> The political reins were held ... by the Departments of Security, Youth, and Agitation in the Central Committee. Thus it was not a homogenous political-bureaucratic apparatus that reigned over cultural affairs, but rather a tangle of administrative agencies, official channels, and commissions, with differing, often even contradictory premises, not infrequently engaged in petty warfare with each other, and united at best by their general incompetence.[24]

An example of the workings of this "ill-functioning, loosely connected network of rival centres of power, ... capable of reversing decisions which other official bodies had taken,"[25] occurred when the television show *Ein Kessel Buntes* (*A Kettle of Color*) barred the Puhdys from playing "Wenn ein Mensch lebt," although the song had already proven popular both on the radio and in the DEFA film *Die Legende von Paul und Paula* (*The Legend of Paul and Paula*).[26] Instances of similar occurrences are innumerable.[27]

Of course, history shows that the aforementioned honeymoon period in Honecker's cultural policy proved short lived, and even the façade of liberalization in the arts disappeared quickly. By 1974, rock musicians and their audiences had increasingly found themselves under attack from the Stasi,[28] and the following year a more severe maneuver occurred: government officials informed the Klaus Renft Combo that they were banned, and that the group in fact no longer existed. Renft's ban was no insignificant act. The group had attained a position as one of the most popular groups in the GDR and had released two of the earliest GDR rock albums, *Klaus Renft Combo* (1973) and *Renft* (1974). The ban on the Renft Combo sent shockwaves around the rock scene, but the deprivation of singer-songwriter Wolf Biermann's citizenship in 1976 far surpassed it in terms of cultural significance. In the aftermath of Biermann's expatriation, cultural lines were drawn as artists from many fields took a stance for or against the government's action. The government could no longer pretend that restrictions were gradually easing or that there were no taboos. The "honeymoon" was over.

By this time, the Puhdys had established themselves at the top of GDR Rock. The group's classic line-up consisted of Dieter Birr, Peter Meyer, Dieter Hertrampf, Harry Jeske, and Gunther Wosylus. This version of the group stayed constant for ten years, from the band's beginning in 1969 until 1979.[29] Klaus Scharfschwerdt replaced Wosylus on drums at that time, in what would be the band's lone personnel change before reunification. The second and latest line-up change occurred when bassist Peter Rasym took over on bass guitar upon Jeske's departure. Birr (guitar/vocals), Meyer (keyboards/saxophone), and Hertrampf (guitar/vocals) remain with the band to this day.

Within two years of its beginning, the band had already achieved a devoted following through their live performances playing cover versions of acts like Led Zeppelin, Deep Purple, and Uriah Heep. It was that following that helped the Puhdys land their first television performance: 154 fan requests for the band led directly to the band's wildly successful appearance on the youth program *Basar* (Bazaar) in 1971.[30] Their career skyrocketed. In 1972, for instance, the Puhdys had enormous success with the song "Geh dem Wind nicht aus dem Wege" ("Don't Go Out of the Wind's Way"), which held the top spot in the charts for months on end.[31]

The group extended its reach into the realm of cinema with *Die Legende von Paul und Paula*, which features three Puhdys songs and boasts an appearance by the band itself. One should not underestimate the importance of this film for the band. Indeed, Rühmann has gone so far as to say that "the Puhdys' career began in the cinema."[32] The band's high-profile performance in this film added an extra dimension to the Puhdy's reception by the authorities and by the public. The film was, of course, a DEFA production, and therefore officially sanctioned by the state. Though some critics condemned the film's negative depiction of life in the GDR, *Die Legende von Paul und Paula* became a blockbuster hit.[33] This movie therefore proves analogous to the Puhdys, the band whose songs play and who appear in it: the state-approved film presents a potential critique of that state, just as the Puhdys' music convey a potentially critical message in several of their releases. Those audience members who appreciated (or were heartened by) the film's critique could also notice the similar position of the band. Furthermore, the concomitant approval of the band and its music within the film would make the band more popular and therefore more difficult to censor and less susceptible to a ban (*Spielverbot*)–if the band were not too emphatic in their criticisms. *Die Legende von Paul und Paula* thus helped cement the band's place with the government as well as the public.

Osman Durrani states that "many groups … proved willing to produce songs that were compatible with the official ideology," and refers to the Puhdys' "Vorn ist das Licht" ("The Light Is Ahead") as an example.[34] The song may be "compatible with the official ideology" as Durrani claims–indeed that compatibility undoubtedly played an important role in the authorities' supporting the song and therefore the group. Nonetheless, even this song–perhaps the key song in terms of establishing the band's viability to the GDR authorities–proves itself an example of the group's ability to come up with a song whose sentiments could either please or frustrate the GDR authorities, depending on which aspects of the song they focus on. Many tracks on the Puhdys' first album, which is largely a collection of the early songs which had established their recording career, performed this same task of creating an ambiguous message towards the East German government. "Vorn ist das Licht," however, merits particular attention, not only because it doubly receives pride of place as both the Puhdys' first single and as the opening track on the band's first album, but also due to its critical reputation as a sell-out move, as demonstrated by Durrani's quote above.

The song's potential pro-government message stands out conspicuously. The title "Vorn ist das Licht" and much of its lyrics carry a resolutely positive message. The voices of the band harmonizing on the title at the beginning of the song and throughout bears an echo which makes it sound like there is a large group of people singing together. This makes the connection to the "tausend Zungen" (thousands of tongues) in the lyrics, as well as to the theme of communal effort that the song as a whole conveys.

The song's notion of movement toward a goal–in fact, of any movement forward–would be a very promising message for the powers that be. The "generation born in the 1950s ... did not share their elders' unconditional belief in the concept of historical progress. As Leeder writes: 'the narrative of history [had] degenerated into almost terminal stagnation.'"[35] The simple use of the word "vorn" (ahead) implies that motion, and the light ahead clearly indicates a positive end result. The Puhdys' use of such an uplifting message would please the authorities who had long realized that rock and roll played a powerful role in the lives, fashion, and outlook of the youth in the GDR, as it did all around the world. If rockers project a bright future in their songs, as the Puhdys do here, that optimism could spread to the youth – a very important point, because "in socialism, people are optimists!"[36]

Despite the apparently clear political message at the surface, "Vorn ist das Licht" is by no means a patently pro-government song. For instance, the optimism within this song may reverberate so strongly due to its religious undercurrent. Indeed, the mention of the actual end of life in the song brings to mind the afterlife and the religious nature of the message that would have been pleasing to many religious people within East Germany who were persecuted or shunned on some level because of their beliefs. And though the GDR desired positive messages like the one in "Vorn ist das Licht," the positivity here is vague. Instead of a communist utopia, the song could depict a simple generic optimism, a Christian version of heaven, or even a day when the stagnant, stagnating East German government collapses.

The lack of political specificity in "Vorn ist das Licht" distinctly weakens any pro-government message contained in the song. The vagueness here does not, however, necessarily constitute a flaw. Indeed, the Puhdys aggressively undercut any messages that could be perceived as government friendly through their multivalent lyrics and music on this and several other recordings from this period. The level of subtlety apparent in this strategy has largely gone overlooked by critics.

The first few seconds of "Vorn ist das Licht" are instructional. The song begins with tympani (or tympani-like drums), in a manner very reminiscent of Richard Strauss's tone poem *Also sprach Zarathustra*. The opening chorus builds upon that resemblance, with the vocals taking the place of the Strauss's brass. The allusion to this Strauss piece works on multiple levels. The opening section of *Also sprach Zarathustra* to which the beginning of the song harkens back is entitled "Einleitung, oder Sonnenaufgang" ("Introduction, or Sunrise"). On the most basic level, this section of "Vorn ist das Licht" is the song's introduction, and the sunrise naturally has connections to the light to which the song refers. Beyond that, the different generations could perceive that reference differently. Members of the older generation, particularly the well-educated ones who yielded the political power, could see how the intertextual allusions to *Also sprach Zarathustra* draw a line to earlier Germans Strauss and Friedrich Nietzsche. These connections emphasize the proud German lineage of the Puhdys, rather than their links to Anglo-American artists to which all rock and roll owes a great debt. While the older generation could make these associations, members of the younger generation potentially knew Strauss's music from Stanley Kubrick's *2001: A Space Odyssey* (1968), and they might find the association to the hominid man-apes smashing around violently among the bones of the dead either amusing or painfully apt.

One also notes the similarity of the guitar entrance here to the opening guitar riff from the 1969 hit "Fortunate Son" by Creedence Clearwater Revival.[37] Again, the intertextual link could produce a message which could please, or disturb, sharp-eared censors. On the one hand, "Fortunate Son" expressly criticized American culture, particularly focusing on the way in which the unequal distribution of wealth in this capitalist nation results in the creation of "have-nots" as well as "haves." On the other hand, however, the anti-authoritarian, anti-government theme shines through as well, something the censors would be loath to propagate.

"Vorn ist das Licht" is only one of the early Puhdys tracks which transmit multiple, conflicting messages which may be dissected in different ways depending on the listener. "Vorn ist das Licht" has a text and music which, on the one hand, convey a surface message that pleased East German censors and has frustrated the large number of rock listeners and critics, yet, on the other hand, simultaneously weakens that message by several different means. "Ikarus" ("Icarus") serves as a counterpart to "Vorn ist das Licht," as it accomplishes much the same feat in reverse.

The song "Ikarus" sketches the mythological story of Icarus and his inventor father Dædalus, who crafts wings so they can escape their imprisonment on Crete. The father tells his son to follow in his path and warns him not to fly too high or too low. Icarus does not listen and flies too close to the sun, whereupon the wax in his wings melts and he falls into the sea and drowns.

The father in the song represents the authority not only of the older generation, but also of the regime. The Icarus myth conveys the message that the young will perish if they refuse to heed the warning of the older generation that knows what is best: a message, of course, that GDR authorities would gladly slip into the consciousness of rebellious young East Germans by means of a popular rock group. While the song does not entirely escape its origins in that myth, however, the band's interpretation of it emphasizes the character Icarus and particularly how he enjoys his freedom. "This text is potential dynamite; it fully endorses the desires of the youth whose home was too 'narrow' for his aspirations. Against the advice of his elders, the young adventurer flies off, and although he is killed, his death is hailed as a victory."[38] Despite its origins in a myth that emphasizes the wisdom and experience of the older generation, "Ikarus" exalts the willfulness of youth. The band holds Icarus up as a role model: "Fliege uns voraus!...Zeige uns den Weg!" and "Doch der erste war er. Viele folgten ihm."[39] In this song, Icarus becomes an archetypal rock and roll hero: he rebels against authority and does exactly what he wants, even if it is to his own detriment. The shift into the present tense in the last verse of the song implicitly extends Icarus's influence to the present, where he serves as a hero to today's youth. With the line "Er heisst Ikarus und ist immer jung,"[40] the lyrics proclaim that his anti-authoritarian message will live forever. The propulsive music, among the best (though not among the best-mixed) of the early Puhdys recordings, carries the listener along as Icarus climbs, flies, and shows us the way.

"Ikarus" is only one of many songs off the first Puhdys album to prominently mention flight. Almost half of the songs (four of ten)[41] contains forms of the word "fliegen" or other allusions to flight. "Von der Liebe ein Lied" ("Lovedreams"), the second song on the album, for instance, begins with the verse "Wieg dich wie ein Segel leicht / Flieg als Vogel unerreicht / Rinn als Sand durch meine Hand."[42] The verse speaks not only of flight, but also of multiple layers of escape. Inasmuch as these last two lines are commands, the band appears to urge its audience to escape. These lyrics do not constitute a particularly GDR -friendly message by a group derided as "*Staatsrocker*" (state rockers).[43]

Of course, other East German rock bands used the theme of flight as a basic metaphor for freedom in their songs: "Over the years, the musicians managed even more successfully to establish a political discourse about society and social realities in the metaphorical lyrics of their songs, such as those about flying, which served as a code to highlight unnatural restrictions against travel."[44] Yet the Puhdys served as the trendsetters, numbering among the first rock groups to so prominently implement the imagery of flight in their songs. They had greater success with this imagery than their contemporaries like the Klaus Renft Combo, whose "... songs about flight, escape, and a meaningless existence did not please the state."[45] The Puhdys possessed the ability to maneuver themselves into a space relatively safe from officially reprisals. Yet such maneuvering does not amount to compromising their anti-authoritarian rock and roll principles. By releasing a song such as "Ikarus," which carries multivalent messages on the topics of freedom and authority, the group could also release a song full of longing like "Von der Liebe ein Lied," peppered as it is with its imagery of flight and commands for the audience to fly and escape.

The song immediately following "Ikarus" on side two of this debut album is one of the Puhdys' best-known songs, and one familiar to the public from *Die Legende von Paul und Paula*. This song, "Geh zu ihr" ("Go to Her"), avails itself of the same flight imagery as "Ikarus," though it uses it in a different way. Whereas the negative aspect of freedom—as depicted in the theme of flight—stays much to the fore in "Ikarus," due to the myth on which it is based, the positive aspects appear more prominent in "Geh zu ihr." Nonetheless, just as the positive aspects of freedom come to light in the first song, the negative aspects of freedom remain present in the second.

"Geh zu ihr" gives the command: "lass Deinen Drachen steigen."[46] In a time and place where artists commonly used metaphors to avoid a direct criticism of state authorities, "Geh zu ihr und lass Deinen Drahen steigen" could mean any number of things: "One could think of all manner of things with that, because thoughts are free. For one person it was simply a love song, for another person the pronounced longing for freedom."[47] Along with the obvious sexual connotations—underlined by the song's placement within the aforementioned movie, the image of the kite summons thoughts of flight and youthful freedom. While the flying of the kite presents such a positive, carefree image, the thought of flight is mitigated, as is the case with the myth of Icarus in the previous song. Kites have to remain tethered down. If not, the kite flies away recklessly, similar to the fall of Icarus into the sea. These images of flight in "Ikarus" and "Geh zu ihr" carry an inherent warning: though free flight is possible, it may also prove destructive, leading inevitably to dire, if not fatal, consequences. This aspect of the flight message could please the government censors who hear and judge the songs. Nonetheless, the very possibility of flight overwhelms and negates any possible consequences, particularly for the group's primarily youthful audience.

"Wenn ein Mensch lebt" ("When a Person Lives") is yet another track which sees the Puhdys treading a fine line with a complex message. It may at first appear odd for one to call the song's lyrics controversial, inasmuch as they are a rather innocuous mixture of the philosophical and the romantic. However, it is not so much their literal meaning, but rather their complex history which would be problematic to GDR authorities. A large part of the text comes from the Bible, specifically from the third chapter of Ecclesiastes in the Old Testament.[48] Having yet another song with religious overtones, along with "Vorn ist das Licht," already presents one strike against the song. On top of this, the Puhdys allude to another text, one potentially more serious in light of the precarious position of rock music in the GDR at that time. The section of Ecclesiastes that appears in "Wenn ein Mensch lebt" had already been used in a rock context, in the song "Turn, Turn, Turn" by the American band the Byrds. The song was a major hit in the United States and Europe in late 1965, and as such could be regarded as a product of the capitalist enemy. A factor mitigating government disapproval may be that "Turn, Turn, Turn" was written by Pete Seeger, a staunchly leftist songwriter who had felt the wrath of the United States because of his political beliefs and had visited East Germany in the late 1960s.

Ulrich Plenzdorf, who wrote the lyrics to "Geh zu ihr" likewise crafted the text to "Wenn ein Mensch lebt." Plenzdorf's most famous work is *Die neuen Leiden des jungen W.*, a politicized update of Goethe's *Die Leiden des jungen Werther*. This work was written in the late 1960s, but could only be published—albeit with significant changes—after the government change from Ulbricht to Honecker. Plenzdorf therefore was both fully aware of the extent to which he could go with his intertextual references before feeling the sting of censorship and also expert in the use of those references.

"Wenn ein Mensch lebt" proves itself to be exemplary of the early work of the Puhdys. Its text provides layered references to multiple texts and themes disfavored by the communist authorities, yet within that text also lies the implicit, redeeming reference to Seeger. The Puhdys' young rock audience would most likely recognize the lyrical similarity to "Turn, Turn, Turn," yet those people who were both in positions of power in the GDR and sufficiently versed in Western rock music to recognize the Byrds' song would likely also be culturally aware enough to know about the song's author. Seeger's leftist credentials therefore sanctify the decadence of the Western pop song to which "Wenn ein Mensch lebt" hearkens back. As with "Ikarus," "Geh zu ihr," and other songs on this album, the Puhdys do not openly question the East German government, its policies, or its authority in "Wenn ein Mensch lebt." Yet with these songs, the Puhdys create a space of rebellion easily comprehensible to its fans. Nevertheless, the songwriters craft lyrics and music so artfully that they do not compel officials to act against them. The album's sequencing merits discussion and should provide insight into the Puhdys and their—at the time still tenuous—relationship to the GDR cultural authorities:

SIDE ONE:	SIDE TWO:
"Vorn ist das Licht"	"Sommernacht"
"Von der Liebe ein Lied"	"Ikarus"
"Mann im Mond"	"Geh zu ihr"
"Vineta"	"Wenn ein Mensch lebt"
"Türen öffnen sich zur Stadt"	"Zeiten und Weiten"

"Vorn ist das Licht" has pride of place as the opening track on *Die Puhdys*. Of all the songs on the album, "Vorn ist das Licht" contains the text most in line with party doctrine. In fact, "Vorn ist das Licht" is arguably the only song of the ten on this album with a message predominantly positive towards the GDR authorities, although even this song contains undercurrents that run contrary to official policy, as shown above. The Puhdys also imbue "Ikarus," "Geh zu ihr," and "Wenn ein Mensch lebt" with multiple meanings, which may be read by the listener as standing for or against the government, depending upon one's perspective. Unlike "Vorn ist das Licht," however, the messages in these three songs tend towards the anti-authoritarian. One cannot help notice that three songs appear on the album's second side—the side generally heard less—despite their popularity. One further notes that the two songs whose lyrics convey a message aimed most specifically at their anti-authoritarian rock audiences—"Türen öffnen sich zur Stadt" ("Doors Open to the City") and "Zeiten und Weiten" ("Times and Expanses")—find themselves buried at the end of each side.

Unfortunately, perhaps, having "Vorn ist das Licht" as the lead track of their first album may have affected the audience's perception of the Puhdys. The song that listeners most frequently hear can, on its surface, sound like a love letter to the regime. Different sequencing may have altered the public and critical reception of the group. If "Zeiten und Weiten" or "Ikarus" led off the album, the audience may more easily notice the anti-authoritarian aspects of some of the band's music.[49] But inasmuch as the track listing obfuscates the relatively controversial and rebellious songs on the albums—and incidentally does so to an even greater degree in CD format—one can easily understand how those listeners began to think of the group as *Staatsrocker*, even though the band forged a significantly more complex relationship to the government—and to its audience—than some would believe. Alternately, the sheer success of the Puhdys may have led to backlash anyway, partially from envy and partially from the idea that no one can succeed without the help of the authorities.

The Puhdys' success stemmed largely from the group's own expertise in communicating multivalent themes in their material. Yet, outside forces did greatly contribute to the band's success, though not necessarily those forces which critics have claimed, that is, that the GDR authorities supported the Puhdys in order to make them pawns. Some of the factors that led to the Puhdys' success do, however, derive from the government's policies and the changes thereto.

As mentioned above, Honecker ascended to the leadership of East Germany in 1971, just as the Puhdys were rising in popularity. The band, like many other artists, benefitted from the honeymoon period in the first half of 1970s when Honecker allowed somewhat greater artistic freedom. As the members of the band had been in the music business for years, however, they knew very well the fluctuations that the GDR authorities—and Honecker in particular—had undergone during the last decade with regard to their stance on so-called "beat music." With that knowledge, they abstained from delivering a one-sided political or social message that could spell the end of the band if history repeated itself—as indeed it did.

The government's subtle but palpable encouragement of GDR radio to broadcast rock music at the very end of the 1960s and in the early 1970s also represented a fundamental, and fortuitous, change that contributed significantly to the Puhdys' success. The 60/40 quota still applied during this time, but since East German rock had been suppressed during the second half of the 1960s, GDR radio desperately needed more domestic product. Recognizing that their inability to deliver the audience's desired music compelled many GDR youths to listen to Western stations,[50] East German radio professionals pushed for bureaucratic changes that would allow them attract and hold an audience. When change came, they were quick to act, with radio taking chances on popular live acts like the Puhdys in order to draw listeners. The AMIGA record label, which had a much firmer grasp on the music buyer than GDR radio had on the music enthusiast, hesitated to make changes which would pave the way for rock acts. This may be a fundamental reason that "in the GDR it was the radio, not the recording studio, which functioned as the first rung on the ladder to fame."[51]

AMIGA lagged behind the times, releasing very little in the way of East German rock, focusing instead on instrumental music or rock groups from the other socialist countries.[52] 1972 was the year when AMIGA finally started incorporating home-grown rock, by which time East German popular radio productions had begun issuing fewer instrumental than noninstrumental tracks.[53] This shift from instrumental rock music to music with lyrics was indeed a tricky one. Bands like the Puhdys had been playing cover versions of Anglo-American rock, and to a certain extent served as a substitute for foreign bands who would never play in the GDR. These East German groups therefore sang English lyrics, something the government would not allow on their records, as English was the language of the enemy. Nevertheless, there not only existed little precedent for German-language song lyrics in a rock context, but also many rockers (and fans) considered English the only language suitable for rock music.

The Puhdys rise to fame occurred at the moment that GDR radio badly needed East German rock music to play on their airwaves. Radio did not just need the relatively nonthreatening instrumental music which had been a significant part of their programs, they needed actual rock songs sung by rock singers, with "the conditions ... that the texts be sung in German and long hair be hidden from view at official public performances."[54] Because the Puhdys commanded a large following at exactly the time when a rock song in German would be both in demand from radio and a point of pride for the authorities, the group was able to play on East German airwaves the song that would become their first hit, "Türen öffnen sich zur Stadt." This song, with its implicit call for freedom,[55] delivered by a relatively unknown band, could not have been released a year or two earlier in Walter Ulbricht's East Germany, nor three or four years later as the Honecker "honeymoon" neared its end.

By Spring 1973 the Ministry of Culture's new Committee for Entertainment Music began to more thoroughly police popular music. This new committee, however, could not immediately function in the more systematic way it would in later years. Even in those later years inconsistencies would clearly remain:

> the hackneyed rhetoric of bureaucratic discourse that prevailed in official channels should not obscure the fact that the constantly invoked unity of the SED, its uniformity of action, was pure fiction. What one authority tolerated or even encouraged could be prevented or even openly boycotted by another. For example, recordings made on the AMIGA label of VEB Deutsche Schallplatten with the permission of the Minister of Culture might be banned for broadcast by the Central Committee's Department of Agitation even before they were released.[56]

In these early years of the Puhdys' career, these rather erratic cultural authorities were trying to find a way to police new artists, while simultaneously heeding the demands of radio and television airwaves for more domestic product. To complicate matters still further for those attempting to keep a tight rein on rock music, this happened at the time when the authorities considered the use of the German language in rock music a triumph. These were the challenges facing the Committee for Entertainment Music, and ones which artists exploited. Few if any recording artists were as successful in navigating—and on occasion circumventing—cultural bureaucratic waters than the Puhdys. Even as the censoring bodies found their footing and began to make their mark, the Puhdys stayed one step ahead of them.

Partially as a result of this political acumen, the band had reached the top of the East German rock world, with their only real competition in terms of popularity being the Klaus Renft Combo. It was at this point that the Puhdys did something incredibly clever: they lay low. They had witnessed the vacillations of the government in its treatment of rock music over the years. Many members of the Puhdys had already been playing together when the government effectively quashed rock music in 1965, and given Honecker's sharp comments at that time, rock musicians did not find themselves on firm ground when he later became the head of state, despite the ostensible freedom and official support. The Puhdys would leave the overt displays of rebellion to the Klaus Renft Combo and let them suffer the consequences.

Renft's ban was a blow to East German rock culture, and a validation of the Puhdy's policy of biding their time and gathering support. Vocalist Peter Gläser from Renft stated: "'We were too confident ... We assumed that we were so popular the government couldn't do anything against us. We obviously overestimated our position in society.'"[57] The Puhdys did not labor under that assumption. Because they became popular and they did not openly rebel against the authorities, the Puhdys got the reputation of being sell-outs and *Staatsrocker*, though a look at the band's early music gainsays these claims, as demonstrated above. The band was expert at walking the thin line between authorities and audience. They were the first group to achieve and sustain such heights of popularity, and, as such, acted as trailblazers for other acts to follow.

The group would act as pioneers in other areas as well. When a West German record executive named Peter Schimmelpfennig was driving between Hamburg and West Berlin, he heard a couple of songs, "Geh zu ihr" and "Wenn ein Mensch lebt," by the Puhdys over East German radio.[58] After considerable effort, Schimmelpfennig managed to bring the band over for their first live shows in West Germany.[59] On the strength of those shows, he got them their first record contract with the class enemy.[60]

The Puhdys' achievements in West Germany opened the doors for other GDR rock bands, and by the 1980s, several artists released recordings in the West. Through their success abroad, the Puhdys earned greater power. The mere suggestion of a Western record contract prompted the authorities to let them perform in the Federal Republic, and after they had that contract in hand, the East German government allowed them ever increasing freedom to travel abroad. There was great reason for the government to do so: money. The GDR consistently suffered under a shortage of hard currency,[61] and foreign record sales provided a significant source of that very substance, as the state collected a hefty 75 percent of the copyright and royalties.[62] Not only the sales, but the fact that an East German rock band was successfully competing in the international music market served as a source of gratification for the government, whether the authorities liked the music or not.

The band's course of keeping their heads down and not stirring up undue trouble had proven successful. Now they were seen as a commodity, with their international record sales bringing the authorities both money and pride. And on the subject of pride, it would have at this point proven very difficult for the government to eliminate the Puhdys because of the many ways it had promoted the band: through records, radio, television, and film. They had also been the de facto representatives of the country on tour in the Soviet Union and other countries in both the West and the East. Dropping the Puhdys would have amounted to a significant loss of face for the GDR, something that its officials were unlikely to undergo without a very, very good reason. Unlike Renft, the Puhdys waited until they had actually amassed enough power before they asserted it.

And assert that power they did. The same year as their first album appeared in West Germany, the Puhdys released *Rock 'N' Roll Music*, a collection of cover versions of American oldies such as "Hound Dog," "Bye Bye Love," and "Good Golly, Miss Molly." This album would not have been possible even a couple of years prior. The band's ability to release an album consisting not merely of English-language songs, but the actual songs that emerged from American culture, prove how much clout they had gained. They were even able to record an album in London containing English versions of some of their biggest hits. Indeed, the sheer amount of material they released speaks highly of their power (as well as their popularity). Not counting re-releases or solo projects, the Puhdys released eighteen albums on the AMIGA record label—in East German terms a huge volume of work. Starting in 1974, the band released at least one album almost every year on a label that only released about twelve to sixteen rock albums by East German artists annually.[63]

As I mentioned at the beginning of this article, and as I have hopefully demonstrated since then, the Puhdys attained and maintained its top spot in the East German rock scene through a mixture of luck, talent, and political savvy. The political savvy demonstrates itself not only in the way the band knew when to exert itself and when to bide its time, but also in the way the band crafted complex music and lyrics that would read differently to different audiences. The luck consists of them having a large enough following during a very brief window in which bureaucratic restrictions were loose and the radio needed more domestic rock music. And a run of success which started with the band playing covers of Deep Purple and Uriah Heep covers in the early 1970s and continued twenty-five years after reunification bears witness to the Puhdy's talent.

JOHN LITTLEJOHN earned his doctorate from the University of Kansas. He is currently Chair of Languages at the Louisiana School for Math, Science, and the Arts, where he teaches courses on German, art, and film. He has published on German hip-hop and Krautrock as well as artists such as Kraftwerk and Rammstein. He co-edited a book on the latter, *Rammstein on Fire: New Perspectives on the Music and Performances* (Jefferson, 2013).

Notes

1. Olaf Leitner, "Rock Music in the GDR: An Epitaph," trans. Margaret A. Brown, in *Rocking the State: Rock Music and Politics in East Europe and Russia*, ed. Sabrina Petra Ramet (Boulder, 1994), 22. All translations are the author's.
2. The band's first two albums are both eponymous works; 1975's *Puhdys* follows their first album, *Die Puhdys*.
3. Patricia Anne Simpson, "Born in the 'Bakschischrepublik': Anthems of the Late GDR" in *Transformations of the New Germany*, ed. Ruth A. Starkman (New York, 2006), 91.
4. Ibid., 90.
5. Osman Durrani, "Language and Subversion in GDR Rock Music" in *Finding a Voice: Problems of Language in East German Society and Culture*, ed. Graham Jackman and Ian F. Roe (Amsterdam, 2000), 146. This opinion may seem as quaint as it is misguided from the eyes of the twenty-first century observer, but one notes similar outrage and fear from the older generation in the United States when rock and roll music first appeared on the scene there. One further notes that the sociopolitical power of rock music would continue to be over-estimated by those for and against the music for decades to come, in the West as well as in the East.
6. Peter Wicke, "Pop Music in the GDR between Conformity and Resistance," trans. Margy Gerber, in *Changing Identities in East Germany: Selected Papers from the Nineteenth and Twentieth New Hampshire Symposia*, ed. Margy Berger and Roger Woods (Lanham, 1996), 28.
7. In fact, "Beatmusik" was a term used in East Germany as a generic term for rock music well into the 1970s.
8. Wicke (see note 6), 29.
9. Beate Kutschke, "Anti-Authoritarian Revolt by Musical Means on Both Sides of the Berlin Wall" in *Music and Protest in 1968*, ed. Beate Kutschke and Barley Norton (Cambridge, 2013), 196.
10. Peter Wicke, "The Times they are a-Changin': Rock Music and Political Change in East Germany" in *Rockin' the Boat: Mass Music and Mass Movements*, ed. Reebee Garofalo (Boston, 1992), 82.
11. Michael Rauhut, *Rock in der DDR: 1964-1989* (Bonn, 2002), 52; Olaf Leitner, *Rockszene DDR: Aspekte einer Massenkultur im Sozialismus* (Reinbek bei Hamburg, 1983), 53.

12. Wicke (see note 6), 30.
13. Michael Rauhut, *Beat in der Grauzone: DDR-Rock 1964-1972—Politik und Alltag*, (Berlin, 1993), 209.
14. Cited in Karl Wilhelm Fricke, *Opposition und Widerstand in der DDR: Ein politischer Report* (Cologne, 1984), 158.
15. Ian Wallace, "The Failure of GDR Cultural Policy under Honecker" in *The German Revolution of 1989: Causes and Consequences*, ed. Gert-Joachim Glaeßner and Ian Wallace (Oxford, 1992), 104.
16. Peter Wicke and John Shepherd, "'The Cabaret Is Dead': Rock Culture as State Enterprise—The Political Organization of Rock in East Germany" in *Rock and Popular Music: Politics, Policies, Institutions*, ed. Tony Bennett et al (London, 1993), 26.
17. Roger Woods, *Opposition in the GDR under Honecker, 1971-85: An Introduction and Documentation* (New York, 1986), 11.
18. Mike Dennis, *The Rise and Fall of the German Democratic Republic, 1945-1990* (Harlow, 2000), 145.
19. Wicke (see note 6), 30.
20. Ibid., 31.
21. Leitner (see note 11), 39.
22. Bernd Lindner, *DDR Rock & Pop* (Cologne, 2008), 92.
23. Timothy W. Ryback, *Rock Around the Bloc: A History of Rock Music in Eastern Europe and the Soviet Union* (Oxford, 1990), 135.
24. Wicke (see note 6), 26.
25. Durrani (see note 5), 146.
26. Michael Rauhut, "Am Punkt Null: Karrierestart im Windschatten Honeckers" in *Puhdys: Eine Kultband aus dem Osten*, ed. Irmela Hannover and Peter Wicke (Berlin, 1994), 30.
27. Ibid.
28. Michael Rauhut, "Auf Silberschwingen durch die Nacht: DDR-Rock in den siebziger und achtziger Jahren," Introduction to Herbert Schulze *Melodie & Rhythmus: Bilder aus 20 Jahren DDR-Rock* (Berlin, 2001), 8-9.
29. An earlier form of the band came into existence in 1965, with Peter Meyer, Udo Wendel, Udo Jacob, Harry Jeske and Dieter Hertrampf, as the Udo Wendel Combo. The name Puhdys evolved from the musician's first names. Peter Wicke, "'Alt wie ein Baum': Die Puhdys im Exklusivinterview" in Hannover and Wicke (see note 25), 142.
30. Ryback (see note 23), 136.
31. Ibid.
32. Ilona Rühmann, "Wenn ein Hit lange Zeit lebt: die Legende von Paula und den Puhdys" in Hannover and Wicke (see note 26), 42.
33. Wolfgang Mühl-Benninghaus, "Die Legende von Paul und Paula / The Legend of Paul and Paula," trans. Christine Maaßen-Wilder, in *The Cinema of Germany*, ed. Joseph Garncarz and Annemone Ligensa (London, 2012), 175.
34. Durrani (see note 5), 150.
35. David Robb, "Political Song in the Herbert Schulze: The Cat-and-Mouse Game with Censorship and Institutions" in *Protest Song in East and West Germany since the 1960s*, ed. David Robb (Rochester, 2007), 235-236.
36. Leitner (see note 11), 120.
37. Thanks to members of my Spring 2014 *German Music and Culture* class who noted this similarity.
38. Durrani (see note 5), 151.
39. "Fly ahead of us!...Show us the way! He was the first. Many followed him." All Puhdys lyrics quoted in this paper are taken from the band's website, www.puhdys.com, accessed 26 April 2017.
40. "His name is Icarus, and he is forever young."

41. A fifth song, "Zeiten und Weiten", begins with the line "Oben auf den Türmen, wo die Tauben sind" (high atop the towers, where the pigeons are), a line that carries with it a less direct, yet still palpable, reference to flight.
42. "Sway like a sail light / Fly as a bird unsurpassed / Run as sand through my hand."
43. Irmela Hannover and Peter Wicke, "Vorwort," in Hannover and Wicke (see note 26), 6; Kate Gerrard, "Punk and the State of Youth in the GDR" in *Youth and Rock in the Soviet Bloc: Youth Cultures, Music, and the State in Russia and Eastern Europe*, ed. William Jay Risch (Lanham, 2015), 159.
44. Wicke (see note 10), 85.
45. Lindsay Hansen, "A Well-oiled Machine: The Creation and Dissolution of East Germany's VEB Deutsche Schallplatten," *ARSC Journal* 43, no. 1 (2012): 10.
46. "Fly your kite."
47. Gunther Emmerlich, "Gedanken eines Zeitgenossen," Foreword, Harry Jeske *Mein wildes Leben und die Puhdys* (Berlin, 1997), 7.
48. Leitner notices similarities to another book of the Bible, The Song of Songs. Leitner (see note 11), 118.
49. The band's first album release in West Germany, *Puhdys 1* (1977), is largely the same as their first East German album, with only three songs being replaced by more recent material. In contrast to this GDR equivalent, *Puhdys 1* features the popular tracks "Geh zu ihr" and "Wenn ein Mensch lebt" in prominent positions, having them open side one and side two, respectively, instead of having them languish at the latter half of side two.
50. Rauhut (see note 13), 230.
51. Durrani (see note 5), 157.
52. Rauhut (see note 13), 269-271.
53. Ibid., 231, 271.
54. Wicke (see note 6), 30-31.
55. One may read "Türen öffnen sich zur Stadt" as a "harmless little song" or a "targeted attack on the leadership of the party and the state," depending on one's perspective. Peter Wicke, "'Wenn Träume sterben:' Die Puhdys und der Alltag in der DDR" in Hannover and Wicke (see note 26), 20-21.
56. Wicke (see note 6), 32.
57. Ryback (see note 23), 138.
58. Irmela Hannover, "Doppelagent in Sachen Deutsch-Rock: Der Musikverleger und -produzent Peter Schimmelpfennig" in Hannover and Wicke (see note 26), 116.
59. Ibid., 118.
60. Ibid., 118-119.
61. Wicke (see note 10), 86.
62. Ibid.
63. Christian Hentschel and Peter Matzke, *Als ich fortging...: Das grosse DDR-Rock Buch* (Berlin, 2007), 232.

Chapter 4

DIY, IM EIGENVERLAG

East German Tamizdat LPs
Seth Howes

For some seventy years, the portmanteau "samizdat" (self published) has been used to designate poems, novels, political essays, manifestos, drawings, maps, or lists of names published extra-institutionally in state socialist societies.[1] While most such works remained in the countries where they had been produced, a significant number were smuggled to the West, where they appeared as "tamizdat" (published over there) and were interpreted, especially in the 1950s and 1960s at the height of the Cold War, as betokening "a rebirth of free speech behind the Iron Curtain, defying ideological brainwashing by the Darth Vaders of the 'Evil Empire.'" Indeed, for Eastern censors and Western readers alike, such things represented what the literary theorist Peter Steiner calls "an obvious challenge (if only by [their] very existence) to the information monopoly enjoyed by the state in a one-party political system."[2]

Well before the Cold War ended, scholars began moving away from reading samizdat in this way, instead posing questions about medium and genre, provenance and canon formation. Focusing on the logistics of tamizdat publicity, some scholars have also examined how works moved on physical media and broadcasts not merely from East to West but from West to East, and how states, exile committees, and NGOs involved themselves in promoting the circulation of tamizdat.[3] Still others have explored how distinctions between the official and unofficial culture in state socialism, which long have informed Western journalists' and critics' definitions of what counted as samizdat, and what did not, were never as clear-cut or as obvious as those living outside state-socialist societies presumed.[4] Far from diminishing in importance as the Cold War recedes into the past, samizdat and tamizdat are anchoring scholarly efforts at advancing what Friederike

---

Notes for this chapter begin on page 81.

Kind-Kovács and Jessie Labov call an "innovative alternative to the Cold War narrative about a strict division of Europe."[5]

Taking its cues from the questions raised by recent scholarship on samizdat and tamizdat, the present article looks at five long-playing records (LPs) recorded in the German Democratic Republic (GDR) that were released unofficially in the Federal Republic of Germany (FRG) during the 1980s. While these were not the first notable tamizdat LPs in the history of Germany's division—Wolf Biermann's *Chausseestraße 131* (1968) preceded them by more than a decade—these five LPs represent intriguing minority reports on the increasing integration of the two German states' pop music industries in the waning years of the Cold War. Because the first of these LPs was released in 1983, and the last one in 1989, a six-year-period in which the East German music industry underwent sweeping economic, political, and cultural changes, they enable us to reconstruct how acts of border-crossing, "do-it-yourself" (DIY) cultural production—in this case, of musical tamizdat—occurred.

Focusing on the tamizdat LPs' configuration of the relationship between aesthetics and politics as an interaction between texts, images, and sounds, and as an encounter between political and economic systems, I show that while the first four LPs clearly positioned themselves in opposition to the East German state as such, critiquing its policies and framing their own interventions as proverbial notes from underground, the fifth record—the self-titled 1989 album by Der Expander des Fortschritts—took a quite different approach. This was in part a matter of genre. The first four were punk and post-punk LPs; *Der Expander des Fortschritts* was not. It was also a question of timing, as Der Expander des Fortschritts was negotiating a very different landscape from the one the punks inhabited in the early 1980s. When examined together, I suggest, these five marginal artifacts, as material traces of cross-border cultural flows in the Cold War's final decade, permit us to reconstruct the institutional and cultural margins of a German music industry whose economic integration had been accelerating for decades.

Industry, Music, and Punk: The First Three Tamizdat LPs

Standing in front of the Schöneberg City Hall on 10 November 1989, Willy Brandt is supposed to have said: "Now let that which belongs together, grow together!" Though now thought to be apocryphal, this statement has often been cited as evidence of Germans' immediate and optimistic embrace of political reunification as the logical, even natural outcome of the Berlin Wall's fall.[6] Even if we are willing to disregard its occlusion of the other options that faced East Germans that November, and willing to indulge the organicist metaphor at its center, the statement suffers from yet another problem: belatedness. For while two distinct German states still existed in early November 1989, the "growing together" that Brandt suggested could "now" begin had already begun at least two decades earlier. Particularly following the ratification of the Basic Treaty in 1972, which normalized diplomatic relations between the Federal Republic of Germany and the German Democratic Republic, economic relations had grown much closer. Despite freezes and thaws in relations between their respective governments, and the East German state's tight regulation of individuals' ability to travel to and from its territory, industrial materials, fuels, agricultural commodities, and refined goods were moving back and forth between the two Germanies in steadily increasing volumes.

Cultural goods were included in this trade. Books, films, magazines, and sheet music produced in one German republic often sold well in the other, and so too did vinyl records, pop music's privileged medium in the 1970s and 1980s. A decade after the Puhdys had sold hundreds of thousands of copies of their eponymous 1974 LP in West Germany, East German bands remained capable of making deep impressions on the West German charts, with bands such as Karat (*Der blaue Planet*, 1982) and City (*Casablanca*, 1987) scoring crossover hits. This westbound traffic had an eastbound complement, as records originally issued in the FRG, the United States, and the United Kingdom were licensed for release in East German editions by the state-owned record company VEB Deutsche Schallplatten, and issued under its Amiga label, responsible for pop and rock. Records by the West German rock singers Udo Lindenberg and Peter Maffay were given Amiga editions, and so were Bruce Springsteen's *Born in the USA*, Billy Bragg's *Talking with the Taxman about Poetry*, and a greatest hits collection by Depeche Mode.[7] By 1989, even the West German punk acts Die Ärzte and Die Toten Hosen had become candidates for licensure. A four-song EP by each band appeared with Amiga that year, joining a small complement of homegrown punk records by bands like Die Skeptiker and Feeling B.

As clear as this trend toward liberalization may seem in retrospect, its ultimate direction was far from apparent in the late 1970s and 1980s, when punk—like new wave, no wave, and goth, post-punk genres that departed from punk's DIY ethos—made it to East German airwaves. Far from embracing the new musical trends as compatible with established East German rock, cultural politicians and Stasi observers alike viewed the unrefined and often experimental sounds of punk and post punk, along with the seemingly clannish behavior of the genres' adherents, as Western initiatives aimed at subverting the GDR's aesthetic and social orders. Commentators in the major East German newspapers had dismissed Western punk in 1977 and 1978 as symptomatic of a specifically capitalist malaise that had little to do with the GDR. By 1981, the Ministry for State Security (Stasi) was directing dozens of surveillance procedures aimed at identifying and punishing East German exponents of this Western behavior. Though punk was never technically made illegal, the Stasi, city police forces, and cultural politicians joined forces to keep punk—and punks—out of city streets, concert venues, and recording studios.

Within a very few years, these efforts culminated in Stasi minister Erich Mielke's infamous 1983 order for "Härte gegen Punk" (hardness against punk). Arrests, preventative detention, prison sentences, military impressments, and, in a few cases, expulsion from the GDR were all designed to intimidate and harm those the Stasi had identified as punks.[8] Just as this anti-punk campaign was ramping up, the first of the five East German tamizdat LPs of the 1980s—a split LP by SchleimKeim (Erfurt) and Vierte Wurzel aus Zwitschermaschine (Dresden/Berlin) was released in West Berlin. Realizing that there was no chance for a punk record to be put out by Amiga, the label for rock operated by state-owned VEB Deutsche Schallplatten, and unsatisfied with continuing to distribute their music via the tape-trading circuit, the two bands smuggled their recordings out of the GDR and to the West. There, an independent label could release the compilation in a print run of a thousand or more copies—tiny by industry standards, but an order of magnitude larger than the circulation the bands could typically reach through audiocassettes.

Originally conceived as a three-band compilation, DDR von unten / eNDe had been recorded near Dresden in early 1983 in the self-designed studio of a blues musician named Anteck Baumgärtel. These initial recordings were converted from the original Tesla tape to a format compatible with West German machines, and smuggled out of the GDR by an employee of the FRG's permanent representation in East Berlin, the so-called Ständige Vertretung. Working with Aggressive Rockproduktionen, Zwitschermaschine co-founder Ralf Kerbach, who had left the GDR in 1982, and so did not take part in the recording sessions that produced his band's side of the LP, arranged for the record's cover images and the graphic design of its lyric insert.[9] Sascha Anderson, the project's organizational linchpin and a Stasi informant, contributed liner notes that frame the record as an attempt to communicate with an East German "generation whose thinking and acting in a society that it rejects was no longer understandable to us."[10] Whatever we might make of Anderson's claims to initiate a dialogue between his own East German generation and a younger one that speaks the language of punk, the record's very title—*GDR from below*—frames its musical contents as notes from underground, traveling from East to West.

In a statement positioned opposite Anderson's remarks in the record's liner notes, Aggressive Rockproduktionen, the West Berlin label responsible for issuing the record, duplicates this framing, even as it comments bitterly on the record's potential to obscure West German concerns: "The exotic sensation of suppressed GDR rock is greedily seized upon and analyzed by West German media. Meanwhile, the Western variant of the underground rock censorship is studiously ignored."[11] Analyses of lyrics by the Hamburg hardcore band Slime, and of FRG government responses to them, follow. In the liner notes to the first issue of any East German punk on vinyl, then, a West Berlin independent label framed the featured musicians' articulation of a suppressed view of the "GDR from below" as one facet of an all-German phenomenon. Common cause appears not only in stylistic parallels between East German punk and post-punk songs and their Western counterparts, but also in resistance to the shared foe of censorship, undertaken by states both capitalist and communist. The concluding lines of Aggressive Rockproduktionen's remarks assert that "in the jargon of the street, this is called the 'pigs' state,' and in the jargon of intellectual critique, an 'authoritarian state.'" Here, it is not clear which German republic, FRG or GDR, is at issue.

The second tamizat release, *"Live" in Paradise DDR*, appeared in 1985, and followed suit in presenting itself as an act of political contumacy. But, while the bands involved in the first project had been willing participants, *"Live" in Paradise DDR* was a compilation of contemporary East German punk and post punk released by Thorsten Philip upon arriving in West Berlin after the GDR government approved his application for permanent resettlement. Before leaving the GDR, Philip had recorded the featured bands in his East Berlin household studio, or live at concerts. Although he neglected to seek their consent for the record's issue, making it essentially a bootleg, he packaged and presented the record as tamizdat—volatile contraband, arriving in the West only after a dangerous journey.[12]

DIY, im Eigenverlag: *East German Tamizdat LPs*

Figure 4.1: The Cover Image for *"Live" in Paradise DDR* (Good Noise, 1985).

Piloted by Lev Kerbel's bust of Karl Marx (Chemnitz, 1971), a makeshift flying machine hangs over a representation of the "death strip" at the center of the Berlin Wall. The Wall itself bisects the record cover as a dull, gray band, interrupting a geometric grid that suggests a depth of field whose vanishing point is occupied by a distant urban landscape, replete with skyscrapers and the cooling towers of nuclear reactors. Standing in the death strip, a sculpted archer bleeding brightly from his heel prepares to defend the border by taking aim at the airship with a bow fashioned from a musical note. Above him, an eye peers out from an irregularly shaped crack. The eye, and the space it inhabits, have a red hue that locates them, chromatically and geopolitically, in socialist space. A dimensional tension pervades the image, threatening to collapse the three-dimensional space into a plane–perhaps a wall–that has obviously begun to crumble.

Distinct in provenance but similar in presentation, DDR von unten / eNDe and *"Live" in Paradise GDR* appeared in West Berlin as containers of contraband from the state-socialist East. In 1986, the Weimar punk band KG Rest released the LP *panem et circensis* on its own label–Rest Records–in West Berlin. Its musical material brought out of the GDR by a member permanently emigrating from the GDR, *panem et circensis* was the first solo LP by an East German punk band released in West Germany. Perhaps because of its bootleg status, the bands featured on *"Live" in Paradise GDR* had avoided negative consequences after that LP's 1985 release. Those members of KG Rest who remained in the GDR were not as lucky, and became subject to redoubled Stasi surveillance in the wake of their departed bandmate's initiative–just as the members of SchleimKeim, unsuccessfully pseudonomized on the *DDR von unten / eNDe* LP as "Saukerle," had experienced three years before.[13] By this point, though, the open repression exemplified by the arrests, impressments, and expulsions during "Härte gegen Punk" had given way to the cultivation of informants in punk bands, the dogged compilation of lists of attendees' names at punk concerts, and the careful perusal of GDR punk lyrics and Western fanzines intercepted in the mail.[14]

Though these initiatives continued through to the end of the GDR in 1989, they became increasingly disconnected from the strategies of the cultural politicians in charge of the GDR's concert venues, recording studios, and airwaves. By 1986, releasing an unlicensed and unapproved record in the West was no longer the only route for East German bands working outside the formal record industry to put their music into a wider circulation than the tape-trading circuit that emerged around 1980 had made possible. In fact, bands could now send audiocassettes to the disk jockey Lutz Schramm, who played them on his radio show Parocktikum, part of the state-owned, youth-oriented broadcasting program DT64, based in East Berlin. Dozens of independent bands from across the GDR leapt at this opportunity, but some were not interested in having a state-run institution broadcast their work, instead remaining separate as a guarantor of their own aesthetic.[15]

L'Attentat was one such band. Formed in Leipzig around 1985 as a successor to the earlier band Wutanfall, L'Attentat adopted an occupied house as its base of operations and took full advantage of the city's book fairs, art shows, concert series, and film festivals to network with punks from elsewhere in the GDR, other state-socialist countries, West Germany, and the United States.[16] During the mid 1980s, the band organized readings, soccer games, concerts, and political discussions within the punk scene–and all this despite having two Stasi informants (IMs), guitarist Imad Abdul-Majid and bassist Frank "Zappa" Zappe, in its membership.[17] Arrested in 1985 after a search of his apartment turned up correspondence with West German fanzine editors, singer Bernd Stracke spent several months in custody before being expelled to West Germany. Once there, he helped organize the release of an LP entitled *Made in GDR* with the label X-Mist, based near Stuttgart, in 1987. First committed to audiocassette in Leipzig, the recordings featured a new singer—Stracke had not participated in the GDR sessions and did not add overdubs subsequently, when the tape made it to the West—and were smuggled out of the GDR by one of the band's many international contacts. Luk Haas, a French citizen who frequently visited Leipzig, then brought out the photos, typed lyrics, and drawings featured in the record's packaging.[18]

Figure 2: Front Image of Sleeve for L'Attentat, *Made in GDR* LP (X-Mist, 1987).

Emblazoned on a crowd shot of a rally in an unidentified but clearly East German city are the name of the band, "L'Attentat," and, in English, "Made in GDR." In an act of genre-authentication linking the record to its punk precursors, all four words are set in the ransom-note pseudo-typography that Jamie Reid had pioneered for the Sex Pistols' records a decade earlier.

Each of the LP's thirteen songs takes its musical structure from the transnational aesthetic of hardcore punk, with its stylistic markers of velocity and ferocity. Two-chord compositions with bridges but no chorus, unchanging propulsive drumbeats, rudimentary arpeggiated solos, doggerel lyric structure—these are the fare on offer. Like the stark blacks and whites of the cover image, these formal elements link L'Attentat's project to international hardcore punk. The lyrics' engagement with state socialism's slow-motion decay also draws on well-established punk critiques of late twentieth-century urbanism, inequality, and perceived social stagnation. The six shrieked couplets of "Heimatlied" don't so much tell a story as paint a picture:

Schau heraus die strassen nass und kalt	Look out there, the streets wet and cold
Die autos dreckig verrottet und alt	The cars dirty, rotten and old
Die häuser verkommen und verfall'n	The houses decayed and ruined
Die gullis stinkende tödliche fall'n	The sewers stinking, deadly traps
Überall dreck lärm und gestank	Everywhere's dirt, noise and stench
Ratten und viehzeug die menschen so krank	Rats and vermin, the people so sick
Die jugend frustriert und absolut leer	The youth's frustrated, a blank generation
Verarscht und gezwungen zum militär	Fooled and forced and forced to draft [sic]
Die ordnung bewacht von der polizei	Law and order preserved by police
Im grundgesetz steht: du bist frei	Fundamental laws say that you're free
Du bist schon tot eh du gebor'n	You're already dead before you're born
Von anfang an bist du verlor'n	Right from the beginning you're lost

Apart from the final two lines' echo of the antifuturist orientation at the heart of global punk rhetoric, what is most striking about this ironic "song of the homeland" is its lack of specificity, its isomorphism with respect to the global corpus of punk lyricism.[19]

Translated into appropriately rough-edged English, these lyrics could just as easily be referring to 1976 London, the city of garbage strikes and the silver jubilee, linked topologically with New York, which together had produced punk in the first place. Or left in German, the grievances listed here could be referring to West Germany instead of East. The architectural and environmental decrepitude of many West Berlin districts was legendary, and the Federal Republic's police bureaus had heavily monitored punk activities. Anchored in a vernacular of punk critique with exponents in dozens of countries, "Heimatlied" is however the only song on the album with lyrics couched in such generalities. "Moskau," "Wo stehst du," "Demonstration," and "Friedensstaat" all borrow from the vernacular of SED power to turn the noble self-descriptions offered at May Day parades and Party functions into petards.

Each song has its lyrics presented in four different languages on the twelve-page lyric insert–the original German, then English, Italian, and French–making the record as a whole maximally legible and comprehensible to an audience, presumably punks, that L'Attentat addresses as transnational. But the photocopied pictures of the band, juxtaposed with magazine and pamphlet cutouts, embed L'Attentat's self-presentation into the body of East German photography, playing up the contrast between the bodies of the band's members and the uniformed, purposive bodies of the soldiers, model citizens, mobilized youth, and politicians critiqued in the lyrics:

Figure 3: Details from Page 2 of the Lyric Insert for *Made in GDR*

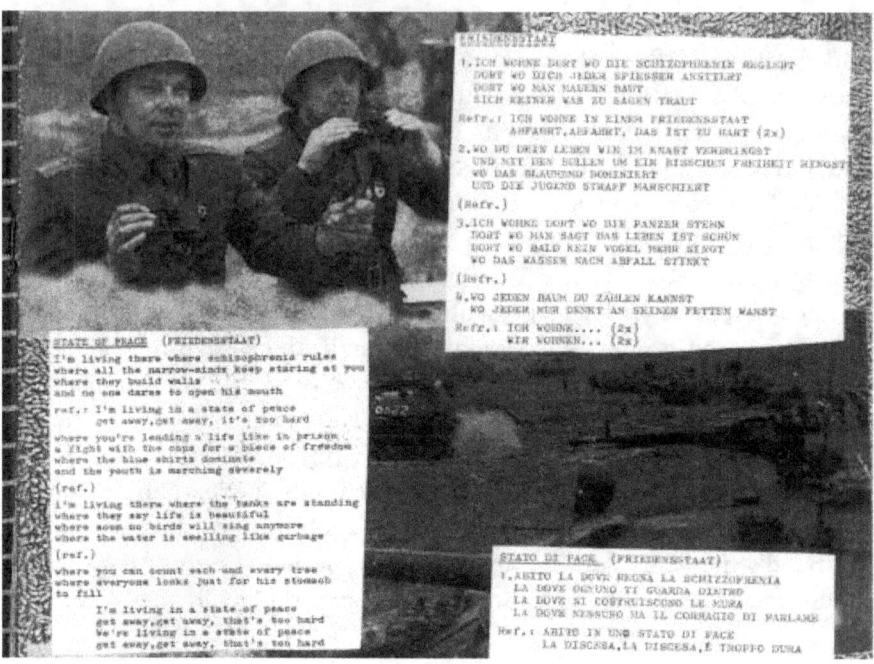

Figure 4: Details from Page 7 of the Lyric Insert for *Made in GDR*

Because there are no captions for the "stock" images, the song lyrics serve as the reader's point of departure for understanding the images, which in turn provide implicit visual corroboration for the objects of the band's critique. The picture in the upper left of East German NVA troops on maneuvers, juxtaposed with a battlefield on the lower right whose context is less clear, visually supports the adjacent text block of "Friedensstaat's" lyrics: "I'm living there where schizophrenia rules / where all the narrow-minds keep staring at you / where they build walls / and no one dares to open his mouth." Similarly, "Ohne Sinn's" straightforward complaint about party discipline ("I don't wanna be commanded / 'cause I am a human being") is outfitted with photographs of Egon Krenz with communist youth organization members (Junge Pioniere), and of a police officer providing directions to smartly attired young women. A reproduction of a pseudo-rustic watercolor of soldiers and young children playing music together further underscores the point.

Finally, as if the didactic and illustrative function of the lyric sheet were not clear enough already, the last page supplies a legend of terms in three of the four languages for listener-readers unfamiliar with the GDR. (For whatever reason, Italian was not used in the glossary.) The excerpts from L'Attentat's lyrics already quoted make it clear that the band is hypercritical of East German politics and society. L'Attentat does not experiment with ambiguity or anonymity, instead maximizing the comprehensibility and clarity of its critique, presumably for the benefit of audiences not just outside East Germany, but Germanophone Europe.

Released in the West in 1987, *Made in GDR* actually appeared after the GDR cultural politicians responsible for scheduling concerts had relaxed their defenses against controversial genres like punk, new wave, goth, and speed metal. In 1988, punk and new wave bands such as Feeling B and Die Skeptiker began recording in Amiga's studios in East Berlin, with the results beginning to appear on vinyl in 1988. As Bernd Lindner, a cultural historian of East German music, summarizes:

> The GDR had to react to the changed youth-cultural scene, because it was slowly losing the youth itself. By the middle of the 1980s, a targeted incorporation [*gezielte Vereinnahmung*] of the punk scene by the state's mechanisms of support took shape. The bands could suddenly obtain professional licensures and play in FDJ clubs and cultural houses.[20]

Opened a crack by Schramm's broadcasts in 1986, the official door swung out even further, as some of what were dubbed the "other bands"–independent groups, typically with years of experience playing concerts outside the government-managed venue system, that drew on the once-disdained, now accepted genres of punk, post punk, new wave, and goth in their songwriting–were permitted to record in state-owned studios.[21]

L'Attentat did not take advantage of these newly available opportunities, instead construing independence from the state as an ethical, political, and aesthetic vantage point from which to critique real-existing socialism from within. Released in the West, and designed as a refined product accessible to hardcore punk fans worldwide, *Made in GDR* was aimed beyond the East German musical landscape, and the borders of the GDR itself, in this sense representing the radicalization, if not the culmination, of East German tamizdat LPs. If *DDR von unten* and *"Live" in Paradise GDR* emphasized their status as bearers of musical reportage from beyond the Wall, *Made in GDR* uses its visual, sonic, and textual aspects to distinguish itself even more explicitly, as a matter of politics, from the state it bitterly notes it hails from. As such, it contrasts sharply with the fifth and final East German tamizdat LP: 1989's *Der Expander des Fortschritts.*

Der Expander des Fortschritts

Der Expander des Fortschritts formed in East Berlin in 1986, and performed for a classification committee in 1987.[22] Between its first concert in

February 1987 and its breakup in 1990, it took advantage of every opportunity to develop and professionally record its music publicly, appearing at gallery openings, house parties, conferences, and other events sponsored by the Berlin Academy of Arts.[23] In early 1988, it performed with the pioneering industrial-electronic band A.G. Geige at the Palast der Republik, the lodestone of East German power and pomp, as part of an event called "Jugend im Palast" (youth in the palace).[24] And when Amiga released the sampler LP *Parocktikum–Die Anderen Bands* in 1989, Der Expander des Fortschritts contributed the song "Fremder Freund."

But in addition to these sanctioned performances in a variety of venues, and to the band's work with the East German music industry, came many performances at unlicensed concerts and the release of self-produced audiocassettes into the then-burgeoning tape-trading circuit, dubbed the *Magnetbanduntergrund* (magnetic tape underground) by Alexander Pehlemann and Ronald Galenza.[25] The band's first self-released samizdat album appeared in 1988 on its own label Irrmenschkassette (crazy man tapes). Entitled *Urknall-Horde-Mensch*–roughly "Big Bang-Horde-Human"–its black-and-white J-card listed the band's membership and division of labor as follows: "Uwe Baumgartner: speaking singing noising, Jörg Beilfuß drumming keying gargling, Susanne Binas: piping tapping puffing, Eckehard Binas: keying clamping piping, Mario Persch: guitaring singing noising, Dirk Pflughaupt: mixing in."[26]

Music journalist Robert Mießner describes the band's action-oriented, as opposed to instrument-oriented, musical practice as follows: "a proprietary montage of rock, improvisation, and electronics, not dissimilar to the British transgressors of style and borders, This Heat."[27] Working with tape loops was not confined to the independent margins of GDR music. The East German composer Georg Katzer, founder of the Studio for Electro-Acoustic Music in East Berlin, had been making tape compositions since the mid 1970s.[28] But Der Expander des Fortschritts combined the use of loops and found-sound with improvisation, interpolating both into compositions also outfitted with rock and pop textures. In this way, the band staged an encounter between rock, reggae, punk, and ska techniques, on the one hand, and serialism, minimalism, musique concrete, and electronic music on the other.[29] As they developed and refined this sonic aesthetic, and incorporated literary material into their lyrical repertoire, the course they charted between music and sound, live improvisation and the pre-manipulation of media, brought them into contact with Chris Cutler.

Cutler was an English musician, popular music theorist, and record producer who founded "Rock in Opposition," a short-lived initiative aimed at countering quietist tendencies in the recording industry. He played in a number of groups, including the Residents, Pere Ubu, Henry Cow, and—from the early to mid 1980s—a band called Cassiber that incorporated punk, jazz, and minimalist influences into an energetic, substantially improvised rock project.[30] A frequent visitor to the GDR, Cutler took part in many roundtable dialogues between scholars and practitioners held as part of the festivals where he and his bands played. He also wrote contributions on the social situation, creative possibilities, and political potential of rock music for *Musik und Gesellschaft*, the GDR's leading journal of music history, music theory, and musicology.

In his 1984 essay "Politicization of Music against Marketing," Cutler identified prevailing modes of producing, distributing, and consuming music in the West as constituting an integrated, profit-driven system that needed to be radically opposed. Rather than simply suggesting that some musicians make anticapitalist music, or listing off the names of a few who did, Cutler imagined a mode of musical production not merely anticapitalist in its sonic and textual composition, but antiprofessional and anti-industrial in its organization.

> In order to set free and develop the new forces of production, and in particular those that are bound up with technological possibilities, musicians *themselves* must become the creators and organizers of sound and unite the compartmentalized functions of the composition, the recording, and performance processes.[31]

Nothing less was needed than musical and medial practices capable of "alienating [the] alienation" (*die Entfremdung entfremden*) inherent to the industrial division of creative labor. Contrasting industry with immediacy, Cutler suggests that those rationalized processes resulting in standardized and technically refined products be supplemented with improvisatory, informal, and fundamentally irrational practices—in short, with samizdat sensibilities that radically level distinctions between performer and audience.[32]

Cutler does not mention the East German recording industry at all, and certainly draws no parallels between the labor arrangements and technologies that had compromised it. But the article does lay out a vision for independent music as an economic practice capable of constituting a new social situation for music, one that could call into question the creative legitimacy of industrial record production undertaken by large labels with a highly articulated division of labor, and also ask whether music produced under such circumstances could ever be truly political. Committed socialist though he was, and someone highly critical of the capitalist recording industry as well, Cutler nevertheless makes an argument in the pages of *Musik und Gesellschaft* that could have served as an ethos for the dozens of bands whose self-produced audiocassettes anchored the tape-trading circuit that had emerged in the early 1980s, and expanded ever since.

Four members of Der Expander des Fortschritts—Susanne Binas, Eckehard Binas, Persch, and Baumgartner—either attended or worked for the Humboldt Universität, with Susanne Binas and Baumgardner attached as student research affiliates to that university's Research Center on Popular Music, directed by popular music theorist Peter Wicke. Here they met Cutler, a frequent attendee of the Research Center's Events, and as a drummer in Cassiber and the Residents a major musical influence for them, at the 1988 event "Musik und Politik," where they gave him audiocassettes of their work—most likely *Urknall-Mensch-Horde*. Unlike L'Attentat's LP, however, these lo-fi recordings were not the basis for the *Expander des Fortschritts* LP that Cutler released on in 1989 on Points East, a sublabel of his larger RER Megacorp record label "dedicated solely to new music from Central Europe." In fact, because of its members' affiliations with Humboldt Universität and with the artists and musicians attached to it, Der Expander des Fortschritts had access to several professional studios, including the ones at DT64 and in the Academy of Arts of the GDR.[33]

Rather than endure an unduly lengthy production process at Amiga, where delays of months and even years could set in, the band sought to expedite the release of their record by having Cutler put it out in England.[34] They therefore gave the completed masters to Billy Bragg's East German translator, Jörg Wolter, who later passed them on to Cutler. The eventual cover art—an abstract, four-color screen-print traversed by drips, streaks, dots of paint, and scratched pictograms that resemble runes—was contributed by Rainer Görß, a Berlin-based performance- and installation artist who worked with the loose collective Autoperforationsartisten. The release was neither organized or supported by the VEB Deutsche Schallplatten and its Amiga label for rock. Nor were the musical compositions on the record officially licensed for Western release by the AWA, the East German composers' clearinghouse and rights agency that worked with the GEMA, its West German counterpart, to secure royalty arrangements and handle currency transfers. And yet, once released on Cutler's Points East Label, with addresses in London, England, and Novi Sad, Yugoslavia, listed on its back cover, rather than being smuggled into the GDR in the lavatory of an interzone train, as *DDR von Unten* had been just four years earlier, the unlicensed record entered entirely legally through the mail.[35]

Besides guitars, bass, and a basic rock drum kit, *Expander des Fortschritts* employs alto and tenor saxophones, flute, keyboards, and tape loops featuring distorted and backmasked found-sound compositions. At the level of composition and arrangement, some songs dispense with rhythmic percussion entirely. Melody is also sometimes left behind, as certain songs head into abstract, ambient territory. "Mond," for instance, lays distorted tape loops of an opera aria across elongated electric guitar notes, as its lyrics—mostly by Mario Persch, though they incorporate a Stephen Crane quote in its original English—are delivered in a tortured, pause-filled declamation addressed to the moon. Other songs, such as "Spätherbst abseits" or "Litanei," are seasoned with bursts of saxophone notes evocative of free jazz. During these disorienting passages, skittering drums, echoing screams, and nervous fumbling along the fretboards of both guitar and bass further the listener's disorientation. Featuring melancholic power chords with a standard rock beat, "Vereinsamt" is built upon a Nietzsche poem, intoned straightforwardly with no modifications made to its text—aside from being subtitled "Lonely Fritz."

Der Expander des Fortschritts incorporates elements from jazz, no wave, funk, ska, industrial music, and punk, but refuses to tarry too long with any of them. The nine energetic works of genre-pastiche emerging from this process are united not by their similarity in sound or rhythm, their adherence to any particular set of genre-bound compositional standards, or their commitment to specific instrumentation, but by their stylistic heterogeneity and dense layering. At one moment, Expander des Fortschritts sounds like the British bands This Heat or Cassiber, or the American Contortions and Pere Ubu. But at the next, the song moves off in another direction. In any case, though the result depends less on tape loops and overdubbing than This Heat's sonic assemblages, and is neither as comic nor as outré as the Residents' work, it plainly shares with these other bands a radically expanded notion of the possible in rock-inflected recordings.

Intoned in a sing-song unison, rather than sung or shouted, the lyrics are entirely comprehensible to the careful listener, but their level in the overall mix is tempered so as not to overpower the musical performances. The lyrics are also united by Mario Persch and Uwe Baumgardner, whose theatrical delivery of the allusive song texts, largely non-rhyming lines that vary in meter and length, requires both singers to play with velocity, muttering some passages in a rush, and elongating vowels into moans as needed. In keeping with this presentational aspect, elements of Sprechgesang and Sprechstimme appear as well. The first song on the first side, "Fatzer komm," displays the centrality of text within Der Expander des Fortschritts' musical arrangements, while grounding the aesthetic in the culture and politics of the late GDR.

The lyrics come from Bertolt Brecht's *Untergang des Egoisten Johann Fatzer*, an unfinished project he assembled a large volume of materials for between

1926 and 1930. Heiner Müller adapted it for the theater in the late 1970s; staged by the Berliner Ensemble in 1986, it perhaps found its widest audience as a radio play called *Radio Fatzer* that Müller produced for the Berliner Rundfunk in 1987.[36] Its broadcast premiere was in early 1988.[37] Loren Kruger has described this production, which incorporated material from two early Einstürzende Neubauten LPs into its soundscape, as "herald[ing] the future, not only through East/West collaboration but also in the deployment of a relatively low-tech and low-profile medium, rather than the dominant institution of television, to realize the drama of the collapsing state."[38] A remediation twice over as a radio production of a stage version of an unfinished philosophico-theatrical labor, Müller's radio play took care to present the "Fatzer, komm" segment as drily and antipathetically as possible, employing multiple takes when Müller's voice shook as he read the lines "Let the order lapse, orderer. / The state needs you no longer / Give it over."

It was almost certainly from Heiner Müller's so-called *Bühnenfassung*, and perhaps *Radio Fatzer* itself, that Der Expander des Fortschritts drew the material. Appropriating the Müller piece's final choral scene, Der Expander des Fortschritts adds a further link to Müller's chain of remediations, by incorporating the last section of Müller's seventy-nine-minute radio play into a song roughly eight minutes in length. This remediation suspends the narrative purchase of Müller's *Fatzer*, deracinating the fifty or so lines, and rescinding the dramatic context they enjoyed in Müller's radio rendering. Instead of entreating the audience to reflect on a plotted work that has come before, the words become lyrics to a song. But this shift in genres, is not so much a simplification or culinarization of Müller's "Fatzer" material as it is a reflection on its transmissibility in a different format.

Der Expander des Fortschritts' "Fatzer, komm" reproduces at the level of composition and musical arrangement many of the defamiliarizing elements that defined Müller's radio play. Echoing and transformed through a number of other effects, nervous guitar riffing stands out most from the instrumental arrangement, giving the song a propulsive, even funky, drum beat. Aside from the insistent, incantatory repetition of "verlass jetzt deinen posten" (leave your post), the song has no lyrical refrain. Instead, a faux-operatic vocalization, mimicked by the instrumentation, creates a pattern of nine rising and following notes. Whispers and shouts modulate the text's delivery, making comprehension difficult. Passages sung solo give way to passages presented by the layered voices of a chorus. Tape loops of varying provenance complicate the soundscape. We hear a conversation between two men about a coming cataclysm whose exact nature is unclear, though it seems the unrest will involve factories. One man's voice matter-of-factly states: "It'll begin soon. We just need to wait it out and hold on." A complicated layering of voices produces not harmonic uniformity or univocality, but polyphony, fragmentation, and discursive space.

If, as Kruger has suggested, Müller took the Fatzer material from the stage to the airwaves to comment on the relative prestige of different media of public address in a decelerating East German socialism, Der Expander des Fortschritts recommits the text—with its repeated injunction to "leave your posts"—to a choral performance with musical structure. By then committing the song to a physical medium—a vinyl record, produced in a tiny pressing in England—Der Expander des Fortschritts subjects a selection of Brecht's Fatzer material, already subject to Müller's tendentious editing for the *Bühnenfassung*, and to Müller's own remediation of it for the radio, to yet another process of aesthetic labor, yet another remediating intervention. In this way, like the album it initiates, Der Expander des Fortschritts's "Fatzer, komm" becomes a palimpsest of Communist narrativity. Recorded just months before the GDR itself dissolved, and sent out as metahistorical Flaschenpost that was not oppositional, but elegiac, the song and the album bear witness to socialism's end, without patently demanding it.[39]

Conclusion

In historical and autobiographical assessments of how independent music scenes were created in East Germany, and what sorts of artistic undertakings and media practices they gave rise to, the metaphor of the *Kassiber* recurs frequently. Derived from Hebrew, this *Rotwelsch* (thieves' argot) word refers to messages passed between prisoners, or given by a prisoner to somebody outside the prison wall.[40] Alexander Pehlemann and Ronald Galenza note that in the East German magnetic tape underground's networks, which initially circulated most of the recordings featured on the tamizdat LPs, "the cassette functioned as the bearer of subversive self-articulations, as Kassiber full of samizdat sounds."[41] Susanne Binas-Preisendörfer has also suggested that the cassettes functioned as Kassiber because they "contained open and clearly formulated critique of the state system of the GDR" not only audible as music, but comprehensible as texts.[42] And as we have seen, even as they moved outside the borders of the state they critiqued, a number of tamizdat LPs conferred the status of risky and risqué communiqué upon themselves. For both DDR von unten / eNDe and Made in GDR, the *Kassiber* sensibility certainly informs their packaging and visual presentation.[43]

However, if the first four LPs present themselves as *Kassiber*, offering clandestine commentary on an intolerable and oppressive state, *Der Expander des Fortschritts* positions itself quite differently. Unlike those unlicensed punk and post-punk bands that did not seek state support for their work, and faced police harassment and recruitment as Stasi informants as a result, Der Expander des Fortschritts worked within and outside of the state-run music industry simultaneously. Recorded in the finest studios in East Berlin, their own tamizdat LP then flouted licensure standards. This decision to produce a record independently across borders, and to rely on tamizdat publicity, resonates with what Cutler, whom the band had known for years, had imagined in his theoretical writing for *Musik und Gesellschaft*—an attempt to avoid not censorship, but the industrial division of labor that (in his view) had effectively alienated popular music from the *populus*.

In a recent essay on the politics of DIY media practices, Kevin Dunn has suggested that insofar as "DIY record labels serve as both a social activity and an anti-capitalist business model," they can be thought of as enacting Walter Benjamin's notion of progressive cultural production.[44] At stake here, Dunn argues, is not so much the lyrical or musical content of individual records produced, distributed, and listened to outside the major label system, but rather their very exteriority with respect to that system. Dunn quotes Benjamin on this point:

> What matters ... is the exemplary character of production, which is able, first, to induce other producers to produce, and, second, to put an improved apparatus at their disposal. And this apparatus is better, the more consumers it is able to turn into producers—that is, readers or spectators into collaborators.[45]

To date, much of the best scholarship on DIY music practices—and Dunn's is surely an example—has focused on their anticapitalist orientation as constitutive of the radical or political aspects of the music. As historians and critics assemble the fossil record of DIY music, and analyze the circumstances under which resourceful musicians have resorted to self-publishing as means for avoiding, challenging, or ignoring prevailing ways of recording and distributing music, the study of non-capitalist, and indeed, non-Western contexts will become increasingly important, and so will the study of how musicians and audiences in capitalist and non-capitalist societies were connected, rather than contraposed, to one another. Examining phenomena like East Germany's tamizdat LPs help us understand how aesthetics and politics intersected in DIY media practices undertaken outside capitalist contexts. We can weigh how recordings produced in *non*-capitalist settings resembled and diverged from generic and lyrical standards obtaining in the

West. And we can see how commonalities or analogies of purpose between contrary media practices in East and West transcended the systemic, macroeconomic differences between capitalist and communist societies enough to be intelligible—and even enjoyable—to listeners on the Iron Curtain's "other" side, and elsewhere.

SETH HOWES is associate professor of German at the University of Missouri, and co-editor of *Beyond No Future: Cultures of German Punk* (New York, 2016).

Notes

1. Friederike Kind-Kovács and Jessie Labov, "Samizdat and Tamizdat: Entangled Phenomena?" in *Samizdat, Tamizdat, and Beyond: Transnational Media During and After Socialism*, ed. Friederike Kind-Kovács and Jessie Labov (New York, 2013), 1-23, esp. 4-8. In addition to thanking Sabine Hake, Alex Fulk, and the University of Texas Department of Germanic Studies for organizing the stimulating colloquium at which I presented an initial version of this article, along with all the attendees at that event, I would also like to thank Candice Hamelin and April Eisman for their shrewd comments on a subsequent version. I am, finally, grateful to Armin Hofmann of X-Mist records for his kind agreement to let me reproduce the images of *Made in GDR*'s packaging.
2. Peter Steiner, "Introduction: On Samizdat, Tamizdat, Magnitizdat, and Other Strange Words That Are Difficult to Pronounce," *Poetics Today* 29, no. 4 (2008): 613-628, here 614.
3. See Muriel Blaive, "The Danger of Over-Interpreting Dissident Writing in the West: Communist Terror in Czechoslovakia, 1948–1968," in Kind-Kovács and Labov (see note 1), 137-155.
4. Serguei Alex Oshakine, "The Terrifying Mimicry of Samizdat," *Public Culture* 13, no. 2 (2001): 191-214, esp. 194-195.
5. Kind-Kovács and Labov (see note 1), 7.
6. On the phrase's circulation in the *Wendezeit* and thereafter, and on its dubious veracity, see Bernd Rother, "'Jetzt wächst zusammen, was zusammengehört'–Oder: Warum Historiker Rundfunkarchive nutzen sollen" in *Wächst zusammen, was zusammengehört?*, ed. Timothy Garton Ash (Berlin, 2001), 25-30. All translation from German by the author.
7. Bragg's record was issued in 1988, albeit as *Billy Bragg*–and thus without the Mayakovsky poem as its title. Springsteen's LP appeared in 1986, and the EPs by Die Toten Hosen and Die Ärzte were released in 1989.
8. Jeff Hayton, "*Härte gegen Punk*: Popular Music, Western Media, and State Response in the German Democratic Republic," *German History* 31, no. 4 (2013): 523-549, here 523.
9. The organizational aspects of the record's production are discussed in Torsten Preuß, "Zonenpunk in Scheiben: Die erste Punkplatte aus dem nahen Osten" in *Wir wollen immer artig sein: Punk, New Wave, HipHop, Independent-Szene in der DDR 1980-1990*, ed. Ronald Galenza and Heinz Havemeister (Berlin, 2013), 126-135; and in Alexander Pehlemann's interview with Zwitschermaschine members Cornelia Schleime and Ralf Kerbach, "Übern Fluß, das Andre suchen," *Zonic* 14-17 (2010): 94-102.
10. Sascha Anderson [credited as S. Anderson], "von einem beteiligten." Liner notes for DDR *von unten / eNDe* LP (Aggressive Rockproduktionen, 1983).
11. N.a., "BRD von unten." Liner notes for DDR *von unten / eNDe* LP (Aggressive Rockproduktionen, 1983).

12. In an interview, members of two of the featured bands–Ronald Lippok (Ornament & Verbrechen) and Bernd Jestram (Aufruhr zur Liebe)–look back on their lack of knowledge about the project. See "Provokation, Paranoia, und Parties" in Galenza and Havemeister (see note 9), 90-107, esp. 101.
13. On KG Rest, see Claus Bach, "Eckermann und das Faustische: Punk in Weimar" in Galenza and Havemeister (see note 9), 312-324, esp. 318. On SchleimKeim, see Anne Hahn and Frank Willmann, *Satan, kannst du mir noch mal verzeihen: Otze Ehrlich, Schleimkeim und der ganze Rest* (Mainz, 2013), 10.
14. As Klaus Michael notes, "In principal, one can conclude that after the year 1986 ... a certain zone of tolerance appeared which only saw state intervention as called for when the productions were interpretable as part of the political opposition or were used by Western media against the GDR." Klaus Michael, "Macht aus diesem Staat Gurkensalat: Punk und die Exerzitien der Macht" in Galenza and Havemeister (see note 9), 136-177.
15. Interview with Lutz Schramm, "Spule, Feedback und Zensur" in Galenza and Havemeister (see note 9), 559-570.
16. Essays on the band's history by its principal lyricist, Ray Schneider–who had also written for Wutanfall–are "Leipzig von unten. Punk- und Independent-Szene, Aktionen, Zeitschriften und Bands" in Galenda and Havemeister (see note 9), 234; "Leipzig in Trümmern" in *Haare auf Krawall: Jugendsubkultur in Leipzig 1980 bis 1991* (Leipzig, 2001), 113-123.
17. Michael (see note 14), 149. Abdul-Majid's file itself is archived as BStU, MfS, BV Leipzig, AIM 2017/88.
18. On the LP's production, see Ray Schneider, "Attentat im Friedensstaat" in *1984! Block an Block: Subkulturen im Orwell-Jahr*, ed. Alexander Pehlemann, Bert Papenfuß, and Robert Mießner (Mainz, 2015), 183-190. See also "Luk Haas: Ein Welten-Erkunder in Sachen Global Punk Phänomen," *Zonic* 20 (2013): 126-131, esp. 129.
19. Seth Howes, "Pessimism and the Politics of the Future in East German Punk," *The Journal of Popular Culture* 49, no. 1 (2016): 77-96.
20. Bernd Lindner, *DDR Rock & Pop* (Cologne, 2008), 169.
21. Ibid.
22. Susanne Binas, "East-West Breakthroughs: The Significance of Pop Underground Today" in *A Sound Legacy? Music and Politics in East Germany*, ed. Edward Larkey (Baltimore, 2000), 26-41, esp. 29.
23. They provided live musical accompaniment to a production at the Theater unterm Dach in a culture house in Prenzlauer Berg in 1987, and performed at the Werkstatt Junge Kunst II in the Academy of Arts in spring 1988.
24. This last event was favorably reviewed in *Neues Deutschland*, 8 January 1989, 8.
25. Alexander Pehlemann and Ronald Galenza, "Ende. Rewind. Play.: Vorwort der Herausgeber" in *Spannung. Leistung. Widerstand: Magnetbanduntergrund DDR, 1979–1990*, ed. Alexander Pehlemann and Ronald Galenza (Berlin, 2006), 6-9.
26. While several different drummers rotated through its lineup, Robert Mießner suggests the initial membership comprised Uwe Baumgartner (vocals and tape loops), Eckehard "Ecke" Binas (keyboards, guitars, and saxophones), Susanne Binas (saxophone, flute, keyboards), Mario Persch (lyrics, guitars), and Norbert Grandl (drums).
27. Robert Mießner, "Das Ende der Larmoyanz: Schreib lauter: Ostberliner Autoren und Musiker" in *Die Addition der Differenzen: Die Literaten- und Künstlerszene Ostberlins 1979 bis 1989*, ed. Uwe Warnke and Ingeborg Quaas (Berlin, 2009), 292-305, here 299.
28. His harrowing 1983 piece on the Holocaust, "Aide Memoire," which incorporates tape loops, was released by Chris Cutler on Georg Katzer, Zygmunt Krause, and Jaroslav Krček, *Aide Memoire, Folk Music, Sonáty Slavíčkové* LP (Recommended Records, 1985).
29. In the GDR, the U and E categories–standing for *Unterhaltungsmusik* (entertainment music) and *ernste Musik* (serious or art music) were not used explicitly to classify musical recordings for marketing and sale, but different labels (e.g., Amiga and Eterna) were used.

30. Cassiber member Heiner Goebbels has commented on the band's approach to performing and recording, and remarked on intragroup dynamics and Cassiber's intellectual influences. See Heiner Goebbels [interview with Stathis Gourgouris], "Performance as Composition," *PAJ: A Journal of Performance and Art* 26, no. 78 (2004): 1-16, esp. 12-13.
31. Chris Cutler, "Politisierung von Musik kontra Vermarktung: Widersprüche und Alternativen kapitalistischer Musikpraxis heute," *Musik und Gesellschaft* 1, no. 84 (1984): 11-16, here 14.
32. Ibid. Cutler also contributed to a roundtable, "Linke Musikkonzepte: Diskussion über eine demokratische und sozialistische Musikkultur," *Musik und Gesellschaft* 9, no. 83 (1983): 524-530.
33. Susanne Binas, interviewed by Alexander Pehlemann, "Der Expander des Fortschritts: Fremdgänger im eigenen Land zwischen Akademie und Untergrund," *Zonic* 14-17 (2010): 84-89, esp. 87.
34. Susanne Binas, "East-West Breakthroughs: The Significance of Pop Underground Today" in Larkey (see note 22), 26-41, esp. 29.
35. On Expander's ease of re-entry, see Binas (see note 33), 87; on the earlier record's difficulty, see Preuß (see note 9), 134-135.
36. In a recent article, Uwe Schütte describes Müller's *Fatzer* as an "*eigensinnige Bearbeitung*"—a processing of Brecht's piece with its own sensibility—pointing to Müller's programmatic statement, in the 1977 address "Fatzer ± Keuner," that "Using Brecht without criticizing him is treason." See Uwe Schütte, "Mit, gegen, und nach Brecht: Heiner Müllers *Fatzer*," *German Life and Letters* 69, no. 2 (2016): 256-268.
37. Judith Wilke notes that Brecht's materials were not published in a curated scholarly edition until the volume of the *Große kommentierte Berliner- und Frankfurter Ausgabe* containing his play projects and play fragments first appeared in 1997. "Fatzer," in *Brecht Handbuch 1: Stücke*, ed. Jan Knopf (Stuttgart, 2001), 167-177, 174-177 focus on its staging and reception.
38. Loren Kruger, *Post-Imperial Brecht: Politics and Performance, East and South* (Cambridge, 2004), 133-170, here 139.
39. As far as end-times discourse in the work of the "other bands" is concerned, an intriguing comparison across historical caesura might be made to the public performances of Die Firma and IchFunktion, stretching from early 1990 (around the time of the currency union) to 1993. See Patricia Anne Simpson, "Soundtracks: GDR Music from 'Revolution' to 'Reunification'" in *The Power of Intellectuals in Contemporary Germany*, ed. Michael Geyer (Chicago, 2001), 227-248.
40. *Duden: Das Fremdwörterbuch*, 10th ed., s.v. "Kassiber."
41. Alexander Pehlemann and Ronald Galenza, "Vorwort: Ende. Rewind. Play" in Pehlemann and Galenza (see note 25), 7.
42. See Susanne Binas, "Die 'anderen Bands' und ihre Kassetenproduktion–Zwischen organisiertem Kulturbetrieb und selbstorganisierten Kulturformen" in *Rockmusik und Politik: Analysen, Interviews und Dokumente*, ed. Peter Wicke and Lothar Müller (Berlin, 1996), 48-60.
43. In producing the *"Live" in Paradise DDR*, Thorsten Philip availed himself of a similar presentation. Of course, the fact that the record was unauthorized means we need to be careful not to ascribe the message of the LP's cover, title, and liner notes to the bands or their members, but rather to Philip himself.
44. Kevin Dunn, "'If It Ain't Cheap, It Ain't Punk': Walter Benjamin's Progressive Cultural Production and DIY Punk Record Labels," *Journal of Popular Music Studies* 24, no. 2 (2012): 217-237, here 217.
45. Ibid., 234.

Chapter 5

POETRY OF AN ALIEN

Black Tape, *Silo Nation, and the Historiography of German Hip-Hop's* Alte Schule

Kai-Uwe Werbeck

The Center Does Not Hold: The Founding Myths of German Rap

𝓘n Sekou A. Neblett's 2015 mockumentary *Black Tape*, three hip-hop activists go on a wild goose chase for the (fictional) German Old School rapper Tigon, whose identity has remained a mystery for almost thirty years. Following coded clues provided by an anonymous source, Neblett and his collaborators, Falk Schacht and Marcus Staiger, decide to retrace Tigon's steps and tell his "story."[1] In *Black Tape*'s alternative historiography, Tigon bum-rushed the stage at a hip-hop jam in Heidelberg's Campbell Barracks in 1986 and dropped a dope verse, ostensibly the first in German. His sudden appearance—the rapper concealing his face with a hoodie and a mask—caused a panic as the G.I.s in the audience assumed a terrorist attack. In the ensuing confusion that the mockumentary gradually establishes, a fire broke out and one person was allegedly trampled to death. While *Black Tape* emphasizes its rootedness in "real" (West) German hip-hop culture, it invents and seamlessly integrates an elaborate founding myth of *Deutschrap* into the narrative.[2] The film thus restages the Big Bang of German rap as a paranoia-infused scavenger hunt in which the journalistic investigation into the events at the U.S. Army barracks three decades ago spurs into action greedy record label executives, nebulous conspiracy theorists, and even the German and American authorities.[3] As fact and fiction become increasingly intertwined, Tigon's identity remains unrevealed, even though Staiger assumes that he must be no other than Frederik Hahn a.k.a. Torch, the charismatic Advanced Chemistry MC and one of the most widely acknowledged pioneers of German hip-hop.[4] That Neblett, Schacht, and Staiger ulti-

---

Notes for this chapter begin on page 96.

mately fail to expose who Tigon "really" is implies that any attempt to locate German-language rap's origin must remain an exercise in futility. The mockumentary's point is precisely that *the* singular moment that signals the emergence of *Deutschrap* exists only as a constellation of postmodern myths that are, however, central to the identity formation and self-understanding of the German hip-hop community.[5]

Black Tape's deliberate non-answer to the question of *Deutschrap*'s origin—despite its many clues as to what, when, and who it *could* be—points research on the topic in a productive direction. In line with the mockumentary's claim, this essay understands *Deutschrap* as a practice of selective cultural adaptation, subtended by internal incongruities, productive animosities, and unexpected overlaps that lacks not only a clear beginning, but also a discernible center. A polyvalent, decentralized, and at times overdetermined subculture on its way into the mainstream demands close-readings of texts—which is to say their styles, sounds, and samples as much as their lyrics—that compliment and at times correct the culture's grand narrative and successfully illuminate "the tensions between local and national identification, nationalism and the hip-hop nation, [...] and claims for realness and the performative."[6] To this end, this essay rearranges rap tracks into heuristically productive constellations and provides comprehensive and comparative analyses of texts that have received less scholarly attention than, let's say, Advanced Chemistry's "Fremd im eigenen Land" or Die Fantastischen Vier's "Die da?!"—even though these seminal texts (and artists) appear as points of reference within a given constellation.[7] Looking at clusters of tracks released by bands that nominally belong to the *Alte Schule* (old school), the culture's pioneers, I examine German hip-hop's cross-pollinations and contradictions during a transitional period from the late 1980s to the mid-90s when the *Alte Schule* was forced to interact with and react to the perceived competition of the nascent *Neue Schule* (new school) as more and more MCs in Germany began flowing in their native language(s).[8] In adopting the strategies of contemporary genre studies writ large, the way in which it "indexes and tracks history within [a genre] via continuities as well as ruptures," it is my goal to "open up history in different ways" and thus permit alternative perspectives on an only selectively mapped-out youth culture that would become the dominant music genre in post-Wall Germany.[9]

To be sure, *Black Tape* interferes into the (academic) master narrative of *Deutschrap* that frames the transition from the Old to the New School.[10] This grand narrative usually begins with hip-hop's reemergence from the underground which then culminated in the forming of two irreconcilable factions, one represented by the white-middle class fun rappers Die Fantastischen Vier from Stuttgart, the other by the politically conscious *Alte Schule*-crew Advanced Chemistry, whose three Heidelberg-based MCs have an immigration background. While Advanced Chemistry—and here in particular Torch as the patron saint of the *Alte Schule*—promoted the culture within the Zulu Nation's strict set of rules as a means to ensure authenticity, Die Fantastischen Vier took a different approach when they infamously performed their break-through hit "Die da" on public television and thus defined German hip-hop for a mass audience.[11] A third power, the Frankfurt-based Rödelheim Hartreim Projekt, added not only a healthy dose of aggressive competition to the game, but also pushed the culture further into the mainstream (as a multi-million D-Mark record business) with their bad boy-image and talent for self-marketing.[12] In 1995, the allegedly apolitical and predominantly white German middle-class *Neue Schule* took over, a changing of the guard, according to hip-hop lore, marked by the releases of the MZEE-label sampler *Die Klasse von 95* (and the tour that preceded it by a year) and Massive Töne's album *Kopfnicker* (1996).[13] The *Neue Schule* in turn provoked the counter-movement of underground battle-rap, in particular associated with the *Aggro Berlin* label and the performance venue Royal Bunker. Out of battle-rap arose Gangsta- and *Straßenrap* in the vein of Bushido and Sido respectively, in which, as Maria Stehle argues, "transatlantic references are superficial, historical references to antiracist struggles are all but absent."[14]

In the context of the culture's muddled historiography, *Black Tape*'s concrete temporal and spatial coordinates, the Heidelberg Campbell Barracks in June of 1986, connect German rap's quasi-mythical *Urknall* to specific discourses on hip-hop's complex identity politics in a way that illuminates important continuities and ruptures.[15] By 1986, hip-hop culture had already been introduced to the West German public sphere (and, what is more, subsequently disappeared from it[16]) not only via the nation's movie theaters but also through public and private television. As the singer Trettmann (Stefan Richter) remembers, "in 1984, the Rock Steady together with the New York City Breakers performed on West German public television, I believe on 'Wetten, dass...?'"[17] The reference to host Thomas Gottschalk's successful prime time TV show is noteworthy since Gottschalk would in hindsight become the inauthentic Other that predated those who took hip-hop culture seriously. Together with his colleagues Frank Laufenberg and Manfred Sexauer as GLS-United, Gottschalk had "translated" The Sugarhill Gang's "Rapper's Delight" into "Rappers Deutsch" in 1980.[18] *Black Tape* acknowledges the existence of "Rappers Deutsch" in a brief clip from a GLS-United live performance on public television, only to reject continuity and date the "true" beginning of German rap six years later, when hip-hop had become a non-topic in the mainstream. In contrast to its original inception in the South Bronx, then, hip-hop in West Germany did not originate as a localized subculture with a relatively well-documented beginning. Instead, it is the product of widely dispersed and, at times, refracted transatlantic (but also inner-European) flows.[19] While German hip-hop certainly evolved via sub-cultural processes until it reappeared in the mainstream again around 1992, it is crucial to understand it as the product of multiple and often contradictory impulses that not only positioned it somewhat awkwardly vis-à-vis what hip-hop originally "meant" as an African-American culture, but also resulted in numerous, disconnected local permutations.[20]

One of these impulses comes from the presence of the U.S. military in West Germany in the 1980s, which ensured that some of the German soon-to-be-hip-hop-heads would be exposed to the music on heavy rotation in clubs frequented by G.I.s, while others found their inspirations elsewhere–for example on TV and on the big screen.[21] One of the most striking details of *Black Tape*'s founding myth in this regard is the reaction that Tigon's unannounced performance caused among the audience as they came face-to-"face" with the intruder and his poetry of an alien.[22] While the narrative in part explains their panic with the anti-American sentiments of the time and the related possibility of terrorist attacks, *Black Tape* also toys with the idea that the unexpected (linguistic) appropriation of African-American culture by the German Other was the trigger.[23] At the same time, a German MC aggressively forces himself into a culture that, it is implied, is not his own. To be clear, my point is not that the film articulates a disregard for the Black Other within the German hip-hop community (or a wholesale rejection of *Amerikanismus*, for that matter[24]), but rather that it allegorizes its struggles for emancipation, legitimacy, and ownership as well as the right to write its own histories.[25] Ironically, *Black Tape* does interfere in the very process of standard historiography it initially undermines. When Tigon ultimately decides against revealing his identity at a highly publicized hip-hop jam, four MCs take the stage in his stead. As stand-ins for the doubly absent Tigon–he is neither physically present nor does he actually exist–the all-male roster of Megaloh (Uchenna van Capelleveen), Afrob (Robert Zemichiel), Max (Maximilian Herre) and Samy Deluxe (Samy Sorge) epitomizes *Deutschrap*.[26] This is not, however, a challenge to the relevance and skills of the rappers who "replace" Tigon, but rather goes to show that *Black Tape* consciously abandons its carefully constructed, heavily coded, and epistemologically elusive postmodern event in favor of a concrete if not necessarily representative cross-section of German MCing. Ultimately, as I show below, Tigon becomes a schizophrenic composite of multiple rappers from different eras and with notably different backgrounds.[27]

In refusing to reveal Tigon's identity—to leave his face blank, as it were—*Black Tape*'s denouement addresses both the issue of cultural appropriation and the related question of who is allowed to shape the subculture's officially sanctioned narrative in Germany.[28] Three of the four ersatz-Tigons are Afro-German, while German-Turkish rappers, to pick one obvious example, are not present on stage. As one of these MCs, Afrob, argues about the black experience inscribed in hip-hop culture, "the right of the Germans to emancipate themselves from where rap actually comes from – and where I come from – is totally legitimate. You just cannot completely negate that part and still claim the rest for yourself."[29] As Afrob's position reminds us, the scene's search for authenticity always also indexes multiple alterities and by default alienations, be it in the context of hybrid identities, marginalized positions, or the narrative of a predominantly white middle-class at the center of 1990's *Deutschrap* vis-à-vis U.S. hip-hop's element of Blackness. Yet, while never explicitly mentioned in *Black Tape*, Karsten Stieneke a.k.a. Aphroe—rather than Torch—provided Tigon's raps for the mockumentary. Born in Herne in the postindustrial Ruhr valley region, Aphroe is a white German MC with no immigration background and, as a lyricist with strong ties to the *Alte Schule*, is quite distinguishable from the styles and pedigrees of the *Neue Schule* MCs Afrob, Samy Deluxe, or Max. Put differently, the phantom Tigon is construed as a site of hybridity that fuses a plurality of (local) identities, ethnicities, and aesthetics into a postmodern myth that raises issues of German-ness. In a sense, then, *Black Tape* challenges histories that compartmentalize German hip-hop into clear-cut categories (including the problematic differentiation between native German MCs vs. rappers with immigration backgrounds[30]), but simultaneously writes its own narrative which in turn creates new blind spots and omissions.[31]

Poetry of an Alien: Case Studies and Constellations

The first set of case studies revolves around aspects of middle-class German-ness in the *Alte Schule*-context and the ways in which specific bands positioned themselves vis-à-vis African-American culture. In 1989, approximately a decade prior to the graduation (or dismissal, depending on one's perspective) of the *Klasse von '95*, the Eifel-based group LSD, short for Legally Spread Dope, had published the "Competent"-EP, which they followed up with their first album, *Watch out for the Third Rail* in 1991—a noteworthy reference to the 1982 movie *Wild Style*. Released on the then Cologne-based label Rhythm Attack Productions, whose owner Stephan Meyner had hitherto specialized in licensing American rap-acts, "Competent" ended up being the only German contribution to the label's *New School*-Sampler—note the moniker—among tracks by African-American artists such as J.V.C. F.O.R.C.E or DJ Duquan & The Wonderluv, which LSD's Future Rock a.k.a. Michael Rick had produced. Performed in English by Ko Lute (Patrick Steffen), the single "Competent," with its meticulously curated samples of James Brown's "Give it up or Turnit a Loose" and Uncle Louie's "I like Funky Music," among many others, explicitly references the U.S. Old School rather than the New School.[32] LSD's sound is thus closer in spirit to the output of Grandmaster Flash and the Furious Five or Afrika Bambaataa than the politically charged noise-sound of Public Enemy or the confrontational hardcore rap of N.W.A. Ko Lute's apolitical lyrics neither refer to the band's West German middle-class background nor do they explicitly address rap in a local context, unless one counts the repeated claim that LSD are, indeed, "competent" despite their visible whiteness, linguistically audible German-ness, and subcultural belatedness.[33] Overall, "Competent" exemplifies a strain of German Old School-rap that seeks to stay as close as possible to the original culture with regard to its aesthetics. Yet, while LSD adopts hip-hop's aural and visual codes, the group does not engage in processes of cultural adaptation as the band seeks to minimize the focus on nationality and skin color.

In 1991, the year in which LSD's *Watch out for the Third Rail* came out, Boombastic Records released one of the first German hip-hop samplers, *Krauts with Attitude – German Hip Hop Vol. 1*. Compiled by the journalist Michael Reinboth and the DJ Katmando—after Rick Ski had left the project due to creative differences—*Krauts with Attitude* contains 15 songs of which only three were performed in German.[34] The track list includes LSD and the pre-fame Die Fantastischen Vier, but also a number of artists with an immigration background such as Brothers Moving Germany or Al Rakhun. The title insinuates a connection between the controversial group N.W.A. (and by extension the Afro-American experience writ large) and German youths, going back to a story in the music magazine *Spex* a year earlier "that announced it luridly on the cover as 'Krauts with Attitude,' but in the issue itself discusses it tamely as 'Eurohop.'"[35] In the sampler's liner notes, we find the following statement: "It is time to counter the self-confidence of the Brits and the Americans. [...]. It was hard enough to be accepted in hip-hop as a non-American and pale face. I believe that the major labels are to blame here as they pretend that they cannot sell hip-hop without a Negro."[36] For Dietmar Elflein, this provocatively phrased proclamation turns a "problematic but still ironically recursive title applied to a globally hallucinated subcultural dissident discourse into a clearly nationalistic statement."[37] Elflein is concerned with the exclusion of immigrant voices in what should be understood as an art form of the disenfranchised on a compilation that prominently features the colors of the German flag on its cover.[38] By reading *Krauts with Attitude* exclusively within the parameters of a specific subset of U.S. hip-hop culture, however, he overlooks not only its deliberate stylistic and topical diversity, but also disregards how specific tracks rethink *Deutschrap*'s own position in the (transatlantic) game.

In this light, consider the contribution of one of the understudied bands on the compilation, the Bremen-based crew Lyrical Poetry, comprised of Matthias Zähler a.k.a. Quick Lyric, Ralf Pauli a.k.a. Nomäd, and Stefan Heilek a.k.a. DJ Goldfinger. The title of the song discussed here, "Poetry of an Alien (Original Mix)," not only evidences a sense of alterity with regard to Lyrical Poetry's whiteness in an African-American culture, but also in the context of their own position within the fragmented national hip-hop scene.[39] Like "Competent," "Poetry of an Alien" is an English-language track by an *Alte Schule*-band that falls into the white German middle-class category.[40] Stylistically and thematically, however, "Poetry of an Alien" differs significantly from "Competent" (or "Jetzt geht's ab" by Die Fantastischen Vier, for that matter).[41] The original mix of "Poetry of an Alien" on *Krauts with Attitude* is hardcore rap, whose industrial one-note sample supports the aggressive beat that drives the raw production and threatens to overpower Quick Lyric's distorted voice. DJ Goldfinger repeatedly scratches parts of Chuck D.'s line from "Welcome to the Terrordome,"–"hear the drummer get wicked"[42]–a song from Public Enemy's third album *Fear of a Black Planet* (1990) and one of the seminal examples of the band's signature sound. Similar to "Competent," "Poetry of an Alien" inscribes itself into the discourse of African-American rap culture via sampling. Yet, whereas LSD frequently rely on funk and soul, Lyrical Poetry cite one of the more contemporaneous voices of "Black CNN" even as they shift the thematic focus away from the African-American experience to their own unclear identity position as white German middle-class hip-hop artists.[43] This contrastive analysis of LSD and Lyrical Poetry is neither meant to assign value, nor does it seek to reframe "Poetry of an Alien" as overtly political rap.[44] Instead it highlights the differences between two texts that tend to be indiscriminately grouped together as the work of white, German middle-class crews that represent the *Alte Schule*– if they become the object of scholarship at all.

In a similar manner, early 90s hip-hop as inscribed in what Sabine von Dirke calls a "discourse and politics of exclusion" is often exclusively negotiated in German Studies through a handful of examples such as "Fremd im eigenen Land" and, to a lesser degree, "Ahmed Gündüz" by Fresh Familee.[45] While, to be clear, the contributions of Torch, Toni-L (Toni Landomini) and Linguist (Kofi Yakpo) are central and critical to an understanding of *Deutschrap*'s trajectory, their *Bildungsbürgertum*-background also sets them apart from the–no less eloquent–Fresh Familee-MCs.[46] This is, of course, not an attempt to dispute Advanced Chemistry's experiences with racism, to challenge their claim to authenticity, or to discredit the quality of their tracks, but rather is meant to allow for a more differentiated look at what has often been lumped together as a separate hip-hop strain shaped by the immigrant experience and as such categorically positioned as a homogenous counter-paradigm to the allegedly all-white middle-class *Deutschrap*. In an essay from 2000, to give a noteworthy counter-example for this tendency toward conflation, Christoph Ribbat engages with the *Ruhrgebiet*-based Sons of Gastarbeita, a band whose core members share, as the deliberate misspelling of the German word for "guest worker" indicates, an immigration background coupled with a hybrid, hyphenated identity.[47] Yet their sound–"a mix of rap, funk, and noisy rock"–sets them musically apart from Advanced Chemistry's discography, for example on a track such as the angry, guitar-heavy crossover "Hardcore."[48] On the other hand, the ways in which Sons of Gastarbeita express the experiences as second- or third-generation immigrants in their lyrics very much evoke the didacticism of many, if by no means all, Advanced Chemistry-releases.[49]

The output of Fresh Familee from Ratingen-West, a 1960s *Neue Heimat*-project near Düsseldorf, further exemplifies the difficulties that arise when certain categorizations are applied too broadly.[50] Fresh Familee's music often differs significantly from that of both Advanced Chemistry and the Sons of Gastarbeita, even if they overlap at times and clearly share an investment in immigrant and hybrid-identity experiences.[51] When Gesa zur Nieden compares Fresh Familee's "Ahmed Gündüz," its first verse deliberately rapped in broken German, to Sons of Gastarbeita's "Söhne der Gastarbeita," she notes that the latter "points to the generational process of cultural rootedness rather than to actual experiences of social, political, and medial discrimination as the reason for rebellion."[52] On "Heimat," Fresh Familee's Suli (Suleman Isak) critically addresses the immigrant experience: "they cannot stay here, but they also cannot go back, they are just without a home and defenseless."[53] In contrast to a track like "Fremd im eigenen Land," however, it is noteworthy that "Heimat" is not a first-person account, but rather narrated in the third person. The decidedly personal points-of-view in Advanced Chemistry's signature track give way to that of an accusing observer, who "lends a voice to his parent's generation."[54] What is more, the lyrics to "Heimat" were in part "ghost-written" by the middle-class poetess Nadia Günther.[55] I do not mean to suggest that Günther's involvement delegitimizes the humanist and pro-refugee impetus of "Heimat," but rather wish to illustrate the permeability of categorical borders in German hip-hop that reconfigured the ways in which authenticity is negotiated. Fresh Familee's own position of alterity within the *Deutschrap* scene of the early 1990s deserves attention in this regard.

In Detlev F. Neufert's 1991 documentary *Fresh Familee: Comin' from Ratinga*, the director explicitly frames the band in the context of ghetto culture. Constructing a clichéd image of Germany's ghetto-scape, Neufert's voice-over ominously intones early on in the documentary: "The children who grew up here lived by their own rules and rejected their environment. In order to escape the isolation of the satellite city, they searched for another identity which they found in gangs and groups."[56] While Neufert's direction irritates with some stilted, scripted skits, he manages to convey a sense of the band members' real-life experiences, including the petty criminal activities of German-Turkish rapper Tahir Cevik a.k.a. Tachi in his younger years. That said, over the course of Neufert's film several band members challenge and even undermine the director's representation of Ratingen-West as a dangerous ghetto. While the social backgrounds of most of Fresh Familee's members arguably resemble the U.S. ghetto experience more closely than that of LSD or Lyrical Poetry–even though comparisons of that kind remain inherently problematic–their music frequently contains strong pop-elements that torpedo an aesthetic comparison to Public Enemy, for example, as they challenge this particular U.S. role-model on the musical level. Fresh Familee's reggae-infused, subversive track "Sexy Kanake," from the major label album *Alles Frisch* (1994) in particular illustrates how the crew also negotiates their alterity through atypical pop-sensibilities.[57] "Memories," a track from the band's first EP *Coming from Ratinga* (1991), includes a melodious and soulful hook by a female singer, a stylistic choice altogether absent not only from "Competent" or "Poetry of an Alien," but also unthinkable in the context of Public Enemy.

In addition, Fresh Familee were one of the first rap crews to be signed by a major label, a move that was met with resistance by large portions of the hip-hop community, especially those who understood themselves as the legit underground opposition to rap's dreaded appropriation by and assimilation into the mainstream even if they hailed from a middle-class background. As Tachi remembers:

> They accused us of never having been at jams. I attended the first jam in North Rhine-Westphalia. Why should I go to Mainz? I didn't have the money to travel there and you also didn't hear about it. I knew early on all the important hip-hop artists from my region, Krefeld, Essen, Oberhausen, and then somebody from Heidelberg tells me years later we weren't real because we didn't go to jams.[58]

Fresh Familee also went on tour with Die Fantastischen Vier, which aligned them directly with the allegedly inauthentic strain of German rap and in turn triggered reactions from the other end of the perceived spectrum, in particular the scenes in Frankfurt and Cologne. This hostility is exemplified by Hans Solo (Frank Schnütgen) from the Cologne-based Äi-Tiem, who raps on "Erbarmungslos" (1993): "Andy Ypsilon, don't think I will spare you, I'm on the microphone and I'm not just threatening you verbally."[59] His juvenile threat toward the sound programmer of Die Fantastischen Vier illustrates well the in-fighting that fueled German hip-hop in the 1990s. The members of Äi-Tiem (such as Ralph Dammers a.k.a. Lord Fader) are white Germans who grew up in Köln-Porz, a neighborhood similar to Ratingen-West in terms of its demographics. Yet, Äi-Tiem, with its often pornographic and violent lyrics, hardly engages with these socio-political realities in a constructive manner and instead utilizes exaggeration as a tool for provocation. As a result, they construct a specific image world of the "ghetto." The crew was also part of the Blitz Mob, a multi-national collective signed on one of the first German independent hip-hop labels, Blitz Vinyl, founded by Rick Ski, among others. In a sense, then, Fresh Familee's social background did little to grant them the seal of authenticity from one of the most middle-class German rap crews, LSD, as the former rejected preconceived notions of what rap in Germany should sound like according to those who had, at the beginning of their career, emulated early African-American hip-hop culture so faithfully.

The complex debate on the German ghetto experience continues across tracks by crews that are not usually associated with this particular aspect of the culture. Combining the political attitude of a track like "Heimat" with the aggressiveness of "Erbarmungslos," the second version of "Rabenschwarze Nacht" by the Dortmund-based *Alte Schule*-formation Too Strong, released on the 1993 EP of the same name, critically engages with xenophobia and racism in the wake of the arson attacks on refugee homes in the early 1990s.[60] In contrast to Fresh Familee's contribution, however, the track maps out the urban night from the perspective of a presumably white graffiti writer. Rapped by MCs Pure Doze and Der Lange, the observant but uninvolved lyrical I exclaims " At 2:30 in the morning, four people died, it was over, hearts were torn apart during the night, nobody was seen, sturdy shoes from the wardrobe of the 1940s, minimal hair, any questions?"[61] In the bleak world of "Rabenschwarze Nacht," right-wing violence is an integral part of German city life, yet one that people choose not to see even if they do witness it. While Too Strong clearly position themselves as opponents of the violence–"When does this nightmare end?"[62]–they do not foresee any change for the better, nor do they actively intervene in the discourse of the Other. The didactic impetus of "Heimat" is replaced by a sense of resignation, while the U.S. projects are restaged as an overdetermined fantasy in the working-class context of the nocturnal Dortmund. While sincere as far as the political position is concerned, Too Strong playfully inscribe themselves into Hollywood's image world of the American ghetto. "Rabenschwarze Nacht," to give one example, opens with a monologue taken from the German dub of George P. Cosmatos's Reagan-era action-thriller *Cobra* (1986), in which Sylvester Stallone plays the gritty LAPD cop Marion Cobretti who cleans out the crime infested urban jungles of Los Angeles.[63] Given Too Strong's own left-wing and even anarchist tendencies, the reference to *Cobra* cannot be read as a blind endorsement of the film's ultra-reactionary politics. Rather, it maps the problematic allure of Stallone's stylized movie vigilante-ism onto the real right-wing violence of burning down a refugee shelter.

Too Strong frequently operate with similar aesthetic strategies to complicate the message of their tracks. The sound of this "Rabenschwarze Nacht"-mix, for example, notably clashes with the brooding lyrics, thus creating tension between form and content. A rap-group that favors funk as the basis for their work, Too Strong sampled "Synthetic Substitution" by Melvin Bliss, a classic South Bronx block-party drum break that adds a club-vibe to the track and draws a direct line from Dortmund in the 90s to New York in the 70s and 80s. Yet, they also add a scratched snippet from a German children's story audio play (the immensely popular *Hörspiele*) that mentions an evil spirit–citing their own German pop-cultural socialization–and eventually sample piano notes from "Matthew Ghost Story," a track on the soundtrack to John Carpenter's supernatural horror film *The Fog* (1980). That Too Strong operate with and merge these pop-culture elements and deliberately superimpose these aural markers over Germany's socio-political landscape becomes even more apparent on the "Empire-Version" to "Rabenschwarze Nacht," released in 1994–but performed live prior to that date on jams as their signature song–on the band's debut album *Greatest Hits*. Rapped only by Pure Doze, this particular remix prominently features a sample of John William's "Imperial March" from the Star Wars-franchise, a leitmotif reserved for the evil Sith Lord Darth Vader.[64] The threatening, horn-heavy melody popularized by a major Hollywood franchise and the powerful beat–that becomes even more pronounced in later versions, such as the 1996 "Empire-Remix"–drastically alter the aural atmosphere on "Rabenschwarze Nacht." As Schacht writes in an online essay, the band wanted "to underscore the political content of the lyrics, an imperial march against Nazis."[65] What is more, Too Strong wrap a political message in an eclectic soundscape that weaves together sci-fi and horror tropes to represent the German city as a phantasmagoric, postmodern pastiche shaped by potentially irreconcilable perspectives.

Despite their reliance on soundtracks, film and music samples, and other pop-culture ephemera, hardly any historian of German hip-hop could deny that Too Strong–in part due to its members' involvement in the Dortmund graffiti scene–are authentic exponents of the culture and, what is more, part of the *Alte Schule*.[66] Yet–to take this discussion full circle–Too Strong also at one point distanced themselves from the values of the Universal Zulu Nation Germany, propagated by Advanced Chemistry, among others, when they proclaimed the "Silo Nation" as a counter-movement that, for example, accepted alcohol and drugs and in which the Silo signified, as Pure Doze points out in the documentary *Silo – Geburt einer Nation*, "receptivity and storage capacity."[67] While initially a beer-infused birthday party gag, the ironic move toward a different interpretation of hip-hop quickly gained traction within certain parts of the community and thus illuminates the culture's localized currents which led Too Strong to define the movement in more concrete terms. As Pure Doze raps on "Dortmund Silo," "Yes, I'm a member of Silo, one million, one trillion, how many are part of this nation? Hard to say, we don't ask questions about rules."[68] While he later positions Die Fantastischen Vier as the paradigmatic Other, it is noteworthy that he also rejects the strict "rules" of Afrika Bambaataa–and by extension Torch–and instead adapts the source culture for his own circumstances.[69] On "Silo Kapitel III," a track from Too Strong's 1996 album *InterCity-Funk*[70]–when Torch and Too Strong had already buried the hatchet–Pure Doze repeats this implied critique of cultural narrow-mindedness and gatekeeping when he rhymes "Silo is a train and you don't need a ticket, nobody will check whether you have one, all you have to do is to get on board," yet at the same time Too Strong not only defend "real" hip-hop against artists such as Die Fantastischen Vier, but further acknowledge the legacy of Advanced Chemistry by using portions of the *Stern-TV* title melody that also features prominently on "Fremd im eigenen Land," which uses it to echo Chuck D.'s idea of rap as "Black-CNN."[71]

Conclusion

On his 2001 zeitgeist track "Gangsta Rap," Curse (Michael Sebastian Kurth) rhymes, "We are the street urchins, the German, Gypsy, Turkish, and Russian children. We are the children of the lower- and the middle-classes, we are the model children. German rap has grown up, plays the guitar, has guns, and unfortunately even listeners among skinheads."[72] Curse not only provides an overview of *Deutschrap*'s diversity and permutations, he also reacts to the culture's paradigm shift toward gangsta-, battle-, and street-rap around the turn of the new millennium that—as the story goes—returned the microphone to MCs with an immigration background. Over the course of the last two decades, rappers such as Bushido, Haftbefehl, or Capital Bra have not only dominated the headlines and charts, but also attracted heightened scholarly interest because of how their songs presumably let the subaltern speak. Yet, these artists do not constitute a homogenous group that necessarily articulates its experiences from the perceived margins of society in comparable fashion. Put differently, scholarly work on Sido and Bushido—to pick the most prominent examples—should take into account the tonal and stylistic differences between the two MCs (Sido's irony, for example, or the samples they use) as much as it acknowledges the fact that Aggro Berlin, the label responsible for their mainstream careers, actively created media personalities for them. The constellations that I have formed in this essay can also be found in the extremely successful *Deutschrap* of the 21st century. Ideally, such constellations would connect the lucrative gangsta-rap with the queer, left-wing raps of Sookee—in part a reaction to both the misogyny and anti-Semitism in tracks by Farid Bang or Kollegah[73]—or the avant-garde, high pitched head-trips of Marteria's mask-wearing alter ego Marsimoto, an aesthetic amalgam of Madlib's Quasimoto and MF Doom. To be sure, there are a lot of flows left to examine in German rap, from the *Alte Schule* to today: the Britcore-inspired songs by bands such as No Remorze, for example, or the psychological horrorcore of Phase V as much as the loudmouthed, feminist trap-tracks of SXTN and SSIO's absurd German-Turkish comedy raps.[74]

KAI-UWE WERBECK holds a Ph.D. from the University of North Carolina at Chapel Hill and is an Associate Professor of German and Affiliate Faculty of Film Studies at the University of North Carolina at Charlotte. He has published on the multi-media poetics of Rolf Dieter Brinkmann, the techno aesthetic in the works of Rainald Goetz, the concept of home in rubble film and literature, subversion in no-budget German horror films, and the interplay between augmented reality and living fiction.

Notes

1. See *Black Tape*, directed by Sekou A. Neblett (2015; Cologne, NRW: Gifted Films,) TV. While never an official member of the Stuttgart-based crew Freundeskreis, Neblett a.k.a. Sekou the Ambassador was featured on many of their songs. Born in Boston, Sekou rapped primarily if not exclusively in English–his native language–both on his collaborations with Freundeskreis and his solo work. Schacht, a.k.a. Hawkeye, is a hip-hop historian, moderator, and activist and Staiger the founder of the Berlin-based battle-rap venue/record label Royal Bunker and a music journalist, among other things.
2. At this point in the narrative, 1986, "Deutschrap" would be an anachronistic term that only emerges half a decade later. The term is a contested one. See Maria Stehle who defines it as follows: "The Deutschrap of the early 1990s did not work with nationalist imagery, but it illustrated a clear move away from the search for forms of identification outside a fixed notion of national identity, which characterized the political hip-hop culture in the early 1990s. Deutschrap is a more commercialized form of rap music, which constructs a new form of national identity." Maria Stehle, *Ghetto Voices in Contemporary German Culture: Textscapes, Filmscapes, Soundscapes.* (Rochester: Camden House, 2012), 141. In a sense, Stehle's definition constitutes a corrective to Elizabeth Loentz's claim that "the moniker Deutschrap had less to do with the music's country of origin or the language of the rap texts but with its young, mostly white 'BioGerman' makers' *post-Wende* search for a new, positive and unapologetic German identity" (quoted in Stehle, *Ghetto Voices*, 141). In this essay, I use it as the catch-all term for "rap made in Germany" that it is today for reasons of economy.
3. As such, it qualifies as one of Hayden White's postmodernist docu-dramas in which "everything is presented as if it were of the same ontological order, both real and imaginary." Hayden White, "The Modernist Event," in *The Persistence of History: Cinema, Television, and the Modern Event*, ed. Vivian Sobchack (New York and London: Routledge, 1996), 19.
4. All translations from the original German are mine unless otherwise stated. As hip-hop activist Ralf Kotthoff claims, "[Torch] is the origin. No doubt about it." Quoted in Jan Wehn and Davide Bortot. *Könnt ihr uns hören? Eine Oral History des deutschen Rap*, 4. Edition (Berlin: Ullstein, 2019), 36. However, see also Rick Ski, who submits that "if you only look hard enough, you will find someone who did it earlier." Quoted in Wehn and Bortot, *Könnt ihr*, 27.
5. This is a complex debate that includes the bold proclamation by Die Fantastischen Vier that they were the "first consequently German-speaking rap recording artists." Quoted in Sascha Verlan and Hannes Loh, *35 Jahre Hip-hop in Deutschland.* (Höfen: Hannibal, 2015), 375.
6. Stehle, *Ghetto Voices*, 131. I follow Ribbat's suggestion that "in-depth research on German hip hop should examine more than just the lyrics of the rap songs and instead provide a comprehensive cultural analysis that also explores the beats, sounds, and samples of the records." Christoph Ribbat. "How Hip Hop Hit Heidelberg: German Rappers, Rhymes, and Rhythms," in *'Here, There and Everywhere:' The Foreign Politics of American Popular Culture*, eds. Reinhold Wagnleitner and Elaine Tyler May (Hanover and London: UP of New England, 2000), 214.
7. This is not to say that these dichotomies–such as party rap vs. authentic rap–are invalid, but rather that they threaten to overshadow a heterogeneous, often schizophrenic scene that at all times constituted a multitude of ideological viewpoints, stylistic preferences, and personal backgrounds.
8. The *Alte Schule* emerged around 1987. As Sascha Verlan and Hannes Loh explain, "usually, Old School denotes the period between the first record releases, which is to say the years before 1991. Those who were already active during that time and built and shaped the scene call themselves old schooler. The formative events for the Old School are the

first trans-regional jams starting in 1986. In contrast, New School are those that joined the hip-hop scene in the 1990s." Verlan and Loh, *35 Jahre*, 293-294. Sabine von Dirke speaks of "adaptations" of the U.S. model and identifies three dominant results of such adaptations: "The Old School, that is the pioneers of hip-hop active since the early 1980s, developed a vague idea of a transnational hip-hop community that was still strongly adapted to the U.S. model of message rap. The New School, which emerged almost concurrently with unification and which became the focus of the music industry's attention, saw itself stepping out of the shadow of U.S. popular culture. [...]. Finally, the second and third generation of immigrants adopted rap music in order to forge an alternative identity in opposition and outside of the confines of ethnicity, race, and nationality." Sabine von Dirke, "Hip-Hop Made in Germany: From Old School to the Kanaksta Movement," in *German Pop Culture: How 'American' Is It?*, ed. Agnes C. Mueller (Ann Arbor: U Michigan P, 2004), 97-98.

9. Jaimey Fisher, "Introduction: Toward Generic Histories–Film Genre, Genre Theory, and German Film Studies," in *Generic Histories of German Cinema: Genre and Its Deviations*, ed. Jaimey Fisher (Rochester: Camden House, 2013), 4.
10. See for example the "Deutschrap Periodensystem" as a creative example. Lili Ruge et al. "Deutschrap Periodensystem," Bayrischer Rundfunk, https://story.br.de/hip-hop-periodensystem/. Accessed 08/06/2020.
11. Their 1992 appearance on Dieter Thomas Heck's *ZDF-Hitparade*, a show that usually featured *Schlager* and, to a lesser, degree German-language pop, arguably constitutes the most singular moment of hip-hop's perceived breakaway from what was considered acceptable cultural practice by what Trettmann sarcastically terms "codex-contaminated real-keepers." Quoted in Wehn and Bortot, *Könnt ihr*, 391. In an interview with Imke Gerriets, Smudo admits that "at first glance, the decision to go to Dieter Thomas Heck in 1992 was stupid. But ten-and-a-half million viewers are quite an audience and we also had to realize that Heck was a real soul-brother behind the scenes." Imke Gerriets. "Smudo: Wir haben schon ein Abschlussbild gemacht," *t-online,* July 7, 2019, https://www.t-online.de/unterhaltung/musik/id_86135630/30-jahre-fanta-4-smudo-spricht-ueber-karriere-kinder-und-kritik.html.
12. See Mark Pennay who delivers one of these scholarly looks from afar and calls "Fremd im eigenen Land" and *Vier Gewinnt* "two catalytic records [that] represent two distinct constellations around which German-language rap has since burgeoned." Mark Pennay, "Rap in Germany: Birth of a Genre," in *Global Noise: Rap and Hip-Hop outside of the USA*, ed. Tony Mitchell (Middletown: Wesleyan UP, 2001), 119. About the Rödelheim Hartreim Projekt he says "their sound is a mixture of rap braggadocio with laid-back grooves and slick production and makes use of their regional accents (a marker of class as well as geography)." Pennay, "Rap in Germany," 124.
13. Von Dirke, for example, claims that the *Neue Schule*–which she lumps together as "middle-class party hip-hops"–was the most critical of the one-to-one equation of the United States with Germany, emphasizing instead the differences between their own social situation and that of African-American youth." Von Dirke, *Made in Germany*, 101. Verlan and Loh, on the other hand, argue that "the Absolute Beginner, Fettes Brot, Freundeskreis, Massive Töne or Fünf Sterne Deluxe were decidedly not of the opinion that the 'rap of the black ghettos' had become German (as Torsten Stecher had claimed in the newspaper Die Zeit). These New School-bands understood themselves in the tradition of the Old School and still saw their music as part of an international movement." Verlan and Loh, *35 Jahre*, 93.
14. Stehle, *Ghetto Voices*, 136.
15. The Campbell Barracks in the South of Heidelberg, in the neighborhood of Rohrbach, were built by the Wehrmacht in 1937, under the name of *Großdeutschland-Kaserne* and as such constitute a transnational space themselves.
16. See Detlef Rick a.k.a. Rick Ski, who argues that after the initial hype "come Winter 1985, rap music was once again considered annoying 'negro music' by the masses and was thus

ignored." Detlef Rick, "Wie Hip-Hop nach Deutschland kam: Der Durchbruch nach dem Hype," *Der Spiegel*, August 8, 2008, https://www.spiegel.de/geschichte/wie-hip-hop-nach-deutschland-kam-a-949537.html

17. Quoted in Wehn and Bortot, *Könnt ihr*, 17.
18. GLS-United's "Rappers Deutsch" is a nostalgic romp through (imported) youth cultures from the 1950s onward that ironically never explicitly mentions hip-hop in the lyrics. Gottschalk, whose verse is actually the last one on the record, rather states that "I am a New-Wave-Man." GLS-United. "Rappers Deutsch" (Hamburg: Metronome, 1980). In this regard it is noteworthy that the Sugarhill Gang also signifies the inauthentic Other in early American hip-hop, as they reportedly appropriated the styles and lyrics of a subculture to produce its first commercial hit.
19. In this essay, I use the term "flow" not only in the broad sense of "informational and interactional links among sets of individuals and institutions" in late-capitalist systems, but also with regard to the vectors of (transatlantic) cultural exchange aligned with it. Michael D. Levin, "Flow and Place: Transnationalism in Four Cases." *Anthropologica* 44, No.1 (2002): 3. As Michael Hoyler and Christoph Mager point out with regard to German rap, "the Federal Republic of Germany was highly integrated in transatlantic flows of people, commodities, and images," which in turn allowed hip-hop culture to migrate to central Europe in multiple adaptations. Michael Hoyler and Christoph Mager. "Hip-Hop ist im Haus: Cultural Policy, Community Centres, and the Making of Hip-Hop Music in Germany," *Built Environment* 31, No. 3 (2005): 237-238. Christoph Ribbat critically intervenes, when he rhetorically asks in the context of *Deutschrap*, "Can we now really view the transfer of American pop music as nothing more than a flow of fashion gimmicks, dollars, and deutschmarks?" Ribbat, "How Hip Hop," 212. Of course, it also refers to the smooth interplay of music and language in rap.
20. See Verlan and Loh, who claim "only with the success of the Fantastischen Vier the question arose, what hip-hop's reason for being in Germany actually was, this protest culture of disenfranchised ethnical minorities from the U.S. big city ghettos. This issue of legitimacy didn't really exist in the scene until then." Verlan and Loh, *35 Jahre*, 272.
21. As living proof, Smudo (Michael Bernd Schmidt), a member of the Stuttgart-based Die Fantastischen Vier, draws a direct line between his career as a rapper and his party nights in the local clubs. As Smudo recalls, "we were socialized in the G.I. clubs: there were four or five big camps in the Stuttgart region, and the soldiers stationed there had a number of clubs they regularly visited. I was there with a female classmate–she because she wanted to chat up men and I because I was interested in the music." Quoted in Wehn and Bortot, *Könnt ihr*, 41. In *Black Tape*, Tobi Tobsen (Tobias Schmidt) from the Hamburg-based band Fünf Sterne Deluxe points out that their rap sounds different from the rest of the republic because they had no such "socialization" as there were no G.I.-clubs in their city. Neblett, *Black Tape*, 2015.
22. *Black Tape* implies that *Deutschrap* aggressively sought to emancipate itself. Thomas D. (Thomas Dürr), as one of the in-the-know, scripted talking heads in *Black Tape*, articulates this explicitly, when he states "they could not accept that there was this German guy who uprooted their very own American culture and threw it before their feet." Neblett, *Black Tape*, 2015.
23. The scene evokes a more lighthearted incident that occurred during a Gang Starr concert in Wuppertal, where a Cologne-based rapper, Ro Kallis (Phillip Löffel), took the mic from Guru and started flowing in German. As DCS (Die Coolen Säue) rapper Schivv (Sebastian Möllmann), a fellow band member of Ro Kallis's, remembers the situation: "Guru thought this was super funny, that someone rapped in German [...]. Shortly after Oliver von Felbert wrote somewhere, that an MC from Cologne 'could not resist the urge to steal the mic from Guru and dawdle into it.'" Quoted in Wehn and Bortot, *Könnt ihr*, 38.
24. In the introduction to their edited volume on *The Foreign Politics of American Popular Culture*, Reinhold Wagnleitner and Elaine Tyler May sum up these debates on *Amerikanismus* as follows: "The massive wave of American cultural products flooding Europe brought

tremendous opposition in its wake. Many experienced it as a cultural invasion of unprecedented proportions. [...] In short, for the European right wing, American popular culture suggested 'racial impurity,' and for the left it evoked *class exploitation*." Reinhold Wagnleitner and Elaine Tyler May. "Here, There, and Everywhere: Introduction," in *'Here, There and Everywhere:' The Foreign Politics of American Popular Culture*, edited by Reinhold Wagnleitner and Elaine Tyler May (Hanover and London: UP of New England, 2000), 6-7. As von Dirke convincingly argues in this regard, "defining Americanization as cultural imperialism is not particularly helpful in analyzing transatlantic transfers of popular music culture." Von Dirke, "Made in Germany," 96.

25. When asked about whether MCs with an immigration background in the *Neue Schule* understood themselves as closer to the socio-political realities of African-American rappers, Rafael Szulc-Vollmann a.k.a. Spax answers, "I never got this impression from any of us. [...]. We never saw these differences. [...] What brought us together was hip-hop culture. We knew about the disparities and understood the problem of racism, but it never played a role for us." (Rafael Szulc-Vollmann, Skype interview with author, June 15, 2020).

26. As Neblett explains in a voice-over in *Black Tape*, "Ironically, entering the stage now were precisely those that Staiger hated: Megaloh, Afrob, Max, and Samy." Neblett, *Black Tape*, 2015.

27. In a video-interview for *Backspin Talk*, Staiger declares that he understands Tigon as a proxy for the multiple, local origins of German rap. In the regional context of Heidelberg, it makes sense to assume that Tigon "is" Torch. *Backspin Talk*. "Hip-Hop-Film: 'Blacktape' – Falk, Staiger und Sekou im Interview mit Niko," YouTube, December 3, 2015, https://www.youtube.com/watch?v=GpssuSrjKtk.

28. Already in 1982, the *Neue Deutsche Welle* rock band Spliff addressed, somewhat ham-fistedly, the element of black culture in their rap-song "Das Blech:" "I notice an elegant black man, he sees a girl and starts talking to her. This is too much. He smiles at me like a radiator grille and looks exactly like James Brown. He asks me: when will you finally stop stealing our black music? He talks at me until my ears bleed and at first I am at a loss for words. Then I say: dude, I happen to like jazz and funk. Wagner makes me puke and Mozart sick." A renunciation of both the *Gesamtkunstwerk* and the German classic tradition as the only acceptable "authentic" means of national sound, the non-black, non-American members of Spliff assert their right to listen to jazz and funk, and, by extension, to rap. Encoded in the lyrics cited above are not only "positive" stereotypes about the "elegant black man," who chats up (German?) women, sports a grille, and looks like James Brown, but also complaints about his incessant talk about the "theft" of Afro-American culture that in turn leads to a sense of annoyance on the part of the "German-Austrian" lyrical I. Spliff. "Das Blech" (Frankfurt a. M.: CBS, 1982).

29. Quoted in Wehn and Bortot, *Könnt ihr*, 181.

30. This debate is complex. Hoyler and Mager, for example, argue that its "political attributes made hip-hop especially attractive to people of migrant backgrounds." Hoyler and Mager, "Im Haus," 234. Gesa zur Nieden goes a step further and claims that rap in Germany was cultivated "mostly by musicians with a migration history." Gesa zur Nieden. "From Sons of Gastarbeita to *Songs of Gastarbeiter*: Migrant and Post-Migrant Integration through Music and German Musical Diplomacy from the 1990s to the Present," in *Popular Music and Public Diplomacy*, eds. Mario Dunkel und Sina A. Nitzsche (Bielefeld: Transcript, 2019), 280. In a more differentiated manner, Verlan and Loh define the Old School as a "colorfully mixed pioneer generation that had made hip-hop big in Germany", but also argue that "more than half of the hip-hop heads were young Turks, Kurds, Yugoslavs, Greeks, or Italians." Verlan and Loh, *35 Jahre*, 96, 315. As manager Götz Gottschalk notes in this context, "at the beginning, hip-hop-music here had a high percentage of middle-class kids." Quoted in Wehn and Bortot, *Könnt ihr*, 88.

31. As Spax argues, "what we have in Germany as the foundation, the birth-form of German-speaking rap comes from completely different classes and from different backgrounds. It

was not just ghetto" (Rafael Szulc-Vollmann, Skype interview with author, June 15, 2020). Spax points out that in particular during the early years "we had an unbelievably high variety of styles," a condition that needs to be taken into account in academic work on the topic (Rafael Szulc-Vollmann, Skype interview with author, June 15, 2020). To be clear, his essay does not seek to erase the immigrant narrative from *Deutschrap*–which would be highly problematic–but rather to diversify and contextualize it through case-studies.

32. LSD, "Competent" (Cologne: Rhythm Attack, 1989). Fast Forward notes that "'Watch out for the Third Rail' did not come across as a mere attempt but was rather professionally made. Nobody would have thought that it was made in Germany." Quoted in Wehn and Bortot, *Könnt ihr*, 23. This said, Ko Lute's lyrics clearly give away that he is not a native speaker of English.
33. The lyrics do, however, tentatively allude to hip-hop's multicultural and anti-racist philosophy: "Don't vote for black or white or any other color, nationalities and other arbitrary [sic] drawn borders." LSD, "Competent, 1989.
34. This is not a surprise. The vast majority of German rap releases between 1986 and 1992 were in English.
35. Dietmar Elflein. "Vom neuen deutschen Sprechgesang zu Oriental Hip Hop: einige Gedanken zur Geschichte von Hip Hop in der BRD," WahreSchule, 1996, http://www.wahreschule.de/Forum/forum_texte1.html.
36. Cited in Hannes Loh, "Tausend Jahre deutscher Hip-hop: Nazimetaphern, Rassismus und neue Härte im deutschen Hip-hop," *Intro*, Januar 17, 2002, https://www.intro.de/popmusik/1000-jahre-deutscher-hiphop.
37. Elflein, "Sprechgesang," 1996.
38. Elflein criticizes that "a copied, adapted style is thus forced into the straitjacket of a national identity that excludes many participants." Elflein, "Sprechgesang," 1996.
39. As Quick Lyric programmatically declares on "Poetry of an Alien," "I say what I want and I do what I like, to community people I'm like a parasite." Lyrical Poetry, "Poetry of an Alien-Original Mix" (Hamburg: Boombastic, 1991).
40. LSD's own contribution to *Krauts with Attitude*, "Accompagnato (Jazzy Muv Part 2)," however, is in German.
41. Quick Lyric in particular was critical of Die Fantastischen Vier. As Verlan and Loh note, "the rapper Quick Lyric from the Old School-crew Lyrical Poetry hoped in vain to meet Smudo in order to show him who has the superior skills." Verlan and Loh, *35 Jahre*, 378.
42. Public Enemy, "Welcome to the Terrordome" (New York: Def Jam, 1990).
43. Lyrical Poetry's 1993 *The S.M.I².L.E. Album* includes the "Poetry of an Alien-Alien Mix" rather than the version released on *Krauts with Attitude*. The album is dominated by slow, psychedelic electro sounds and distorted, hypnotic vocals and differs from LSD's up-tempo, funk-infused b-boy homages to U.S. hip-hop from the 1980s. Informed by the esoteric theories of American psychologist and "neuronaut" Timothy Leary–*S.M.I².L.E.* stands for "space migration // intelligence increase // life extension"–Lyrical Poetry display an almost avant-gardist move away–in form and content–from both the dominant American influences and their German epigones. In the album's liner notes, we find shout-outs not only to Aleister Crowley, but also "all cyber punks or intelligence agents, all extra-terrestrials and post-larvals." Lyrical Poetry, *The S.M.I².L.E. Album* (Bremen: O-Ton Musikverlag, 1993).
44. Lyrical Poetry's later output is largely in German. Tracks such as "Vom Teufel bessessen" and "Illusion oder Vision" feature cerebral lyrics that continue the band's investment in topics such as drug-related mindfucks and futurity.
45. Von Dirke, "Made in Germany," 103.
46. Torch grew up in "a liberal, open-minded home in the 1970s." Verlan and Loh, *35 Jahre*, 148. As Verland and Loh further note, "in Heidelberg, he grew up in the shadow of the old university and, early on, had access to education through his parents." Verlan and Loh, *35 Jahre*, 162.

47. When Ribbat published his article, the Sons of Gastarbeita, founded in 1994, consisted of the rappers Bünyamin Aslan and Gandhi Chahine, as well as the musicians Germain Bleich, Mustafa Sarac, and Frederik Lubitz.
48. Ribbat, "How Hip Hop," 208.
49. See zur Nieden, who submits that the texts of Sons of Gastarbeita "were embedded into the rise of rap and rock as media of antiracist commitment and of what was commonly referred to as Germany's 'multicultural' identity after the many racist arson attacks on refugee centers in 1991 (Hoyerswerda), 1992 (Rostock-Lichtenhagen), and 1993 (Solingen)." Zur Nieden, "Sons of Gastarbeita," 282.
50. As one of the Fresh Familee MCs, Tahir Cevik a.k.a. Tachi, states, "we didn't know that we were a multi-cultural band. […]. The media told us." Quoted in Verlan and Loh, *35 Jahre*, 93.
51. The term "Oriental Rap" is frequently used to describe the output of artists such as Cartel, Islamic Force or Asiatic Warriors. Yet, Tachi, for example, wonders how to explain to people "that you don't do 'Oriental hip-hop' just because you sample a Saz (a Turkish string instrument) in one of your songs or use uncommon melodies." Verlan and Loh, *35 Jahre*, 382.
52. Zur Nieden, "Sons of Gastarbeita," 281.
53. Fresh Familee, "Heimat" (Cologne: Phonogram/Mercury, 1992).
54. Verlan and Loh, *35 Jahre*, 362.
55. As the director Detlev F. Neufert notes about Günther's class affiliations in his documentary 1991 *Fresh Familee: Comin from Ratinga*, "this is family life in Ratingen-West as well. The idyll of a bourgeois private home." *Fresh Familee: Comin' from Ratinga*, directed by Detlev F. Neufert, (1991; Cologne, NRW: WDR), TV.
56. Neufert, *Fresh Familee*, 1991.
57. Von Dirke notes how "Already in 1994, the band Fresh Familee […] problematized the term *Kanake* and German stereotypes about immigrant men with their rap," but has little to say about the song's musical form and the irony that the MCs hide in their deceptive pop sounds to reclaim the derogatory term. Von Dirke, "Made in Germany," 103.
58. Quoted in Verlan and Loh, *35 Jahre*, 360.
59. Äi-Tiem. "Erbarmungslos" (Cologne: Holy Chaos Recordings, 1993).
60. At the time when "Rabenschwarze Nacht" was released, Too Strong consisted of the MCs Der Lange (Lars Gurofski) and Pure Doze (Michael Fritze), and the DJs Zonic (Martin Brockbalz) and Broke (Markus Brockbalz).
61. Too Strong. "Rabenschwarze Nacht-Original Mix" (Frankfurt a. M.: Tribehaus, 1993).
62. Too Strong, "Rabenschwarze Nacht-Original," 1993.
63. On "Rabenschwarze Nacht," Thomas Danneberg, the German voice of Stallone, monotonously intones, "there is […] a violent crime every 25 seconds, a murder every 24 minutes." Too Strong, "Rabenschwarze Nacht-Original," 1993. This in turn links the track to the cinematic representations of New York in the 1980s. As Verlan and Loh write about the interlinking of the Bronx as a real place and its cinematic representation, "Only with the Cross Bronx Expressway the Bronx became what movie and television audiences know: an apocalyptic urban landscape dotted with abandoned factory buildings, rugged, dilapidated tenements, and dirty backyards. A location made for brutal gang wars and end time scenarios à la Hollywood." Verlan and Loh, *35 Jahre*, 274.
64. "Rabenschwarze Nacht" itself is a reference to the German title of Tom Holland's 1985 vampire-horror *Fright Night* in which a suburban neighborhood in the US is haunted by an undead creature.
65. Falk Schacht, "Too Strong: 'Rabenschwarze Nacht' – die Evolution," Red Bull, June 8, 2019, https://www.redbull.com/de-de/too-strong-90er-deutschrap.
66. Verlan and Loh note that "until now, the founders of the Silo Nation haven't managed the great break-through even if Too Strong are way up on the realness chart." Verlan and Loh, *35 Jahre*, 413.

67. Goreminister. "Silo – Geburt einer Nation (Goreminister Cut)," YouTube, July 22, 2020, https://www.youtube.com/watch?v=ruHSXQLcBZk.
68. Too Strong, "Dortmund Silo" (Frankfurt a. M.: Tribehaus, 1993).
69. Pure Doze's diss is relatively tame, compared to, for example, the Hans Solo one cited above: "we are four, but not fantastic, elastic indeed and sarcastic, mostly bombastic. Too Strong does not show you the way, because you have to find it for yourself." Too Strong, "Dortmund," 1993.
70. While the titular Inter City refers to a specific type of long-distance train that old-school hip-hop activists frequently used to travel across Germany and Europe, it is also a reference to Marvin Gaye's seminal song "Inner City Blues (Make me wanna holler)" (1971). On this track, Gaye moved away from the Motown "pop" and took a much more "conscious" and open stance toward the Civil Rights movement. Marvin Gaye, "Inner City Blues (Make me wanna holler)" (Detroit: Tamla, 1971).
71. Too Strong, "Silo Kapitel III" (Frankfurt a. M.: Tribehaus, 1996).
72. Curse, "Gangsta Rap" (Stuttgart: Four Music, 2001).
73. After Kollegah and Farid Bang had received the "Best of Hip-Hop/Urban, National"-award at the 2018 Echo Music Awards, they were criticized for their song "O8/15," on which Farin Bang raps "My body more defined than that of Auschwitz-inmates." Kollegah and Farid Bang, "0815" (Berlin: BMG, 2017). The controversy eventually led to the discontinuation of the award and triggered a heated debate on anti-Semitic tendencies among German rappers.
74. Props go out to Spax who agreed to do a lengthy Skype-interview and provided me with thoughtful insights and comments, Jörg "Q" Querbach who not only attended all these hip-hop jams with me back in the day, but also used his connections to dig up some hard-to-find info, and Doris Werbeck who searched the attic for my long-forgotten *Deutschrap*-CDs and sent me her archaeological findings via Messenger.

Bibliography

Äi-Tiem. "Erbarmungslos." Cologne: Holy Chaos Recordings, 1993.
Backspin Talk. "Hip-Hop-Film: 'Blacktape' – Falk, Staiger und Sekou im Interview mit Niko." YouTube, December 3, 2015.
https://www.youtube.com/watch?v=GpssuSrjKtk.
Cosmatos, George P., dir. *Cobra*. 1986; Los Angeles, CA: Cannon Group, et al. Film.
Curse. "Gangsta Rap." Stuttgart: Four Music, 2001.
Elflein, Dietmar. "Vom neuen deutschen Sprechgesang zu Oriental Hip Hop: einige Gedanken zur Geschichte von Hip Hop in der BRD." WahreSchule, 1996.
http://www.wahreschule.de/Forum/forum_texte1.html.
Fisher, Jaimey. "Introduction: Toward Generic Histories–Film Genre, Genre Theory, and German Film Studies." In *Generic Histories of German Cinema: Genre and Its Deviations*, edited by Jaimey Fisher, 1-26. Rochester: Camden House, 2013.
Fresh Familee. "Ahmed Gündüz." Self-Released, 1991.
—. "Heimat." Cologne: Phonogram/Mercury, 1992.
—. "Memories." Self-Released, 1991.
—. "Sexy Kanake." Cologne: Phonogram/Mercury, 1994.
Gaye, Marvin. "Inner City Blues (Make me wanna holler)." Detroit: Tamla, 1971.

Gerriets, Imke. "Smudo: Wir haben schon ein Abschlussbild gemacht." t-online, July 7, 2019. https://www.t-online.de/unterhaltung/musik/id_86135630/30-jahre-fanta-4-smudo-spricht-ueber-karriere-kinder-und-kritik.html.
GLS-United. "Rappers Deutsch." Hamburg: Metronome, 1980.
Goreminister. "Silo – Geburt einer Nation (Goreminister Cut)." YouTube, July 22, 2020. https://www.youtube.com/watch?v=ruHSXQLcBZk.
Hoyler, Michael, and Christoph Mager. "Hip-Hop ist im Haus: Cultural Policy, Community Centres, and the Making of Hip-Hop Music in Germany." *Built Environment* 31, No. 3 (2005): 237-254.
Kollegah, and Farid Bang. "0815." Berlin: BMG, 2017.
Levin, Michael D. "Flow and Place: Transnationalism in Four Cases." *Anthropologica*, 44, No.1 (2002): 3-12.
Loh, Hannes. "Tausend Jahre deutscher Hip-hop: Nazimetaphern, Rassismus und neue Härte im deutschen Battle-Rap." *Intro*, January 17, 2002. https://www.intro.de/popmusik/1000-jahre-deutscher-hiphop
LSD, "Competent." Cologne: Rhythm Attack, 1989.
Lyrical Poetry. "Poetry of an Alien-Alien Mix." Bremen: O-Ton Musikverlag, 1993.
—. "Poetry of an Alien-Original Mix." Hamburg: Boombastic, 1991
—. *The S.M.I².L.E. Album*. Bremen: O-Ton Musikverlag, 1993.
Neblett, Sekou A., dir. *Black Tape*. 2015; Cologne, NRW: Gifted Films. TV.
Neufert, Detlev F., dir. *Fresh Familee. Comin' from Ratinga*. 1991; Cologne, NRW: WDR. TV.
Pennay, Mark. "Rap in Germany: Birth of a Genre." In *Global Noise: Rap and Hip-Hop outside of the USA*, edited by Tony Mitchell, 111-133. Middletown: Wesleyan UP, 2001.
Public Enemy. "Welcome to the Terrordome." New York: Def Jam, 1990.
Ribbat, Christoph. "How Hip Hop Hit Heidelberg: German Rappers, Rhymes, and Rhythms." In *'Here, There and Everywhere:' The Foreign Politics of American Popular Culture*, edited by Reinhold Wagnleitner and Elaine Tyler May, 207-216. Hanover and London: UP of New England, 2000.
Rick, Detlef. "Wie Hip-Hop nach Deutschland kam: Der Durchbruch nach dem Hype." Der Spiegel, August 8, 2008. https://www.spiegel.de/geschichte/wie-hip-hop-nach-deutschland-kam-a-949537.html.
Ruge, Lili et al. "Deutschrap Periodensystem." Bayrischer Rundfunk, https://story.br.de/hip-hop-periodensystem/.
Schacht, Falk. "Too Strong: 'Rabenschwarze Nacht' – die Evolution." Red Bull, June 8, 2019. https://www.redbull.com/de-de/too-strong-90er-deutschrap.
Spliff. "Das Blech." Frankfurt a. M.: CBS, 1982.
Stehle, Maria. *Ghetto Voices in Contemporary German Culture: Textscapes, Filmscapes, Soundscapes*. Rochester: Camden House, 2012.
Too Strong. "Dortmund Silo." Frankfurt a. M.: Tribehaus, 1993.
—. "Rabenschwarze Nacht-Empire Version." Frankfurt a. M.:Tribehaus, 1994.
—. "Rabenschwarze Nacht-Original Mix." Frankfurt a. M.: Tribehaus, 1993.
—. "Silo Kapitel III." Frankfurt a. M.: Tribehaus, 1996.
Various. *Krauts with Attitude*. Hamburg: Boombastic, 1991.

Verlan, Sascha, and Hannes Loh. *35 Jahre Hip-hop in Deutschland.* Höfen: Hannibal, 2015.

Von Dirke, Sabine. "Hip-Hop Made in Germany: From Old School to the Kanaksta Movement." In *German Pop Culture: How 'American' Is It?*, edited by Agnes C. Mueller, 96-112. Ann Arbor: U Michigan P, 2004.

Wagnleitner, Reinhold, and Elaine Tyler May. "Here, There, and Everywhere: Introduction." In *'Here, There and Everywhere:' The Foreign Politics of American Popular Culture*, edited by Reinhold Wagnleitner and Elaine Tyler May, 1-13. Hanover and London: UP of New England, 2000.

Wehn, Jan, and Davide Bortot. *Könnt ihr uns hören? Eine Oral History des deutschen Rap*, 4. Edition. Berlin: Ullstein, 2019.

White, Hayden. "The Modernist Event." In *The Persistence of History: Cinema, Television, and the Modern Event*, edited by Vivian Sobchack, 17-38. New York and London: Routledge, 1996.

Williams, John. "Imperial March (Darth Vader's Theme)." Los Angeles: RSO, 1980.

Zur Nieden, Gesa. "From Sons of Gastarbeita to *Songs of Gastarbeiter*: Migrant and Post-Migrant Integration through Music and German Musical Diplomacy from the 1990s to the Present." In *Popular Music and Public Diplomacy*, edited by Mario Dunkel und Sina A. Nitzsche, 277-300. Bielefeld: Transcript, 2019.

Chapter 6

DEATH IN JUNE AND THE APOLITEIC SPECTER OF NEOFOLK IN GERMANY

Mirko M. Hall

– "We aim to please with constant unease!"[1]

The post-punk genre of neofolk or apocalyptic folk–with its melancholy lyrics, acoustic melodies, and martial beats–has been an enduring feature of the dark alternative music scene of the past thirty years. Drawing upon Germanic and Celtic paganism, *völkisch* mysticism, and antimodernist imagery including National Socialism, neofolk is perhaps most noted for its (supposed) association with a nebulous web of right-wing ideologies. According to its many critics, the genre celebrates the establishment of a new "European conservative cultural avant-garde"[2] that is based upon egoistic individualism, ethnocentrism, nationalism, and revolutionary traditionalism.[3] Given these controversial ideologies, especially against the backdrop of modern European history, it is rather surprising that neofolk has found–since the mid 1990s–its strongest fan base in Germany and Austria (and to a lesser extent, Italy), where albums have "repeatedly achieved impressive sale figures."[4] Although many Germanic bands are active in the scene and worthy of scholarly attention,[5] they are still–to riff on A. N. Whitehead– merely a series of footnotes to their fabled progenitors, the English band Death in June and its charismatic front man Douglas Pearce.

While it is true that the neofolk scene is an ideologically diverse subculture not necessarily defined by extreme right-wing politics, and only united by its elective affinity for dark romanticism, the suggestive musical and visual aesthetics of Death in June continue to exert–in the popular imaginary of fans and critics alike–an overarching presence on the German-speaking scene. Pearce's use of politically charged (proto) fascist aesthetics and themes has served as a highly affective source of debate for fans, antifa activists, and scholars of the arts, humanities, and social sciences: opinions

Notes for this chapter begin on page 122.

of the band tend to range from dangerously racist to entirely innocuous. On one side of the debate, fans insist that the band simply appropriates contradictory right-wing messages (if at all) as a form of artistic creativity and provocation. On the other side, a significant portion of the academy, along with its partners in journalism, have aggressively argued that the band's use of antimodernist images and tropes is a veiled philosophical program to create acceptable social spaces for fascist cultural ideals. Unfortunately, both of these analyses foreclose a more nuanced reading by foregrounding the absoluteness of two key questions: Are they Nazis or not? Is this (valuable) art or not?

My chapter seeks to investigate some of the National Socialist references within Death in June's oeuvre to problematize attempts to unequivocally characterize neofolk as "hipster-fascism."[6] Drawing largely upon the scholarly work of Anton Shekhovtsov, Marcus Stieglegger, Peter Webb, and Maciej Zurowski, I investigate the band's critical reception in Germany by undertaking a select rhetorical reading of interviews with Pearce as well as the critique of his critics. In exploring whether the band might have *völkisch* affinities without necessarily engendering the specter of an aestheticization of politics, I hope that my discussion can also serve as a primer for Anglophone Germanists, who are largely absent from this discussion.

Philosophical Orientations

Death in June is presently the exclusive musical project of openly homosexual singer-songwriter Douglas Pearce (born in 1956 in working-class London).[7] Formed in 1981 as a trio, the band arose out of the ashes of the anarcho-punk band Crisis (1977-1980), when guitarist Pearce and bassist Tony Wakeford left to form Death in June with friend Patrick Leagas. Over the next thirty-five years, the band's output consisted of some twenty albums and numerous compilations and include such well-known experimental musicians as Leagas (later Sixth Comm/Mother Destruction), Rose McDowall (Strawberry Switchblade), Boyd Rice (NON), David Tibet (Current 93), and Wakeford (later Sol Invictus). Since its inception, the band's signature sound has moved from angular guitars, melodic bass lines, and militaristic percussion and brass—via historical samples and industrial noisescapes—to acoustic guitar, sorrowful keyboards, chime percussion, and neoclassical elements (especially, piano). Pearce's vocals, which are mixed forward, are reminiscent of iconic singers Scott Walker and Leonard Cohen. His songs tend to harmonize dark romantic themes with guitar melodies that are "at odds with the melancholy of the words."⁸ For Pearce, music is the "most instant, evocative and magickal of all art forms"⁹—and, as we shall see in the following pages, his musical enterprise is equal parts nonmainstream artistic creation and a politically influenced *Weltanschauung*.¹⁰

Many critics insist that the band's name deliberately refers to 30 June 1934, the "Night of Long Knives," when Hitler had Ernst Röhm and other leaders of the Sturmabteilung murdered. As such, they contend that this name serves as a kind of political nostalgia for the purged "left-wing" elements of Nazism. Pearce, however has always insisted that "Death in June" resulted from mishearing a phrase in a telephone conversation during the band's first recording session in 1981. According to Pearce, it "came about purely by chance and then we realised the 'significance'."¹¹

In order to better contextualize Death in June's aesthetic trajectory, it is imperative to first review Pearce's participation in Crisis. This band made an important contribution to the post-punk scene by critiquing—through revolutionary fervor—the neoconservative substratum of late 1970s England. Crisis was, according to Pearce, an "unashamedly left wing … [band that] wanted to be taken seriously politically."¹² During this time, Pearce was a member of the International Marxist Group, a Trotskyist organization led by Tariq Ali. He also played with the band at numerous events sponsored by the Anti-Nazi League, Right to Work, and Rock against Racism. The band's famous antifascist rallying cry was the song, "White Youth" (1978-1979) with its memorable image of black and white solidarity being "dynamite."¹³ Not surprisingly, Death in June's first gig was a benefit concert for Workers against Racism, which was sponsored by the Revolutionary Communist Party, at Central London Polytechnic in late 1981. In clear solidarity with left-wing causes, Crisis was already engaging with the legacy of National Socialism through their lyrics. It is for this reason that the band's two retrospective albums were entitled "We Are All Jews and Germans" (1997) and "Holocaust Hymns" (2005).

Although left-of-center, Pearce and Wakeford soon became disillusioned with the dogmatic interpretations of (far) left-wing ideologies and began looking for new answers and identities outside of the strict dichotomy of left and right. In the pursuit of a cosmopolitan, multicultural identity, these interpretations often worked to devalue national cultures and made people "feel guilty about their cultural identity rather than emphasising the positives within it."¹⁴ Through the new musical incarnation of Death in June, their interest in the historical past of war-torn Europe continued, but one that moved in an entirely new direction: away from practical politics to an aestheticized realm that was more conducive to open experimentation and exploration. In the summation of one observer, it was a movement that transitioned from a "pro-worker Leftist punk orientation to an esoteric, occult Right-wing position."[15] By the mid 1980s, this new position would lead to unrelenting accusations of neofascist sympathies.

Instead of pursuing his "vague plans to go to University to study to be a teacher of Economic and Social History,"[16] Pearce became an autodidactic historian of the Third Reich—although he once insisted that he had "still read more pages of 'Das Kapital' than ... 'Mein Kampf'!"[17] In a revealing biopic, "Death in June–Behind the Mask" (2006), Pearce talks about his morbid attraction toward the "ultimate tragedy of that period,"[18] which was influenced by his upbringing in the immediate postwar era and being surrounded by militaria as a child as his father was an RAF pilot in the war. In his search for a "political view for the future,"[19] Pearce explained—in several interviews from the mid 1980s—how he became drawn toward the left-wing factions of National Socialism, especially Röhm's Sturmabteilung and Gregor Strasser's Black Front. This attraction originated from a keen historical interest in exploring what this "tainted ideology which has been so powerful had to say in the beginning."[20] He stressed that this attraction proceeded solely "from identification with or understanding of the leftist elements of the SA which were purged, or murdered, by the SS."[21] Unfortunately, Pearce never comments on the ideological implications of this identification: namely, whether or not the core ideals of National Socialism—notwithstanding their "erroneous" application—are still correct. As critics have pointed out, valorizing the Sturmabteilung (a paramilitary organization known for liquidating the opposition and implementing *Kristallnacht*) is extremely problematic: its members are "make no mistake ... still fascists."[22] It appears that—at this particular moment in the band's history—National Bolshevism, which aimed to unite anticapitalism with popular nationalism, offered Pearce a more plausible political alternative.

Complementing this engagement with National Bolshevism, Pearce's aesthetic project also critiqued the rationalization, capitalist destruction, and Christianization of modern society, which destroyed traditional European cultural bonds. This critique followed, for example, Oswald Spengler's thesis on the "decline of the West" and Max Weber's on the "disenchantment of the world."[23] This epistemic viewpoint, which pervades much of the neofolk scene, can be understood as a fundamental "cultural longing for things that seem to be lost (as in community) or things that ... are in short supply (e.g., honour, respect, heroism)."[24] In addressing this longing, many neofolk musicians became interested in thinkers as diverse as Friedrich Nietzsche (and his "will to power"); Ernst Jünger (and his "Waldgänger" as sovereign figure); and Julius Evola (and his defiant traditionalism). Despite being initially more attuned to the National Socialist past, Pearce's aesthetic and philosophical interests eventually aligned more with Germanic paganism in the late 1980s together with strains of dark romanticism that were influenced by the homoeroticism of Jean Genet and the warrior fetishism of Yukio Mishima.

In an effort to re-enchant contemporary life, Pearce advocated a valiant struggle (as represented by his frequent use of the Death's Head, a "sign of total commitment"[25]) against today's modern headwinds. His search for a new transcendental anchor amidst the ruins of those "spiritual and traditional values unique to Europe"[26] led him directly to northern Germanic paganism. In fact, he argues that Death in June is "part of a European cultural revival" and that he is "pleased that the Old Gods [and old symbols] are being resurrected, for want of a better word."[27] Pearce, thus, elevates his interest in paganism into a kind of art religion (*Kunstreligion*) that becomes a thoroughly aestheticized practice, which unites and glorifies–through artistic and musical expression–the sacred with "deep *völkisch* essences."[28] Here, neofolk is a "realm of reconciliation and redemption that [strives] to suspend the negative side-effects of the functional and social differentiation of society."[29] As a result, Pearce's musical project is viewed by his critics as an attempt to reclaim the supposedly redemptive power of a "long-lost imagined past ... between the Middle Ages and National Socialism"[30]–a past not necessarily marked by enchantment, honor or nobility, but a undeniable historical movement toward the Holocaust. Likewise, the band's use of the ancient Germanic rune "Life" (*Algiz*) or the occult Merovingian symbol "Black Sun"–which were valorized by the Nazis as markers of "community, order, identity ... competence [and] legitimate authority"[31]–have greatly contributed to the accusations of harboring neo-Nazi sympathies.

The Antifa Critique

Despite being always qualified by critics as a relatively small and little-known cohort, neofolk musicians and fans have received a rather surprising amount of scholarly and journalistic attention. And no other band has been the "subject of so much writing, discussion and speculation"[32] as to whether or not it harbors fascist proclivities than Death in June. Although preliminary discussions about Pearce's "intention of demystifying fascism"[33] began in the mid 1980s in the English alternative music press (e.g., *Sounds*), concerted efforts to decode–from a critical perspective–the band's extensive use of fascist imagery first occurred in the mid 1990s. This latter period notably corresponded with the beginnings of a "New World Order" that had seen the collapse of communism in eastern Europe, shifting patterns of noncontinental immigration to Europe, and rapidly expanding globalization. According to Emily Turner-Graham, a historian of right-wing extremism, these critiques of Death in June and other bands tapped into a number of "popular dialogues" at that time that addressed "European identity, its composition and the way in which Europe's cataclysmic past and connections to fascism and Nazism contribut[ed] to Europeans' understanding of their selves."[34]

The ideological critique of Death in June has fallen into three general camps. The first group consists of enthusiastic fans, who have strongly defended the band's aesthetic practices along the lines of *l'art pour l'art* and, thereby, refuted any pro-Nazi readings. The second group consists of a number of scholars–such as Turner-Graham, Anton Shekhovtsov, Marcus Stiglegger, and Peter Webb–that work within the academy proper, namely, in the fields of history, media studies, political theory, and sociology. These individuals take a critical, but more nuanced approach to questions about the right-wing fascinations of neofolk. They have largely focused on rhetorical analyses of the band's aesthetics, while more or less keeping open a door to a number of pluralistic readings. Webb, a sociologist of music subcultures, is by far the most generous interpreter here. He argues that the band, like many others from the post-punk era, attempted to "enliven, question, re-examine, and provoke a response by juxtaposing many symbols, aesthetics, music, and lyrics that in their new context ... take on new meaning and provocation."[35]

The third group consists of another alliance of scholars–mostly antifa activists such as Andreas Speit and left-wing journalists such as Maciej Zurowski–who strive to unmask the band's hidden fascist sympathies. Many of these scholars, including those hailing from the "anti-German Left" (i.e., post 1989 activists that are both pro-U.S. and pro-Israel), view the band strictly through an analytical lens that seeks to "detect 'fascism' and 'anti-Semitism' everywhere."[36] A prominent example of such a predetermined conclusion is *Ästhetische Mobilmachung* (*Aesthetic Mobilization,* 2002), a volume edited by Speit and published as part of a series of antifascist texts by UNRAST Verlag. This volume alleges a direct infiltration of right-wing national ideologies into the German dark music scene (featuring, no less, a central essay on Death in June), but it fails to offer a convincing analysis of how this infiltration works as a demonstrable mechanism. The work merely lists the origins, influences, and effects of these ideologies.

The heightened scrutiny given to Death in June by fans and scholars–regardless of their individual assessments–is the result of two key problems:

(1) the cognitive dissonance of the band's radical juxtaposition of music, performance, and semiotics (e.g., the recent addition of the Death's Head, now redesigned with a faint, awry smile, to a rainbow pride flag); and (2) concerns about the band's interest in the leftist factions of National Socialism given that regime's morally repugnant and incomprehensible atrocities. Here, it is essential to highlight that this second problem is continuously understood through the first. Death in June's visual aesthetics have always served as the catalyst for understanding its cultural politics. As Robert Forbes, an early fan and commentator suggested, this may be, because "[n]one of their lyrics [could] be interpreted as fascistic, unlike their imagery, which *could* be" (emphasis in original).[37] If one surveys the lyrical content of the band's entire oeuvre, one can find a large number of songs about alienation, desperation, loss, love, and solitude–alongside surprising indictments of colonialism, genocide, sexism, and war.[38]

Consequently, analyses of the band have tended to focus on decoding its striking visual aesthetics (with lyrics and interviews relegated to a secondary status) through an interpretative lens that deliberately sought to prove right-wing sympathies. But, paradoxically, the ambiguous nature of these recontextualized visuals pulled critics and fans alike toward the need for expressions of authorial intention to help resolve this dilemma. This desire, however, was exacerbated by the fact that–until the rise of social media–Pearce rarely gave interviews or defended himself against criticism. If he did participate in these forums, he made, in the words of his critics, little sense or "positively enjoy[ed] sending out contradictory messages and fabricating ambiguous sound bites."[39] These exacerbations only fueled more intrigue and speculation.

The engagement of those scholars, who critique Death in June for its fascist sympathies, is complicated by the fact that direct references and appeals to fascism are now "only rarely found in the Neofolk realm."[40] Even for Pearce, any interest in National Bolshevism, as a political ideology, "lies in the past."[41] Indeed, this ideology has not played a significant role in his work since the 1980s. Yet, much of today's criticism of the band still actively revolves around the implications of its continued existence. What is so challenging about all of these assessments (whether positive or negative) is how so many erudite scholars–operating in good faith with similar critical-analytical tools–can arrive at such different conclusions about the band. My intent in this article is not to provide a definitive critique of the band's aesthetics, or question Pearce's or these critics' integrity, but rather to provide an investigatory perspective that may be less black and white as suggested by some.

The desire to categorize Pearce as a fascist sympathizer appears to proceed out of the motivation to refute more generous interpretations of the band's aesthetics by supporters and, more importantly, to unmask the band's "true" ideological proclivities. This former position, which is best exemplified by political journalist Maciej Zurowski, argues that the band's aesthetics are misunderstood by fans to be a "mere flirtation with taboo subjects: a desire to shock, a morbid fascination with the dark side of history, or … [the sublimation of] fetishistic sexual fantasies into art."[42] Zurowski further argues that these fans are falling for a classic marketing gimmick: that of the "glamour of [a] culturally subversive work."[43] In other words, by creating perpetual controversy through a mysterious artwork, whose messages are never fully clarified, Pearce's strategies of mystification "keep people [forever] guessing: is he 'really' a fascist?"[44] As the antifa organization Midwest Unrest adds, fans become thereby mesmerized by a form of "fascist pornography" that "garner[s] attention and sales" and keeps the band financially secure in its established countercultural niche.[45] Unfortunately, in advancing these conclusions, other commentators–particularly, agit-prop artist and activist Stewart Home–have resorted to launching *ad hominem* attacks on fans and more generous critics like Webb, accusing them of irrational biases and psychological delusions.[46] Even institutional scholars have not been immune to using the language of psychoanalysis to pathologize the "[d]efense reaction rhetoric" of individuals, who complicate the aforementioned conclusions.[47] Some neofolk fans have likened these actions to a kind of "neo-McCarthyist hypersensitivity."[48]

The ideological critique of this latter position argues that Pearce in fact supports fascist cultural policies, but cleverly uses strategies of rhetorical evasion and obfuscation (in addition to historical misreadings) to avoid any negative judgments. Many of this position's adherents believe that Pearce has "always been careful to conceal his true political beliefs and avoid controversy" and that only a "close examination of [the band's] interests and activities reveals where his loyalties lie."[49] Or, stated from a complementary perspective, the band uses the supposed political ignorance of its fans–who like the subcultural capital of wearing military uniforms and playing with runes–to clandestinely provide them with a framework of experience that makes them highly susceptible to right-wing ideologies.

This argument regarding the ideological susceptibility of the neofolk scene was first advanced by Anton Shekhovtsov, a political scientist, who conducts research on the new right in eastern and central Europe. What makes Shekhovtsov's work attractive for some commentators is that his critique is grounded in comparative historical analysis and, unlike other critics, he does not subscribe (as we shall later see) intentional malice to neo-folk musicians and fans. He suggests that bands like Death in June produce apoliteic music: a "type of music in which the ideological message contains obvious or veiled references to the core elements of fascism but is simultaneously detached from any practical attempt to implement that message through political activity."[50] By "core elements of fascism," Shekhovtsov draws upon historian Roger Griffin's definition of fascist ideology as an instance of a revolutionary ultranationalism, which originated in the early twentieth century and sought to "combat the allegedly degenerative forces of contemporary history ... by bringing about ... a 'new order' ... based on the rebirth, or palingenesis, of the nation."[51] This orientation creates a kind of political religion, where individuals are imbued with "heroism, the spirit of sacrifice, mass rituals, the cult of martyrs, [and] the ideals of war."[52] Shekhovtsov concludes that, although "by no means the *sine qua non* of fascism ... [these ideals] are indicative of fascism's commitment to the aestheticization of political life, extreme activism and spectacular politics."[53] Whether or not the band supports the conclusions of these core elements, however, remains open to debate. He further argues that, while ultimately supporting fascist ideals and goals, such music does not directly recruit supporters nor affiliate itself with radical right-wing organizations, tendencies, or violence.[54]

Responses to the Antifa Critique

In response to the above accusations, Death in June has experienced its fair share of canceled concerts by venues and staged protests by antifa groups (who have called for violent direct action) in Europe and the United States–although these occurrences have sharply decreased in recent years. Most notably, two of the band's albums–*Brown Book* (1987) and *Rose Clouds of Holocaust* (1995)–were indexed in 2005 and 2006 by Germany's Federal Review Board for Media Harmful to Minors for their "National Socialist tendencies" (i.e., banned from public display and purchase by minors).[55] With reference to *Rose Clouds of Holocaust*, Pearce vehemently denies that its title and signature song of the same name are connected to the Holocaust in any way. Instead, both refer to a solstice celebration at the Blue Lagoon in Iceland, where Pearce and a friend spoke of "Life and its disappointments," reflected on "lies about a particular [personal] relationship," and were surrounded by a "freezing cold landscape, coupled with the strange rose/purple colour of the sky [that] gave the whole scenario a 'holocaustic' atmosphere ... 'Rose Clouds of Holocaust' ably describes that scenario." Here, he emphasizes that his use of "holocaust" is derived from the ancient Greek word for "burnt offerings."[56] Despite its etymological roots, this term is now forever associated with the unspeakable crimes of the Nazi regime: one can only conclude that—if not specifically referring to this historical event—its usage is a deliberate provocation that ultimately dishonors the victims of the *actual* Holocaust.

Following the advice of the band's German music distributor TESCO to clarify his work, in 2006 Pearce offered an unusually candid explanation—in light of his previously ambiguous interviews—of the origins and meanings behind his indexed works. His clarifications are prefaced by a statement as to why he has refused to explicitly explain his band's music, aesthetics or politics. In this declaration, he follows a rather traditional argument of artistic license and privilege, where the "author" operates beyond mere politics:

> In the 24 years of Death In June's existence I have never explained my work. I feel that would make my art ordinary and stillborn and panders to elements within society that seek to control freedom of expression and thought, abstract or otherwise. All art, whether it be in the form of music, literature, painting etc. worth a grain of salt should be open to interpretation. In turn, this also makes it open to misinterpretation; sometimes good, sometimes bad. It is in the nature of art that "challenges" or "confronts" the consumer, or potential consumer, to be misunderstood ... I am a musician and I do not involve myself in politics and I refuse to be forced into becoming involved in politics.[57]

In interviews from the 1980s, Pearce is already cognizant of this metonymic slippage of signification as it pertains to ideologically tainted symbols. He is aware that individuals could "either interpret or misinterpret [these symbols] in whatever way they see fit" by falling into the "trap of taking [them] on a surface value"—something that is solely "their problem."[58] This position will have clear implications for my later comments on artistic responsibility.

Pearce has been more forthcoming in addressing his critics' concerns about the band's aesthetics promoting right-wing ideals that might be predicated on the violent exclusion of the Other (similar to political theorist Carl Schmitt's famous friend/foe distinction). When asked in a 1993 interview in the fanzine *Glasnost Wave-Magazin* about the increase in antiforeigner violence in Germany (a period noted for several high-profile attacks on immigrants in an environment aggravated by the difficulties of reunification), he comes out unequivocally against racial violence in all its guises:

> Why should Death in June or I have anything to do with these asinine skinheads or neo-Nazi shit? Is there something about my music that could make one think that I may have an interest in these people ... For 11 years, I have said that skinheads, neo-Nazis, and violent criminals are complete assholes and I say that again still today![59]

Likewise, when discussing the band's withdrawal from the Dark X-Mas Festival in Hamburg in 1992 (along with popular left-oriented band Project Pitchfork), because of its overt politicization in support of Germany's asylum policies, Pearce reiterated the band's "abhorring [of] all forms of violence directed at anyone regardless of race, religion or sexuality"[60] in an official statement.

Fans and more sympathetic critics have welcomed these unambiguous declarations. Given the band's contested history, though, it is not surprising that Death in June has also been accused of supporting genocidal violence—one of many claims that critics allege, but do not substantiate with corroborating evidence. The most widespread claim is that the band performed a special benefit concert for the national-conservative Croatian Defense Forces (HOS) in Zagreb in the midst of the Yugoslav Wars in 1992. Croatian DJs and concertgoers, who saw the band live, have now come forward and stated that Pearce actually played in a series of independent (even antifascist) clubs—without "any kind of 'Nazi-Ritual'"[61]—for members of the country's dark wave scene. Furthermore, the proceeds from a double album of acoustic songs did not go to the militia, but rather to the Klinički bolnički centar Zagreb, the largest state hospital in Croatia, which provided rehabilitation services to a multiethnic cohort of soldiers and civilians, who had lost their limbs. Although Pearce did visit the headquarters of the HOS, it seems that its former location as a popular gay club was a determining factor (as his professional entourage since the days of Crisis has always included members of the gay community).[62]

Unlike some of Death in June's critics, I am inclined to give these quotations a more generous reading: one that is properly contextualized by knowledge of the band's inherent contradictions. Although I acknowledge that it is difficult to know Pearce's true intentions, the now popularized critique that he has been playing a dangerous game of deliberate obfuscation—over a period of some thirty years to secretly indoctrinate his audience seems to be an unnecessary expenditure of psychical energy on his part. Additionally, such a program of mystification would ultimately be a cowardly position given Pearce's fascination, for example, with the warrior ethic of his favorite author, Mishima, which demands telling the truth without any deceptive intention.

"Runes and Men"

To better understand the poetics of Death in June, it is helpful to briefly look at the music and lyrics of its most iconic song, "Runes and Men," from the

Brown Book album. With its allusion to Evola's bestselling antimodernist book, *Men Among the Ruins*, the song has courted a significant amount of controversy for its supposed (crypto) fascist content. It has also been covered by a number of German-speaking neofolk and independent artists, most popularly by Von Thronstahl. The song features elements of the band's now classic soundscape: melodic guitar work with simple chord progressions, trumpet fanfare, martial beat, singer Rose McDowall's "la-la-las in the background," and a very notable Nazi-era looped speech sample.[63] This loop features the voice of Munich Gauleiter Adolf Wagner (which was often mistaken for Hitler's, because of its uncanny resemblance) and was taken from Leni Riefenstahl's propaganda masterpiece, *Triumph of the Will.* Here, Wagner talks about how the elimination of the Sturmabteilung was a revolutionary act designed to prevent "'total anarchy'."[64] Accompanying this sample, Pearce sings a much-cited stanza in the antifa literature. It describes a lyrical I, who is overcome with loneliness and—under the influence of a German wine—slowly surrenders to "dreams of ... greater times."[65]

For critics like Shekhovtsov, there is a palpable fear that listeners will "eventually become involved in attempts at the practical implementation of those [fascist] 'dreams'"—that is, for a violent return to the "greater times" of premodern, precapitalist Europe.[66] For other critics, the deliberate use of Wagner's speech trivializes, and even aestheticizes National Socialism, by giving listeners the "proxy thrill of listening to a track of Hitler speaking."[67] Some interpreters, however, have also argued that—when considered as part of the larger lyrical text—this stanza might denote something entirely different: a simple lover's serenade. As Forbes has suggested, the "drunken thoughts" of runes and men, while indeed referencing pagan Germania, could very well be that mythical space, where the lyrical I is reunited in a singular moment of ecstasy with his lover, who has hair of "flaming blooms," eyes of "flaming roses," and the kiss of "Medusa's touch."[68] This interpretation becomes more plausible when properly contextualized: this period is marked by Pearce's thematic transition to Germanic mythology, his literary engagement with Genet and Mishima, and the ending of his long-term relationship with a (male) partner.

In talking about his lyrics, Pearce has always highlighted how different readings, influences, and life experiences affect his compositional method. It is an oneiric-like process that involves a cut-and-paste approach to writing, which is very similar to that of William Burroughs. In fact, he claims that this process is "not completely straight forward not even for [him]."[69] Yet, in response to early fascist accusations, Pearce "deliberately set a trap for the conceited and self-righteous"[70] by working with ambivalent textual material on *Brown Book*–hence, the sampling of Wagner for both shock value and pure aesthetics. Nevertheless, the use of highly charged signifiers like the Wagner sample raises important questions about the responsibility of artists to use controversial materials "ethically" (a topic that is worthy of a separate investigation).

Death in June's unique juxtaposition of (proto) fascist, pagan, and homosexual imagery has often been compared to the Slovenian avant-garde band Laibach's own manipulation of seemingly incongruent symbols. According to philosopher Slavoj Žižek, Laibach's aesthetic provocation resulted from an "aggressive, inconsistent mixture of Stalinism, Nazism and *Blut und Boden* ideology,"[7] in which symbols were carefully altered to imbue them with new, unexpected meanings (such as artist Kazimir Malevich's substitution of black crosses for swastikas). This provocation frustrated the conventional semantic system *"precisely insofar as it is not* [an] *ironic imitation* [of totalitarian ritual], *but represents an over-identification with it"* (emphasis in original).[72] In other words, the band exposed the "obscene superego underside" of totalitarianism:[73] not its superficial mask of benevolent populism, but rather its true character of political terror. Consequently, as the theory goes, the audience is compelled to question their own cultural and political biases and positionality while interpreting these symbols.

In comparing both bands, media theorist Marcus Stiglegger offers the arguably most persuasive argument for understanding Death in June's aesthetics in this "atmosphere of momentary euphoria."[74] (Many critics never undertake a close theoretical reading of the band's juxtaposition of symbols, but rather insist, from the very onset, that its motivations are to paradoxically "obscure actual fascist and neo-fascist sentiments."[75]) Although both bands use similar iconography, Stiglegger argues that they diverge in their "intended effect:" whereas Laibach wants to elicit political ambivalence, Death in June wants to promote a kind of "'negative poetics'."[76] Here, the "often-criticized National Socialist motifs (photos, camouflage, daggers, death's head) are ... transferred into a new context–the hermetic DEATH IN JUNE universe."[77] Likewise, cold wave musician Sean McBride argues that such a poetics is a "self-conscious ... strategic move to maintaining a hermetic underground and allowing the debate to thrive."[78] This transfer creates a strangely depoliticized and ahistorical universe of "militarism, homosexuality, mysticism, world weariness, and romanticism,"[79] which provides Pearce with his very own private world of meaning–one that requires, given its politically fraught material, a "high degree of abstraction and differentiation"[80] on the part of the audience to decode.

Engaging Right-Wing Populism

As central and eastern Europe re-experiences a wave of right-wing populism, citizens need to once again be vigilant against manifestations of nationalist authoritarianism. The ultimate fear of Death in June's critics is that the popularization of fascist aesthetics, in whatever guise, may in fact recruit real-life neo-Nazis. That is to say, the band's idealization of protofascist images and tropes "can eventually lead ... listeners to contribute to the *political* cause, even if such bands—perhaps honestly—do not mean to" (emphasis in original).[81] At the very least, it can lead to the denial or trivialization of the violence of existing fascist regimes. Pearce, however, has never denied wartime atrocities or the existence of the Holocaust.[82] For sociologist Christian Dornbusch (the pseudonym of Martin Langebach, an expert advisor at Germany's Federal Agency for Civic Education), the former outcome is already a foregone conclusion, because neofolk bands always play with "pre-fascist symbols and motifs" in such a way that directly stages a "'fascist synthesis.'"[83] At the same time, some critics argue that if these bands were to truly engage in a negative critique of fascism, this act would be a clear game changer—but their refusal to do so is "[a]t best ... irresponsible, at worst reprehensible."[84]

Is such a political mobilization a reality? Speit, for example, contends that key characteristics of the gothic and dark wave scenes—such as the sense of "individual pessimism and collective melancholy" and the accompanying ideals of "death, decay, loyalty, love, purity, and simplicity"—can easily be channeled through an "aesthetic mobilization" into "moral concepts and attitudes toward life ... against humanism and emancipation."[85] And even Stiglegger wonders what might happen if the band's symbols are removed from their hermetic context by fans. Judging from online forums and fanzines, supporters of Death in June, while being clearly aware of the above concerns, are largely apolitical with regard to the band's aesthetics. They simply enjoy the music's dark romantic sounds. In fact, Speit has pointed out how the neofolk scene has been surprisingly immune to polarization and right-wing radicalization.[86] Cultural critic Dominik Tischleder has even noted (referencing a post on the U.S. white supremacist website "Panzerfaust") that self-professed neo-Nazis tend to hate Death in June, not only because of its "'queerness'" and "'Jewish' play with Nazi symbols," but also because of its refusal to take a clear ideological position.[87]

It has always been easier to ascertain the general contours of Pearce's cultural views—especially, when he refers to himself as a "Euro-centric Englishman"[88]—than how this perspective might materialize as a concrete politically actionable orientation. It may be that Pearce is not a "politicized, extreme right-wing voice," but rather one that holds a "conservative though more esoteric perspective," which critiques contemporary Europe as a neoliberal bastion run amok.[89] In other words, he may see himself as part of a revolutionary or avant-garde conservatism: a position that is "simultaneously ... to the right regarding a certain number of topics [i.e., nationalism when compared to the radical left] ... and on the avant-garde regarding the acceptance of countercultures [i.e., post-punk critiques of society eschewed by the classic right]."[90] Finally, Pearce has never advocated for the construction of a new fascist order or encouraged violent or discriminatory "solutions" to societal issues—unlike a visible portion of the U.S. electorate that threw its support behind Donald Trump's 2016 successful presidential candidacy.

Sapere aude!

Given the pathos-ridden arguments on both sides of this controversy, and the continual metonymic slippage of meaning in Death in June's works, a definitive assessment of Pearce's aesthetics is difficult to stake out. In light of this conclusion, it might be better to explore how observers of the band—including fans—can be empowered to think critically about its aesthetic program.

The specter of fascist thought and its present-day resurgence on the continent still haunts the Central European imaginary. As intellectual historian Sander Gilman has argued: National Socialism's horrific apex, the Holocaust, is the "central event of modern German culture, the event toward which every text, every moment in German history, and, yes, culture moved inexorably."[91] This event remains, to this day, a key interpretive lens for German cultural and political analysis. It goes without saying—once again—that vigilance against totalitarian systems of thought is an epistemic necessity in the ongoing fight for justice in the world. At the same time, however, one needs to be more careful about not falling into the trap of equating traditional political orientations (as more militant antifa activists tend to do) with the most repugnant forms of right-wing thought. Whether Death in June's cultural politics are purely ludic, apoliteic or conservative-national, one needs to be very mindful about hurling accusations of "Nazi" sympathies—a rhetorical strategy that has become an unfortunate feature of modern polemics. Such discourse runs the risk of resulting in an ideological inflexibility that is likely to lead toward intense political polarization. This inflexibility, in turn, not only stifles careful rational inquiry, but also dishonors the real victims of a singularly unfathomable act through its constant desemanticization.

Given the troubled historical context of various European runes and occult symbols, "[n]eo-folk is easily absorbed into mainstream and normative modes of dissemination."[92] These modes instantly equate primordial symbols with their later fascist incarnations. A simple way for Pearce to avoid this problem, as well as the ensuing controversy, is to not indulge in this type of provocative semantic play, regardless of his beliefs in artistic license. If Death in Junes' "initial objective"[93] was indeed a critical strategy of defamilarizing the aforementioned symbols, this position would have removed–following the methodology advocated by Walter Benjamin's famous theses "On the Concept of History"–these prefascist symbols from their fascist contexts and reassembled them into new critical constellations.[94] Although never fully elucidated by Benjamin, this technique would require Pearce to combine the powers of critical intelligence and aesthetic-technical precision to unlock the transvaluative potential of these symbols (whatever that may be) to create a left-revolutionary understanding of history that both remembers and overcomes Europe's poisoned connection to fascism. As suggested by Stiglegger's thesis above, such a conclusion seems rather improbable given the hermetically sealed world of the band.

Even if Death in June uses fascist images and tropes in a non-critical way, avid listeners of the band can still take measures to prevent aesthetic experiences from becoming a political mechanism that could actualize dangerous *völkisch* impulses. As with all artistic expression, listeners of Pearce's music need to actively engage in a careful critique of the band's aesthetics–and work through their own desires and ambivalences. As one commentator states: "Some dark art is beautiful and much of it is compelling, but it requires confrontation and self-analysis if you're to avoid succumbing to the bullshit [i.e., melancholy and politically suspect actions] that comes along with it."[95]

Listeners cannot always rely on artists and bands to explicitly explain their aesthetic program; they need to create their own conclusions through a self-reflective listening that carefully oscillates between identification and detachment. Unfortunately, this perspective is more challenging for the casual listener, who will most likely encounter the band without the necessary background knowledge and interpretive tools to understand the contradictory aesthetics of the band.

The hermeneutic challenges posed by analyzing bands like Death in June is a forceful reminder that music is foremost a discursive practice. Its consumption, production, and reception is not wholly determined by musicians or listeners themselves, but is rather made "meaningful"–in part–through its ever-changing cultural, historical, and political recontextualizations. To fully understand music, and listen through attempts at its rhetorical manipulation, one must always engage in its careful discernment. Only such a critical consciousness can answer the question posed by the title of the band's 1992 album: *But, What Ends When the Symbols Shatter?*

MIRKO M. HALL is Professor of German Studies and Chair of Languages, Cultures, and Literatures at Converse College. He is the author of *Musical Revolutions in German Culture: Musicking against the Grain, 1800-1980* (Basingstoke, 2014) and co-editor of *Beyond No Future: Cultures of German Punk* (London, 2016). He is an intellectual historian, who explores music as a site of cultural creativity, critique, and resistance.

Notes

1. Death in June, *Nada!*, New European Recordings, LP, 1985. I would like to thank the participants of the German Studies Workshop at The University of Texas at Austin, my darkwave collaborator Naida Zukić, and an anonymous reviewer for their constructive comments and suggestions. This article is a minor revision of the version that was previously published in *German Politics and Society* 35 (2017): 60-79.
2. Andreas Speit, "Einleitung" in *Ästhetische Mobilmachung: Dark Wave, Neofolk und Industrial im Spannungsfeld rechter Ideologien*, ed. Andreas Speit (Münster, 2002), 8.
3. Stéphane François, "The Euro-Pagan Scene: Between Paganism and Radical Right," trans. Ariel Godwin, *Journal for the Study of Radicalism* 1 (2007): 35-54.
4. Andreas Diesel and Dieter Gerten, *Looking for Europe: The History of Neofolk*, trans. Markus Wolff (Wittlich, 2013), 28-29.
5. See, for example, such ideologically diverse bands as Allerseelen, Darkwood, Falkenstein, Jägerblut, Jännerwein, Von Thronstahl, and Waldteufel.
6. Alexander Reid Ross, "Fighting the Trojan Horse of Hipster-Fascism," *Counterpunch*, 14 November 2014; available at http://www.counterpunch.org/2014/11/14/fighting-the-trojan-horse-of-hipster-fascism, accessed 1 December 2015.
7. For two excellent biographical surveys of Death in June, see Diesel and Gerten (see note 4), 82-107 and *Death in June–Behind the Mask*, directed by Darryl Hell (Boston, 2006), DVD.
8. Peter Webb, "Neo-Folk or Postindustrial Music: The Development of an Esoteric Music Milieu" in *Exploring the Networked Worlds of Popular Music: Milieu Cultures* (New York, 2007), 62.
9. Douglas Pearce quoted in "Interview: 2010–Depkac.com English," *Death in June*, 12 March 2010; available at http://www.deathinjune.org/wiki/index.php/Interview:2010-Depkac.com_English, accessed 1 December 2015.
10. Webb (see note 8), 73.
11. Pearce quoted in Robert Forbes, *Misery and Purity: A History and Personal Interpretation of Death in June* (Amsterdam, 1995), 13.
12. Pearce quoted in Brian Clark, "The March of Man's True Destiny," *Occidental Congress*, January 2006; available at http://www.occidentalcongress.com/interviews/intdoug_06.htm, accessed 1 December 2015.
13. Crisis, *UK '79 B/W White Youth*, Ardkor Records, 7", 1979.
14. Webb (see note 8), 86.

15. Sean McBride quoted in Michael Giebel, "There is Freedom in the Minimum," *skug: Journal für Musik*, 27 March 2010; available at http://www.skug.at/article4852.htm, accessed 1 December 2015.
16. Pearce quoted in "Article: Death in June Demystified," *Death in June*, 27 October 2008; available at http://www.deathinjune.org/wiki/index.php?title=Article:Death_in_June_Demystified, accessed 1 December 2015.
17. Pearce quoted in ibid.
18. Pearce quoted in Hell (see note 7).
19. Pearce quoted in Forbes (see note 11), 15.
20. Pearce quoted in ibid., 36.
21. Pearce quoted in ibid., 15.
22. Midwest Unrest, "Death in June: A Nazi Band?," *Libcom*, 19 November 2006; available at http://libcom.org/library/death-in-june-a-nazi-band, accessed 1 December 2015.
23. This critique is best summarized by the title of Sol Invictus' 1994 album, *Death of the West*. Wakeford founded this band after leaving Death in June in 1984 due to musical differences and his deliberate removal by Pearce for membership in the far-right National Front (UK). "[H]e started to bring [right-wing leanings] into the group and we couldn't have that, we're not like that." Wakeford has long since regretted and disavowed this affiliation. Pearce quoted in Forbes (see note 11), 31.
24. Webb (see note 8), 98.
25. Pearce quoted in "Interview: 1998–Scapegoat," *Death in June*, 5 March 2010; available at http://www.deathinjune.org/wiki/index.php/Interview:1998-Scapegoat, accessed 1 December 2015.
26. François (see note 3), 49.
27. Pearce quoted in "Interview: 2005–Heathen Harvest," *Death in June*, 28 October 2008; available at http://www.deathinjune.org/wiki/index.php?title=Interview:2005-Heathen_Harvest, accessed 1 December 2015. See also Nicholas Goodrick-Clarke, *Black Sun: Aryan Cults, Esoteric Nazism and the Politics of Identity* (New York, 2002).
28. Stefanie v. Schnurbein, "Germanic Neo-Paganism—A Nordic Art-Religion?" in *Religion, Tradition and the Popular: Transcultural Views from Asia and Europe*, eds. Judith Schlehe and Evamaria Sandkühler (Bielefeld, 2014), 256.
29. Jochen Schulte-Sasse, "The Prestige of the Artist under Conditions of Modernity," *Cultural Critique* 12 (1989): 87.
30. Jan Raabe and Andreas Speit, "L'art du mal–Vom antibürgerlichen Gestus zur faschistoiden Ästhetik," in Speit (see note 2), 66.
31. Susan Sontag, "Fascinating Fascism" in *Under the Sign of Saturn* (New York, 1980), 99.
32. Diesel and Gerten (see note 4), 82.
33. Stewart Home, "We Mean It Man: Punk Rock and Anti-Fascism, or, Death in June Not Mysterious," *Stewart Home Society*, n.d.; available at https://www.stewarthomesociety.org/dij.htm, accessed 1 December 2015.
34. Emily Turner-Graham, "'Keep Feeling Fasci/nation': Neofolk and the Search for Europe" in *Monsters in the Mirror: Representations of Nazism in Post-War Popular Culture*, eds. Sara Buttsworth and Maartje Abbenhuis (Santa Barbara, 2010), 205.
35. Webb (see note 8), 79.
36. Maciej Zurowski, "Of Runes and Men," *Who Makes the Nazis?*, 22 December 2011; available at http://www.whomakesthenazis.com/2011_12_01_archive.html, accessed 1 December 2015. Some critics argue that attempts to deny the band's (supposed) fascist tendencies–by highlighting their work with Jewish musicians, playing concerts in Israel, and supporting the State of Israel–is disingenuous, since "countless far-right parties in Europe [are] gaining international legitimacy from Zionist claims [of protecting the Judeo-Christian worldview of Europe] while retaining and supporting anti-Semitism in Europe." Ross (see note 6).
37. Forbes (see note 11), 36.
38. Diesel and Gerten (see note 4), 86, 91, 392.

39. Zurowski (see note 36).
40. Marcus Stiglegger quoted in Diesel and Gerten (see note 4), 415.
41. Pearce quoted in Diesel and Gerten (see note 4), 86.
42. Zurowski (see note 36).
43. Ibid.
44. Ibid.
45. Midwest Unrest (see note 22).
46. Stewart Home, "The McGonagall Syndrome: Peter Webb and 'Intellectual' Decomposition at the University of Birmingham," *Stewart Home Society*, n.d.; available at https://www.stewarthomesociety.org/webb.htm, accessed 1 December 2015.
47. Anton Shekhovtsov, "Apoliteic Music," *Anton Shekhovtsov's Blog*, 13 December 2009; available at http://anton-shekhovtsov.blogspot.com/2009/12/apoliteic-music-comment-1.html, accessed 1 December 2015.
48. Clark (see note 12).
49. Midwest Unrest (see note 22).
50. Anton Shekhovtsov, "*Apoliteic* Music: Neo-Folk, Martial Industrial and 'Metapolitical Fascism'," *Patterns of Prejudice* 43 (2009): 439.
51. Quoted in ibid., 436. Roger Griffin, *Modernism and Fascism: The Sense of a Beginning under Mussolini and Hitler* (New York, 2007), 181.
52. Quoted in ibid., 436. Emilio Gentile, "Fascism, Totalitarianism and Political Religion: Definitions and Critical Reflections on Criticism of an Interpretation," *Totalitarian Movements and Political Religions* 5 (2004): 338-339.
53. Shekhovtsov (see note 50), 437.
54. Ibid., 432.
55. The task of this Federal Review Board is to protect minors from harmful media content that may endanger their development as socially responsible citizens.
56. Douglas Pearce, "Statement 2," *Death in June*, 29 November 2010; available at http://deathinjune.org/wiki/index.php?title=Article:Statement2, accessed 1 December 2015.
57. Douglas Pearce, "Statement 1," *Death in June*, 29 November 2010; available at http://deathinjune.org/wiki/index.php?title=Article:Statement1, accessed 1 December 2015.
58. Pearce quoted in Clark (see note 12) and Forbes (see note 11), 36.
59. Pearce quoted in Speit (see note 2), 20 (my translation).
60. Pearce (see note 57).
61. Concertgoer Tomi Edvard Šega quoted in Diesel and Gerten (see note 4), 97.
62. See Diesel and Gerten (see note 4), 96-97 and a detailed comment by reader "Someone in Europe," 3 October 2011 in Midwest Unrest (see note 22).
63. Diesel and Gerten (see note 4), 94.
64. Adolf Wagner quoted in ibid., 94.
65. *Death in June*, "Runes and Men," on *Brown Book*, New European Recordings, LP, 1987.
66. Shekhovtsov (see note 50), 456.
67. John Madziarczyk, "Laibach and Neofolk Fascism ... A Relationship with Some Responsibility," *Lost Highway Times ... Paths in Oblivion*, 7 March 2011; available at http://www.losthighwaytimes.com/2011/03/laibach-and-neofolk-fascisma.html, accessed 1 December 2015.
68. Forbes (see note 11), 106-108 and Death in June, "Runes and Men" (see note 65).
69. Pearce quoted in Webb (see note 8), 78. See also Forbes (see note 11), 106-107.
70. Pearce quoted in "Interview: 2006–Orkus," *Death in June*, 28 October 2008; available at http://deathinjune.org/wiki/index.php?title=Interview:2006-Orkus, accessed 1 December 2015.
71. Slavoj Žižek, "Why Are Laibach and the *Neue Slowenische Kunst* Not Fascists?" in *The Universal Exception*, eds. Rex Butler and Scott Stephens (London, 2006), 65. See also Alexei Monroe, *Interrogation Machine: Laibach and NSK* (Cambridge, 2005).
7. Žižek (see note 71), 65.
73. Ibid., 65.

74. Stiglegger quoted in Diesel and Gerten (see note 4), 390.
75. Madziarczyk (see note 67).
76. Stiglegger quoted in Diesel and Gerten (see note 4), 392.
77. Ibid.
78. McBride quoted in Giebel (see note 15).
79. Stiglegger quoted in Diesel and Gerten (see note 4), 392.
80. Diesel and Gerten (see note 4), 16.
81. Shekhovtsov (see note 50), 456.
82. Pearce (see note 56).
83. Raabe and Speit, "L'art du mal," in Speit (see note 2), 110.
84. Midwest Unrest (see note 22).
85. Raabe and Speit (see note 83), 110. See also Gabriele Eckart, "The German Gothic Subculture," *German Studies Review* 28 (2005): 547-562.
86. Speit (see note 2), 10.
87. Dominik Tischleder quoted in Diesel and Gerten (see note 4), 411.
88. Pearce (see note 9).
89. Turner-Graham (see note 34), 206.
90. François (see note 3), 41.
91. Sander L. Gilman, "Why and How I Study the German," *The German Quarterly* 62 (1989): 200-201.
92. McBride quoted in Giebel (see note 15).
93. Ibid.
94. See Michael Löwy, *Fire Alarm: Reading Walter Benjamin's "On the Concept of History,"* trans. Chris Turner (New York, 2005).
95. othiym23, "Death in June Are or Are Not Nazis," *A Year of Music*, 14 March 2008; available at http://driftglass.org/music//2008/03/13/death-in-june-are-or-are-not-nazis, accessed 1 December 2015.

Chapter 7

KNITTED NAKED SUITS AND SHEDDING SKINS

The Body Politics of Popfeminist Musical Performances in the Twenty-first Century

Maria Stehle

Since her first, now classic album *The Teaches of Peaches* [Peaches] uses her lyrics to confuse the symbolic matrix in which gender attributes are organized and which orients the respective gendered scripts for men and women. Her playful approach to the clichés we understand today as heteronormativity are sometimes blunt, sometimes smart, sometimes rebelliously post-pubescent, sometimes adult-ironic, but most of the time funny. That her music is a mix of punk, techno, and R'n'B serves her anti-rock and anti-essentialist purpose. The real site of her attack on heteronormativity, however, is her body—as topic of her songs but also as a tool for her performance.[1]

In a role-play between naked alien and red-glittery glamour queen, McGowan takes five different forms of identity. Each of her disguises stands symbolically for facets of self-perception and self-depiction: "all characters are variants of myself, are parts, that make a whole: artist, public persona, and—most importantly—just human," says McGowan. This anti-"dream-factory" video is drastically gaga-esque: an optical dream with the message of a nightmare.[2]

Glitter Skins and Penis Suits

Within a few days of one another, the German pop-music magazine *Spex* published articles about the 2015 musical releases of Peaches and Rose McGowan.[3] Both emphasize how Peaches' album and McGowan's single centrally address questions of gendered bodies and identities, while the respective authors express their admiration as well as their confusion about the diversity of expressions in the works of these artists. Peaches' work illustrates an aggressively joyful approach to questions of gender and sexuality while McGowan's debut single offers a more tentative but clearly troubled perspective on the public perception of female artists and of their bodies as marketing tools.[4]

Notes for this chapter begin on page 141.

The very fact that popfeminist musical performances trigger such responses is the starting point for my theorizations of popfeminist music as a form of political intervention into gender and body politics in the twenty-first century. Since the 1960s, the "pop" prefix in the German context has been used to denote a specifically "German" subcultural phenomenon floating on the surface of global mass culture.[5] In the 1990s, pop-theorists of the so-called pop-left (often in the then still independently owned magazine *Spex*) have attempted to claim pop as a theoretically informed form of cultural-political intervention. Understood as such, pop recodes signs of popular culture through quotations, pastiche, and cut-up methods, resignifying and redefining the original subject in a manner that reflects, exposes, and even problematizes superficial aspects of everyday reality. In their foreword to *Pop seit 1964*, Kerstin Gleba and Eckhard Schumacher explain that pop is a way to remake and remodel culture, utilizing artificial exaggeration in its approach to reproduction and copying: "Pop is ... a strategy, a posture, an attitude."[6] First theorized by Sonja Eismann in the 2007 edited volume *Hot Topic: Popfeminismus heute*, popfeminism provides a feminist approach to pop culture, but it also critiques and redefines both feminism and pop culture: "Pop culture [should] be perforated and rocked by feminist strategies."[7] In Eismann's volume and in her subsequent publications, the concept of popfeminism offers a way to define a new form of feminism against the lifestyle or postfeminisms of the early twenty-first century, as well as against persisting ideas of feminism as defined by the concerns of second-wave feminists.

Body politics, as defined by Hester Baer, here functions as a term to describe "a heuristic for considering the disputed status of the (female) body within both neoliberalism and feminism today."[8] Relying on the work of Alison Phipps,[9] Baer posits the "emphasis on self-optimization, personal responsibility, and individual choice" as the way in which "neoliberalism recasts the body as a key site of identity, empowerment, and control."[10]

These definitions of pop and popfeminism are the point of departure for the two songs I discuss in this article, Peaches and Rose McGowan's 2015 releases. Both artists are not just—and sometimes not even primarily—musicians; they are also activists, performance artists, actors, or fashion designers, and their work relies on visual projections and disseminations. The larger political landscape, where protest actions such as the performances of Pussy Riot are music, protest art, and political resistance, where actions such as FEMEN's topless protests are pop, performance, and media spectacle, have muddied the lines between musical and pop performances and—in this case feminist—politics in new ways.[11] Popfeminist music emerges within forms of digitally as well as DIY (Do It Yourself) inspired political protest acts—for example, feminist twitter hashtags or feminist flashmobs—that collide feminist theory and action, digital realms and physical bodies and worlds, and transnational and local contexts.[12] These new intersections and collisions in expression, form, and dissemination require us to find new ways to theorize the politics of pop culture and to describe their political interventions.

Pop music is a site of cultural exchange, collision, and assemblage.[13] Reading popular culture allows us to examine "affectively complicated relation[s] to commodities, information, and performing, the ways in which we labor, exchange, and consume"[14] in late capitalism. By creating such sites of collision, popfeminist music participates in a defiant act that messes with the logic of neoliberal consumption of gendered, racialized, and sexualized bodies and transgresses the boundaries of national or ethnic identity categories. This disruption might not happen in or because of a single song but by reading these songs as part of a media landscape that includes a range of artistic expressions: eerie artistic videos and playfully silly songs, artist-collaborations and artists that inhabit multiple personas as well as various forms of assemblages of bodies, sounds, and images in digital and analog forms. Ideas of so-called mainstream pop cultures shift as neoliberalism appropriates alternative cultures at increasing speeds and on a transnational terrain.[15] Rather than the "permeation of mainstream culture"[16] as a development of popfeminist musical performances from the 1990s into the early twenty-first century, musician-performers-artists in the twenty-first century self-confidently place themselves, however queerly or awkwardly, in the global pop mainstream. The politics of popfeminist music cannot adequately be described by reading for alternative or subcultures; rather I suggest we read for social aesthetics that form communities within and across the commercial mainstream and niche markets, across the national and the transnational.

The transnational, in line with Sabine Hake's definition, is a "constitutive part of the national."[17] This emphasis on the entanglement between the national and the "trans" calls attention to the sociopolitical contexts in which these artistic expressions emerge and circulate, are consumed and tinkered with. This article develops reading strategies that allow us to read for specifics without falling back onto (often imprecise) categories of the national, international, or global, or vague concepts of various forms of trans. The fact that none of the two examples I discuss here are "German" but both are certainly part of the pop-culture scene in Germany and have various connections to German-specific contexts illustrates this entanglement.

Thus, my main goal is not to interpret specific songs, music, or their visual-auditory elements as "culture," "pop," or specifically "German pop culture" but to offer a theoretical reflection on how to read politically inspired pop in the twenty-first century. For my theorizing, I chose the examples of Peaches' and McGowan's 2015 releases, two musical events which, on first impression, could not be more different. Peaches' song and video "Dick in in Air" from her 2015 album *Rub* is a rather simply composed song with a playful-DIY video of U.S. comedian Margret Cho and Canadian Berlin-based artist Peaches roaming the streets of (presumably of L.A./Hollywood) in knitted penis suits. At the beginning of the video, a man exits a Victorian house dumping a pile of clothes on the side of the road. Out of this pile, Peaches and Cho pick the knitted penis suits that they then wear throughout the video; Peaches wears a bright pink and Cho a bright yellow suit to mirror and mock their respective racialization.[18] Electronic dance music accompanies Peaches' roughly rhymed raps in her typical electro-trash style. Containing the signature explicit lyrics of a Peaches song, Peaches raps in a sultry voice:[19] "Drop, give me eight inches a pop/stop, you've gone numb, you need a lift/ use a thumb, or take a fist." The beats of the song and the rap lyrics are interrupted only once by bits of diegetic sound as the two stop at the Hollywood Walk of Fame to specifically honor Barbara Streisand with Peaches singing the first lines of her song "The Way We Were." The chorus of "Dick in the Air" consists only of the words "dick in the air, let me see you put your dick in the air. Dick, dick." And later "balls balls dick dick balls and dick," at which point the song most certainly elicits awkward smiles. Scenes such as Peaches giving a "blow job" to Cho only to struggle with the yellow fuzz stuck in her mouth afterwards are comical and further enhance the goofiness of the video and the spontaneously awkward feel of the song as a whole.

Rose McGowan's first single "RM486,"[20] also released in September 2015, develops complex electronic soundscapes accompanied by a highly stylized video produced by Jonas Åkerlund.[21] Aside from vague references to Madonna and Lady Gaga, McGowan's video and her music evoke artists such as Björk, Sinéad O'Connor, and David Bowie; they allude to early electronic music such as the minimalist soundscapes of Anne Clark.[22] The video positions her figure, visible only from the waist up and in close-ups of her face, in a non-space as she sheds skins and morphs through a range of personas. The characters in the video are "alien," "dark beauty," "green hair Hollywood," "needles," and "red glitter bomb."[23] The glittery character appears as both a person with a layer of brittle glitter covering and a sort of sphinx-figure wearing knife-like headgear. The video, depicting McGowan's figures in stop motion movements combined with the lyrics sung with her almost whispering voice, creates a sense of fragility and danger while at the same time, the presence of the artist and the way in which she seems to fixate the camera, project power and assertiveness. As the speed and the beat pick up in the second half of the song, her presence and her voice become more stable. Similarly, the lyrics of the song intermingle ideas of empowerment with concepts of pain, hurt, and insecurity. While the intro ends with the line "time to die", the first verse asserts: "Held my hand up to the stars/Gilded lilies driving cars/ It's time to say it so I will/ I can, I do, I vow to live/ To all of us lost in time/ To those waiting to be picked up/ And those who cry, bleed and die/ To those with the unnatural sighs." The chorus repeats two lines that read "only here to paint color in the sun/ Only here to see the fire run." Bridge and Outro consist of only one command: "Run!"[24]

In both of these examples, Peaches' "Dick in the Air" and McGowan's "RM486," the format of the song offers the temporal and auditory frame for reflections about bodies physically being in this world and about how to be in the contemporary world. These aesthetic products address the question of how we—our gendered and racialized bodies— are impacted by our surroundings and how, in turn, we impact these surroundings. According to Lauren Berlant, aesthetics "provide metrics for understanding how we pace and space our encounters with things, how we manage the too closeness of the world and also the desire to have an impact on it that has some relation to its impact on us."[25] When Ben Highmore writes about how aesthetics posit "our most subjective experiences as social,"[26] he offers a further way to read aesthetics not as the exceptional and/or beautiful, but instead as defining how the ordinary resonates in our senses and emotions and turns these emotions into collective experiences.[27] Similarly, Sianne Ngai describes "vernacular aesthetic categories" as not only calling "forth specific subjective capacities for feeling and acting but also specific ways of relating to other subjects and the larger social arrangements these ways of relating presuppose."[28] According to Ngai, "aesthetic categories ... do nothing less than reorganize the relations of subjects to a postmodern geopolitical reality."[29] Defined in such terms, attention to aesthetic form offers avenues to tackle questions about our relation to our surroundings, to the local and the global, to neoliberalism and its discontents.

The focus here is on feminist and popfeminist politics; however, a similar strategy of reading pop also applies to, for example, politics of religious belonging or of ethnic identification as they are manifested and constructed in pop and media productions in examples such as Arabic language rap or Christian rock music. In such musical productions, a sense of belonging, articulated on a personal level, intends to create social community, often one that includes but is not limited to national categories, and one that codes belonging in terms of religious, gender, and/or ethnic identities.

Rather than a direct call for political action, such pop musical productions are political in their imaginations of social communities. Tools of neoliberal globalization, mainly access to digital media and digital proliferation, enable such communities; in turn, in the face of neoliberal capitalism, a sense of community that goes beyond the borders of the national or local also offers an increasingly important space for the formulation of political alternatives.[30] Such neoliberal circularities, "cycles of resistance and consumption, meaning making and undoing, action and reaction ... recalibrate time, perception, and visibility."[31]

Feminisms: Gender and Neoliberalism

Popfeminists imagine feminist communities in the face of a neoliberal economic reality where, together with social class, race, and religion, gender remains one of the main sites for identification, self-regulation, and discipline. As Rosalind Gill and Christina Scharff have argued, in neoliberalism, "it is women who are called on to self-manage, to self-discipline. To a much greater extent than men, women are required to work on and transform the self, to regulate every aspect of their conduct, and to present all their actions as freely chosen."[32] This rhetoric of free choice is a crucial part of the postfeminist backlash that McRobbie describes in her work. Based on Beck and Giddens, McRobbie describes neoliberalism as a system that requires individuals to project a sense that they

> choose the kind of life they want to live. Girls must have a lifeplan. They must become more reflexive in regard to every aspect of their lives, from making the right choice in marriage, to taking responsibility for their own working lives, and not being dependent on a job for life or on the stable and reliable operations of a large-scale bureaucracy which in the past would have allocated its employees specific, and possibly unchanging, roles.[33]

McRobbie describes the "regulative dimensions of the popular discourses of personal choice and self improvement" where "the individual is compelled to be the kind of subject who can make the right choices."[34] According to McRobbie, "by these means new lines and demarcations are drawn between those subjects who are judged responsive to the regime of personal responsibility, and those who fail miserably."[35] Neoliberalism produces power relations that "work ... effectively at the level of embodiment" and that "are productive of new realms of injury and injustice."[36]

Both artists discussed in this essay understand their work in a specifically feminist context, meaning that they try to address the gendered aspects of such embodiments and the injury and social injustice they produce. An interviewer asked Rose McGowan about her "ideas of female empowerment and sexual liberation" and specifically about if she feels "a responsibility to create a feminist dialogue." McGowan responded: "Yes I feel like it's my duty and other people who have a voice, it's their duty as well. We're told from when were very young: 'don't upset anybody, don't rock the boat.' Why not?"[37]

Evading an answer to the question about voice and empowerment, McGowan turns to the concept of "upsetting" people, of creating disturbance, as a way to create feminist political interventions. To "rock the boat," then, means to work against what McRobbie describes as regimes of discipline and personal responsibility and towards new and different kinds of embodiments.

Peaches, in an interview with German pop-magazine *Spex*, also defines feminist political acts as acts of disturbance but more directly connects them to questions of embodiment and the body when she asserts: "It is not just about sex. The point is not to be afraid any more, of one self and one's body. It is a political act to ask people to be comfortable with who they are."[38] In their work, artists such as McGowan and Peaches take on and reveal neoliberal mechanisms and their potential for injury and injustice and try to disrupt and counter them with their lyrics, musical style, and visuals. Their musical performances show how concepts such as free choice and self-improvement are tools for disciplining people into smoothly functioning neoliberal subjects.

Media reception of Peaches and McGowan in Germany focuses on their respective feminist messages. Since "RM486" is her first single, McGowan is mainly known as an actress and for her activism against sexism in the Hollywood film business. Anke Westphal in the *Berliner Zeitung*, for example, described how McGowan gave advice on how to counter gender injustice in the world of film: "Her most important advise: 'Be bold,' which means 'be daring and direct'."[39] In interviews in the U.S. music press after the release of her single, McGowan emphasized her attempt to create statements in her music that playfully take on the way in which bodies are "inscripted." Even her title, her initials with the number, which references the controversial morning-after pill (or "abortion pill"), is an attempt to take back the power of writing your own, in this case, codes and numbers: "Something I've always felt in public, they put a number on you and I reject that number. So, I decided to put one on myself–take back the power of it."[40] This statement might be the most direct reference McGowan makes to a neoliberal and consumerist coding in late capitalism, including physical bodies. In this way, McGowan creates a sensual relation between ordinary aesthetics and collective experience that manages, to use the concept of Lauren Berlant, the too closeness of the world, and creates disruptions that directly shed light on the political power of aesthetics.

Peaches is always too close; her lack of distance, especially when it comes to questions of sexuality, the body, and normative bodies, has paved the way for other artists to lift non-normative depictions into the mainstream. Peaches understands the fact that she lived and worked in Berlin since 2000 as a key factor in her development towards breaking this path to the mainstream. In interviews in German media, Peaches is often cast as an expert on post-wall Berlin, its alternative cultures and the forces of gentrification. As a pioneer of queer pop, interviewers confront Peaches with questions such as:

> When you started fifteen years ago, your openness regarding sex and gender questions was new. You lifted Madonna's work up to a new level. Today, sexiness/sex is a requirement for pop as one can see in artists such as Nicki Minaj and Miley Cyrus. Do you see them as your followers and how are they doing their job?[41]

In her answer, Peaches does not mourn the fact that her work has entered the mainstream and that she has become an idol for younger artists who are often more commercialized and more commercially successful. This, for Peaches, is a sign of progress and does not mean that her current work has lost its feminist and aesthetic power. Yet, she describes her 2015 album *Rub*, which contains the song "Dick in the Air," as her angriest album to date. In her art, Peaches aggressively counters physical norms and gender norms, while McGowan displays the body as injured and fragile but also as a body that can disguise, arm, confront, and/or simply run away.

The 2015 releases of McGowan and Peaches illustrate that postfeminist currencies of the 1990s, as discussed by McRobbie, have, at least in some spheres of popular culture, made way to new forms of aesthetic expression. In 2004, McRobbie saw an emergence of pop culture that created new sites of critical engagement with how neoliberalism employs (not always subtle) mechanisms of oppression and physical discipline to construct its gendered subjects. While postfeminist productions often evoke specters of second and third wave feminism, feminist activisms and performances only to undo them and consider them no longer necessary, popfeminism twists these previous forms to bring them into a material aesthetic context, to make them present in new—sometimes joyful sometimes troubling—ways. The current historical moment allows artists such as McGowan and Peaches to work with and through gendered, queer, and drag performances and (re) insert political currency into such representations also because in light of global financial crises and in the face of terrorism, war, and violence, neoliberalism has become a more and more difficult concept to sell ideologically. This, however, stands in tension with a socioeconomic reality where neoliberalism remains a stubbornly persistent force.[42]

Social Aesthetics: Songs and Bodies

The political currency of these performances does not lie in their provocation or in their extraordinariness. To try to answer the question of whether or not it is outrageous to knit a penis suit and make a video about it or if McGowan's naked, painted body is or is not a provocation runs the risk of constructing far too generalized sites of resistance that are, in fact, a (in some cases rather calculated) part of neoliberal, commercial spectacles. Rather, a focus on the formal, aesthetic, and material—in this case, the performing body and the song—tackles how such aesthetic expression functions, interacts, and intervenes in specific political contexts. Music paces and spaces bodies in this world and negotiates sensual encounters with our surroundings, meaning also with the material world. More than mirror experiences of being in this world, popfeminist songs seek to shape and disrupt physical and sensual structures of being.

Performance theorists emphasize the material presence of the body. In his "manifesto" on performance and popular culture, Philip Auslander attempts to bring together performance and music study by arguing that "despite the physical absence of the performer at the time of listening, listeners do not perceive recorded music as disembodied."[43] Auslander aims to encourage "close readings of performances by popular musicians, readings that attend to the particulars of physical movement, gesture, costume, and facial expression as much as voice and musical sound."[44] The fact that bodies are always also digital image, costumed in layers of fabric or "skins," and, maybe most importantly for the context of this workshop, bodies produce sounds—they sing, play instruments, manipulate sounds, or, in some cases, even wear instruments, further complicates the question of the physical body in contemporary pop music. Thinking about the bodies of the performers in such terms broadens our thinking about the material context of this kind of, often digitally produced and disseminated, pop music. The body, its skin and clothes, voice, make-up, and costumes, mark race, gender, class, and sexual identity. And it is precisely these markers that the performers of interest in this essay engage with—joyfully but also by pointing to their troubling readings, appropriations, and exploitations. Peaches' and McGowan's songs, for example, rewrite tropes of the racialized body, the sensory and boundary organ skin, and of discourses of porn and queer identification.

McGowan performs skin as layers of make-up, as body armor, and as bare-nakedness. Maybe ironically, while reviews of her single emphasize her being nude, naked, or natural in the video, her skin never appears without thick make-up, clothing, or other kinds of covers on screen. In the beginning of the video, she sheds skins, literally peeling layers of her body at the beginning of the video, reminiscent of the classic German feminist novel by Verena Stefan *Häutungen* (Shedding Skins) published in 1975. For McGowan, however, shedding skin is not a process that reveals a more authentic or core self nor is her bear-breasted chest an act of political protest in the tradition of bra-burning and second-wave feminism, or, to give a more contemporary example, akin to the feminist protest group FEMEN. McGowan's body in the video morphs into a range of selves that all face the world in their own vulnerable, armored, and simultaneously confrontational ways. While each of McGowan's characters is alone on screen, they respond to and communicate directly to a social context by confronting the viewer face-on. The body armor, the make-up, and the various kinds of skins and veils the singer wears are simultaneously defensive and offensive; they protect her and allow her to assert her various presences. The slow and fragile beauty of the music and the characters of the first half of the song speeds up into electronic beats as the skins of the characters harden into armor and towards the almost omnipresent power of the sphinx character. The final character wears a body armor made of feathers and her skin is colored in chalk-like red and pink paint. The fast cuts between close ups of her face and chest and portrait style images of the dancing bird-woman end in a close up of McGowan's face with a tear running over her messily painted face, a reoccurring image in the video. The close-up of her face in sadness that ends the video leaves a troubled impression, rather than an eerie, freaky, jarring, or creepy one, as some critics claim.

Peaches' art and aesthetics relate to feminist discourse in different ways than "RM486." Her sex-activist, sex-positive, and feminist porn-inspired aesthetics update the pro-sex activism from the 1970s to the 1990s, which evokes names such diverse artists as Valie Export, Annie Sprinkle, and Sandra Bernhard. The video to her 2015 album cover song "Rub" appears censored on video channels online due to its explicit depiction of lesbian sex. "Dick in the Air" also connects to the history of feminist protest art and naked protests and to current feminist activisms but also departs from there. The bright colors of the penis suits reference the masks, shirts, and tights of Pussy Riot protesters (not the least also since Peaches made a song and video in support of Pussy Riot while they were in prison, "Free Pussy Riot" that uses a similar color scheme).[45] Rather than protesting, however, the performers run around and have fun; rather than exposing their own skins, they wear a different layer of skin, a drag-skin or, what can paradoxically be described as a naked-suit. The video does not document a political happening or a public disturbance since its focus is not on other peoples' reaction to the artists but on their very own joy and sense of wild and fast-paced experimentation. The penis-suit performance together with the lyrics and the danceable beats of the song simultaneously mock and assert masculine sexual postures. Cho and Peaches joyfully embrace being "men" with their dicks in the air while at the same time they critique this very image of masculinity by mocking it. This leads to a complex politics where it is not the gender-transgressive body that is mocked but the gender-conforming one. Their joint gender transgression, the closeness of their naked-suited bodies, and their collective queerness, here, are acts of joy and mockery. Violent male gestures are appropriated, exposed, and mocked.

For both artists, the format of the song and its video clip offers the aesthetic frame for visual interventions into body politics. Gender-normativity is the foil for their popfeminist interventions and connects each production to a larger pop-cultural landscape. Pop music is an active site of feminist theorizing and for the development of new forms of body and material politics in a complex multi-media world, also precisely because pop-music is the site for some of the most normative depictions of gender, race, sex and the body. These songs make discourses about the body present and intervene with these discourses. In her re-reading of Walter Benjamin, artist-theorist Hito Steyerl offers a definition of this kind of re-presencing: "Things are not being represented, they represent themselves. They actualize themselves in the present."[46] This actualization is an inherently social act–to represent to and for an implied spectator. Peaches' video displays and includes a viewer in collective silliness and joy; McGowan's social presence, in contrast, is troubling since a viewer is directly confronted with her simultaneously assertive and fragile personas. Identification is one response to her presence; another one is to feel challenged by her vulnerability, her body armor, her peeling skins, and her defenses. Her order "Run!" that is repeated often in the song's lyrics is equally ambivalent since it can either mean to run from or with her. Similarly, Peaches order to "put your dick in the air" is an invitation to join their explorations but also a challenge to do just that–ambivalent in its assertive gesture towards women and in its mocking tone towards cis-gendered males. In both songs, bodies represent and actualize themselves; in their aesthetic re-presencing, they address presupposed social relations and suggest new ways to relate and, to return to Ngai, not "organize" but confuse and disturb the position of the subject in a geopolitical reality.

Re-Presencing: Gender and Drag

Performance as a form of re-presencing means that the focus is not primarily on "the sociological, institutional, and policy contexts in which popular music is made" but on "finding ways of discussing what popular musicians do as performers—the meanings they create through their performances and the means they use to create them."[47] Gender in these videos is not a performance in the ways in which Butler's theories were often (mis) read in the 1990s, but the performing bodies make present the discourses that shape, form, and cast bodies in social contexts (which also includes the national) and, possibly, cast them/think them/do them in new ways. Pop music in the twenty-first century connects material cultures, images, and projections and presents us with a heightened focus on the too-closeness of things through aesthetic form.

Rachel Devitt reads Butler's theories of drag and performative, theatrical citation not simply as ways to subvert norms, but emphasizes how "Butler locates both power and pleasure, critique and celebration in the cracks and slippages, in the 'out of syncness' of a system predicated upon the appearance of fixity and impenetrability." In Butler's theorizations,

> sex and gender are ... naturalised through the reiteration of their naturalness but, paradoxically, they are also perpetually destabilised by this dependence on repetition. ... Drag and other forms of "gender insubordination," Butler argues, can powerfully wallow in these gaps and fissures, troubling the cohesiveness of systems of gender, sex and identity and highlighting their "flaws" and failures.[48]

By playing through and with this "naturalness"—in the case of McGowan and Peaches images of the "naked" body—and ideas of fixity and appearance, and by repeating and by creating fissures, Peaches and McGowan, in their respective ways, highlight flaws and failures and critique oppressive systems of gender without devaluing or disregarding the body as material and the material as the site of political agency.

Peaches' video is awkward;[49] it erases distancing and suggests connection. The video displays the flaws and failures of the artists' imperfect performance of "Dick(s) in the Air" as a disruption of gender binaries that present themselves as cohesive. Peaches displays the joy of queerness by mocking the normative gaze. She takes apart and reassembles ideas of masculinity and assertive sexuality while she plays through and with ideas of subversion and cooption, comparable maybe to drag-performers (think, for example, of the actor Divine). The way in which the normative gaze is assumed, maybe even a prime means of luring in a viewer and listener, but then thoroughly disturbed, is also a strategy that artists such as Lady Gaga and, in the German context, Lady Bitch Ray, use.

Drag in McGowan's video functions differently. Katrin Sieg describes drag, in her work applied to race, as including "not only cross-racial casting on stage, but, more generally, the performance of "race" as masquerade."[50] Gender and self, in McGowan's video, are masquerade, but the affective responses to these masks are valued and central to McGowan's work. Her forms of drag are not representing anything per se, but they are making present the various masks in which the body exists. Sieg describes the complexity of these interventions when she defines drag "as a symbolic contact zone" that "facilitate[s] the exercise and exchange of power,"[51] which can be used in the service of dominant ideologies as well as in ways that challenge the very essentialisms—and I would add material exploitations—of these normative bodies. In McGowan's video, it is not just gender that is drag, but being in this world is presented as always relational to perception and potential disturbances in and of such perception. The material, the body, then only exists as a social relation; there is no "naked self" outside of perception. What the song re-presences is the body in a close, albeit in some cases antagonistic, relation to a social reality. The white-face and the glittery skins McGowan is wearing reveal the white female body as vulnerable, as racialized, as masked, even or maybe especially in its most "naked" appearances.

In Peaches' song, gender is masquerade in a rather direct way; it estranges and denaturalized, but it also unveils drag as a strategy that is in itself flawed. According to Sieg, "[a]s a technique of estrangement, drag denounces that which dominant ideology presents as natural, normal, and inescapable, without always offering another truth."[52] Drag in "Dick in the Air" challenges essentialisms but rather than offering another truth, it shows an excessively awkward act of collective gender defiance. Similarly, in "RM486" taking off masks and shedding skins does not reveal another truth; it exposes the very process of revealing the "naked" or "true" self as flawed and troubling. These videos do not draw attention to what gender is, but to what it does and how it is operating. Wendy Hui Kyong Chun in the introduction to a special issue on "Race and/as Technology" of the journal *Camera Obscura*, reads "race as technology," which "shifts the focus from the *what* of race to the *how* of race, from *knowing* race to *doing* race by emphasizing the similarities between race and technology."[53] Thinking of gender and race as technologies, to follow Chun's argument further, means to displace the gendered or racialized body as purely cultural or purely biological, because, as Chun argues, "technological mediation ... is always already a mix of science, art, and culture."[54] Thinking about race and gender as technologies allows for the possibility of making gender and race "do different things."[55]

With artists such as Lady Gaga, drag has entered the commercial pop mainstream. This does not mean, however, that gender normativity has disappeared as part of a social, aesthetic, and material reality. On the contrary, neoliberalism has produced some of the most clearly gendered, violent, and gender-oppressive systems. To (re)politicize drag, popfeminist artists show how acts of (gender and also race as) drag and masquerade can be part of a gender-normative system; a system that is exposed as troubling but also as, when it is materialized, disturbed and disturbing. If drag and masquerade are part of our ordinary experiences of and in the aesthetic, Peaches as well as McGowan, in their respective ways, make this very fact present. This act of re-presencing, however, I argue with Devitt, "creates temporal and aesthetic spaces in which other meanings, other futures, and other relationships with popular music and identity might be imagined."[56] This means that re-presencing, as a way to make the body, however "precarious"[57] it may be, do different things, to create aesthetic relations to the material worlds that surround it, exposes a fissure between an aesthetic present that commercializes displays of gender non-conformativity and a social reality that continues to seek and enforce clearly marked gender lines. As such, aesthetic demonstrations of social relations are always interventions into a lived presence as well as explorations into how we might live differently in the future.

What remains—and has to remain—an open question is who this "we" might be. When Peaches performs in Berlin or L.A., her two respective places of residence, or when she performs on tour in Texas, the imagined futures evoked by her work clearly look different. A sense of community forms among Peaches' fans that is based on re-presencing, on making present different ways of living in and relating to bodies; however, this community is not one of physical proximity or connection. Similarly, global circulation of McGowan's video via very different video sharing sites, such as messy youtube channels or the artsy site "Nowness.com," ensure global accessibility of her song and video, but also imply that reception in a postcapitalist context is complex in that it also, similar to the messages of her video, creates spaces of connection as well as fissure and division. The powdery white skin and masks of McGowan certainly take on different meaning depending on whether they are viewed in Kenya, Japan, or Germany, for example.

Shifts and Fragile Bonds

Popfeminist music and the minor/vernacular aesthetics it produces as a social aesthetics and collective experience intervene in the body politics of the current, neoliberal moment. Reading for vernacular aesthetics offers ways to uncover how artists re-presence the experience of physically being in a postcapitalist, neoliberal world. McGowan and Peaches' musical productions address the "too closeness" of the world, too closeness also (but not only) in a physical and material sense that bodies are controlled and affected, while at the same time imagining spaces for different kinds of social community and connection. Both artists suggest ways of relating to the world and of being in this world that are not oriented directly towards political or economic change but towards creating new social futures by forming joyful and/or troubling relations and connections, in spite of and in the face of persistent and violent neoliberal gender regimes.

There is certainly no clear line between neoliberal spectacle and feminist political intervention and often artists not only accept this very blurriness but welcome and foster it. This means that my argument is not about judging Peaches, McGowan, Lady Bitch Ray, or even Lady Gaga or Miley Cyrus' feminist politics; rather, it illustrate strategies to read for the political in a shifting aesthetic landscape of pop. By reading for social aesthetics, I try to avoid generalizations based on categories such as the national, local, or global, which do not seem to hold when we regard the globally circulating images and sounds that form our aesthetic registers. Pop music and music videos offer the vernacular aesthetic form for popfeminist interventions. The songs call for us to stay with both, the joy of the playfully provocative and the social act of sharing—maybe the joy of—being in trouble together.

MARIA STEHLE is Associate Professor of German and faculty in Cinema and Women, Gender, and Sexuality Studies at the University of Tennessee Knoxville. She is the author of *Ghetto Voices in Contemporary German Cultures* (Rochester, 2012), co-author of *Awkward Politics: The Technologies of Popfeminist Activism* (Montreal, 2016), and has published widely in the fields of German, cinema, media, and gender studies.

Notes

1. Ulrich Gutmair, "Peaches–Zeit, die Stellung zu wechseln," *Spex: Magazin für Popkultur*, 9 December 2015; available at http://www.spex.de/2015/12/09/peaches-zeit-die-stellung-zu-wechseln-tourdaten-feature-aus-spex-n-363: All translations from the German in this article are my own.
2. Maxi Zingel, "Gaga-esk: Rose McGowan setzt feministisches Ausrufezeichen mit neuem Video 'RM486'," *Spex: Magazin für Popkultur*, 23 September 23, 2015; available at http://www.spex.de/2015/09/23/gaga-esk-rose-mcgowan-setzt-antisexistisches-ausrufezeichen-mit-neuem-video-rm486.
3. Rose McGowan, "RM486," Single released in September 2015. Official video available at https://www.youtube.com/watch?v=w1Wq5Tt-op8 and Peaches, *Rub*. Album released 2015.
4. This essay engages with the concept of "trouble" borrowed from Donna Haraway, *Staying with the Trouble: Making Kin in the Chthulucene* (Durham, 2016) and relies heavily on Carrie Smith-Prei and Maria Stehle's *Awkward Politics: The Technologies of Popfeminist Activism*, (Montreal, 2016). Smith-Prei and Stehle develop strategies of reading for the political in popfeminist art and use the concepts of joy and trouble in various ways. This essay applies these two concepts specifically to pop music.
5. See Heinz Ludwig Arnold and Jörgen Schäfer, ed., *Pop-Literatur* (Munich, 2003) and Maggie McCarthy, *German Pop Literature: A Companion* (Berlin, 2015).
6. Kerstin Gleba and Eckhard Schumacher, ed. "Vorwort" in *Pop: Seit 1964* (Cologne, 2007), 11-14, here 12.
7. Sonja Eismann, ed., *Hot topic: Popfeminismus heute*, (Mainz, 2007), 10. For a more detailed exploration of these discussions, see Smith-Prei and Stehle (see note 4), 56-57.
8. Hester Baer, "Redoing Feminism: Digital Activism, Body Politics, and Neoliberalism," *Feminist Media Studies* 16, no. 1 (2016): 19.
9. Alison Phipps, *The Politics of the Body: Gender in a Neoliberal and Neoconservative Age* (Cambridge, 2014).
10. Baer (See note 8), 19.
11. For a detailed discussion of pop-political feminist protest and art, see Smith-Prei and Stehle (see note 4).
12. See Rachel Devitt, "'Keep the best of you, "do" the rest of you': passing, ambivalence and keeping queer time in gender performative negotiations of popular music," *Popular Music* 32, no. 3 (2013): 427-449, here 428. Devitt's argument is that music is not just a way to make political interventions but that often politics use music to convey a message. Reading for social aesthetics emphasizes that the spheres of politics and music are intricately entangled.
13. For an introduction to the cultural study of music also see Martin Clayton, Trevor Herbert, and Richard Middleton, *The Cultural Study of Music: A Critical Introduction*, 2nd ed. (New York, 2011).
14. Sianne Ngai, *Our Aesthetic Categories: Zany, Cute, Interesting* (Cambridge, 2012), 242.
15. For more detailed discussions of feminist politics under neoliberalism, also see Baer (see note 8).
16. Maria Stehle, "Pop-Feminist Music in Twenty-First Century Germany: Innovations, Provocations, and Failures," *Journal of Popular Music Studies* 25, no. 2 (2013): 222-239, here 237.
17. Sabine Hake, "German Cinema as European Cinema: learning from Film History," *Film History* 25, nos. 1-2 (2013): 110-117, here 116.
18. Zoe Camp, "Peaches and Margaret Cho Don Fuzzy Genitalia In 'Dick In The Air' Video," *Pitchfork*, 9 September 2015; available at http://pitchfork.com/news/61125-peaches-and-margaret-cho-don-fuzzy-genitalia-in-dick-in-the-air-video/.

19. The songs that made Peaches famous are "Fuck the Pain Away" (2000) and "Impeach my Bush" (2006).
20. Before the release of her first single, McGowan was an actress and directed the short film *Dawn* (2014); available at https://www.youtube.com/watch?v=RQ41Y2Gp4io.
21. Åkerlund also produced videos for Lady Gaga and Madonna, among others.
22. For a detailed discussion of Lady Gaga's art see: Martin Iddon and Melanie L. Marshall, ed., *Lady Gaga and Popular Music: Performing Gender, Fashion, and Culture*. (New York, 2014).
23. See http://genius.com/Rose-mcgowan-rm486-lyrics for a brief discussion of the song/video also see Jon Blistein, "Watch Rose McGowan's Jarring, NSFW 'RM486' Video," *Rolling Stone*, 22 September 2015; available at http://www.rollingstone.com/music/news/rose-mcgowan-shares-jarring-nsfw-rm486-video-20150922.
24. See ibid.
25. Lauren Berlant, *Cruel Optimism* (Durham, 2011), 12.
26. Ben Highmore, *Ordinary Lives* (New York, 2011): 11.
27. Ibid., 21
28. Ngai (see note 14), 11.
29. Ibid., 14.
30. Smith-Prei and Stehle (see note 4) describe this neoliberal circularity in greater detail.
31. Hester Baer, Carrie Smith-Prei, and Maria Stehle, "Digital Feminisms and The Impasse: Time, Disappearance, and Delay in Neoliberalism," *Studies in Twentieth and Twenty-First Century Literature* 40, no. 2 (2016); available at http://newprairiepress.org/sttcl/vol40/iss2/3/
32. See Rosalind Gill and Christina Scharff, *New Femininities: Postfeminism, Neoliberalism, and Subjectivity* (New York, 2011), 7.
33. Angela McRobbie, "Post-Feminism and Popular Culture," *Feminist Media Studies* 4, no. 3 (2004): 255-264, here 261.
34. Ibid., 261.
35. Ibid.
36. Ibid.
37. "Rose McGowan: RM486: A Look at the inimitable actor's first musical performance," Interview, 21 September 2015; available at https://www.nowness.com/story/rose-mcgowen-rm486-jonas-akerlund-b-akerlund.
38. Gutmair (see note 1).
39. Anke Westphal, "Männer und Frauen," *Berliner Zeitung*, 6 May 2015).
40. Blistein (see note 23).
41. Nadine Lange, "So wütend war ich noch nie," *Der Tagesspiegel Online*, 25 September 2015.
42. Peaches and McGowan are but two examples of these new critical currencies in pop music and culture. As Carrie Smith-Prei and Stehle (see note 4) argue, the performance-artist collective Chicks on Speed, for example, is working through concepts of gender and the body in neoliberalism by experimenting with clothes as instruments, with bodies, technology, and cyber-bodies. Similarly, for German performer and rapper Lady Bitch Ray, costumes and fashion are a key part of the performance and of her multimedia presence. Lady Bitch Ray's art addresses questions of racialized and gendered violence in her assertive representation of female sexuality and voice–similarly, in a troubled but joyful manner.
43. Philip Auslander, "Performance Analysis and Popular Music: A Manifesto," *Contemporary Theatre Review* 14, no. 1 (2004): 1-13, here 5.
44. Ibid., 3.
45. For a more detailed reading of this video see Smith-Prei and Stehle (see note 4).
46. Hito Steyerl, *Die Farbe der Wahrheit: Dokumentarismen im Kunstfeld* (Vienna, 2008), 122.
47. Auslander (see note 43), 3.
48. Devitt (see note 12), 444.
49. See Smith-Prei and Stehle (see note 4).
50. Katrin Sieg, *Ethnic Drag. Performing Race, Nation, Sexuality in West Germany* (Ann Arbor, 2002), 2.
51. Ibid., 2-3.

52. Ibid., 2.
53. Wendy Hui Kyong Chun, "Introduction: Race And/as Technology; Or, How to Do Things to Race," *Camera Obscura* 24, no. 70 (2009): 7-35, here 8, emphasis in the original. For further reading, also see Beth Coleman, "Race as Technology," *Camera Obscura* 24, no. 70 (2009): 176-207.
54. Ibid., 8.
55. Ibid., 8.
56. Devitt (see note 12), 446.
57. Baer (see note 8), 30.

Chapter 8

SEARCHING FOR THE YOUNG SOUL REBELS

On Writing, New Wave, and the Ends of Cultural Studies
Richard Langston

> We found writing to be the most important thing.[1]
>
> Already in school I found it amusing to hear that one could read and interpret an author—for instance with the help of Lukács—against himself or, as it were, "behind his back." I simply never thought that I would eventually do that very thing to an author I knew inside out, namely myself...[2]

Looking Back at the Late 1980s

𝓑eginning in the late 1980s, a paradigm shift among North American Germanists gained momentum to renegotiate the German literary canon, expand the text's boundaries, and invigorate critical methodologies in the name of setting their work apart from a perceived stagnate continental European *Germanistik*. Around the same time, a coterie of vanguard West German music journalists was tapping into the very same toolbox developed by Anglo-American Cultural Studies in its own battle against complicity and cultural barbarism brought to light, in part, by the string of xenophobic riots in the early 1990s. As will be established over the course of this chapter, what may have looked in the moment like two parts of the same tectonic shift in thinking were in fact two very different phenomena. This distinction was especially oblique thanks to their identical traffic in new cultural theory. While some North American scholars sought out, for example, "overlaps" between or even a grand "synthesis" of their tried-and-true Frankfurt School and theoretical innovations coming out of Anglo-American Cultural Studies, others called for throwing old ballast overboard in order to decenter the field entirely by transcending its literary biases,

---

Notes for this chapter begin on page 160.

remedying its cultural omissions, and facilitating a politically engaged scholarship.[3] Meanwhile in newly reunified Germany, a small group of music journalists and cultural critics reached for some of the very same cultural theorists like Judith Butler, Henry Louis Gates, Jr., and Homi Bhabha (as well as Jacques Derrida, Gilles Deleuze, Félix Guattari, and Michel Foucault).[4] At roughly the same time Cultural Studies seemed like a transatlantic panacea capable of remedying the dearth of attention to diversity and difference plaguing niches in the North American academy and swaths of everyday life in unified Germany oblivious if not hostile to the emergence of "new political subjectivities."[5]

In spite of manifest theoretical correspondences and shared political commitments, there is much that separates these two synchronous appropriations of Cultural Studies. For one, the location of their political aspirations could not have been more different. Whereas German Studies aspired to make its work in the ivory tower more socially relevant by shifting its focus and broadening its scope, a cadre of music journalists turned their eye to cultural theory with the hope of educating it readership on the perils of mass culture and the promise of subversive consumption.[6] (An established discipline within the North American academy when its influence waxed in the humanities, Cultural Studies as Richard Hoggart and Stuart Hall nurtured it at the Birmingham School found virtually no resonance at universities in the Federal Republic.[7]) One unforeseen outcome of this extracurricular appropriation in Germany was its far-reaching transmission. Not only did mainstream music magazines like the German edition of *Rolling Stone*, lifestyle magazines like *Tempo*, and even traditionally conservative German daily newspapers like the *Frankfurter Allgemeine Zeitung* eventually secure a younger generation of columnists capable of emulating this highfalutin discourse on pop music, but some of these writers then went on to become best-selling prose authors in their own right, whose literary works have, in turn, garnered the attention of German Studies scholars. Although both the North American and German appropriations of Cultural Studies led to new modes of writing, the American phenomenon remained wholly academic while the German one wound its way from countercultural subcultures to mass-market print media to belles lettres. Of concern here is both how these two strains of Cultural Studies eventually meet and why misrecognition played a central role in German Studies' appreciation of German "pop literature" steeped in Cultural Studies. Unmasking this misrecognition upon which an entirely new literary canon has emerged requires stepping backward in time from that moment when contemporary German literature donned Cultural Studies' mantle and to that earlier point in time when the transgressive consumption of popular culture required no theory.

Neither mass-market paperbacks nor top contenders on *Der Spiegel*'s influential weekly list of bestsellers, German pop literature has often been described sociologically as a generational tendency within a cadre of mostly male, affluent authors largely born in the 1960s and intent on advancing new, more entertaining modes of storytelling influenced in part by Anglo-American models.[8] Not only did leading representatives like Christian Kracht and Benjamin von Stuckrad-Barre follow in the footsteps of illustrious West German pop critics from the 1980s (who later heralded the arrival of Cultural Studies) by cutting their own teeth as culture journalists, but their literary debuts in the mid 1990s also trafficked heavily in pop music and even paid homage in a few exceptional instances to some of music journalism's heroes of yore.[9] For German Studies scholars on both sides of the Atlantic, the evidence was clear that the tools of Cultural Studies were best suited for grasping the subversive agency at work in the cultural consumerism featured in these works as well as their alleged forerunners from the 1980s.[10] After calling the literary canon into question, German Studies assembled entirely new ones. Yet, the remaining few, still active music critics from the 1980s responsible for bringing Cultural Studies to Germany in the first place were quick to shake off any such genealogy: "Contemporary pop literature," contested one writer, "couldn't be any more removed from the concept of literature [that arose] in the eighties milieu of pop music."[11] What separates these corpuses, above all, is the intervening need for Cultural Studies, that theoretical toolkit for unlocking the deeper political potential within popular culture. Prior to the arrival of Cultural Studies, West German music aficionados discovered in writing a means for giving political expression to the music they believed was capable of bestowing form on the abstract contingencies of modern life. It was in this vein that the very same critic asked in 1982: "How can I write about the deepest depths of the ... pure soul?"[12] Unlike the commercial interests typical of mainstream music journalism, this idiosyncratic writing found in only a few cultish magazines was thoroughly essayistic in nature and as such aspired to that which the young Georg Lukács concerned himself with in 1910: though no work of art, "the essay is an art form, an autonomous and integral giving-of-form to an autonomous and complete life."[13] As explained below, this Lukácsian renaissance intent on giving expression through writing to the transcendental soul–a "fast, intense, rebellious life" just like the songs by the band Dexys Midnight Runners–only lasted a couple of years.[14] By 1984, commercialism quickly encroached so far and fast that more arcane academic discourses became necessary for articulating the everyday politics of life to be found in popular music. It eventually did so by inoculating itself with theories taken from Cultural Studies. Tracing Cultural Studies' assent from the travails of music writing in the early 1980s shall provide the necessary foil with which to identify just how much the concerns of the soul get lost on the pop literature of the 1990s and just how little German Studies has understood what makes this literary corpus unique, namely its aversion to death.

Problems with Writing circa 1982

Writing in September 1981, the first anniversary of the founding of the fledgling Cologne-based music magazine *Spex: Musik zur Zeit*, co-editor Clara Drechsler qualified her and her colleagues' successes and failures at producing a grassroots counter-public sphere for music criticism in terms of authenticity. Good writing about underground post punk and emergent new wave, like good music itself, steers clear of diversionary, self-indulgent flourishes and instead lays bare honest truths regardless of just how awkward or flawed their expression. Consider Drechsler in her own words:

> We only measure our contributions according to the same standards applied to the music we write about. For this reason, a scrappy article that presents a correct message or an honest concern is for us always preferable to a stylistically perfect bubble or some tortured parlance. We are not, after all, experienced rock journalists. Rather, we all have our problems with writing that we wish not to cover up.[15]

Given the magazine's early admiration for the bristling rawness of post-punk bands—issue 1 hailed, for example, Joy Division as having come closest to capturing "our 'modern' soul"—it is perhaps not unreasonable to conclude that this sought-after authenticity was a function of a revered mimesis between music and essay.[16] Good writing, like the sounds brought forth by post punk, was simple and unpolished and therefore emotional and real.[17] We would fall, however, woefully short of comprehending the "problems with writing" were we to grasp them as a mere sign of *Spex's* antijournalistic ethos, namely its animus toward editorial dictates and slick writing set on selling stuff. In fact, the problems with writing for *Spex* authors like Drechsler were indices of something much deeper. Yet, Drechsler's account skirts around what exactly made writing so difficult for these "enthusiastic consumers" of music and it never adequately addresses what truths their good writing aspired to uncover. What exactly makes a music essay's message true and right? What deems its claims to be honest?

Truth, honesty, unpretentiousness, objectivity and, above all, a sober commitment to, if not critical engagement with the contemporary affairs of the world: these core ingredients in Drechsler's recipe for good writing were certainly not at odds with the subjective factor. In fact, her divisive penchant for incorporating aperçus, jokes, personal confessions, digressions, and free associations—all in the name of doing records justice—attest to her conviction in the writer's own irrefutable place in the writing process.[18] What her occasional statements on the "problems of writing" refrain from articulating explicitly (for doing so would violate her prohibition against biographism) is the precarious task of positioning the essayist's life in the encounter with a work of art such that the relevance of that work for everyday life is rendered legible. Drechsler goes on to describe her writing method thusly:

> Sometimes it's impossible to explain why I hold Grandmaster Flash's "The Message" in the same high regard as Human League's "Mirror Man," Yazoo's "Don't Go" and Gil Scott-Heron's "B-Movie." Escapism, a sense of reality, resistance, and letting oneself go. I feel all these things at different times. And stumbling upon one's many different needs, discovering contradictions within oneself, that's what pop music is all about.[19]

In other words, the problem of writing boiled down to the problem of identifying for works of popular music literary forms with which both the essayist and her readers could make sense of their lives in the contemporary world. Unlike the majority of music journalists who merely depicted their own solipsistic mental states when listening to music, Drechsler's "explosive fantasy"—triggered by the works themselves—unveiled the contradictory nature of life and this discovery, in turn, pointed toward modes of conduct and forms of praxis vis-à-vis the world for both the writer and reader. What ultimately made the task of writing especially "problematic" was maintaining the right ratio between life and the work of art. Oddly reminiscent of Adorno's own edict from over a decade and a half earlier that "thoroughgoing critique of identity gropes for the preponderance of the object," the music essay for Drechsler ultimately erred on the side of too much art.[20] "Records containing reality [should] go on the [good] list," she declares. Those who conflate the panoply of pop music into "soundtracks for acting out different identities" deceive themselves, however, for any agency found in such play is peanuts when cast against the backdrop of the annihilatory power of NATO's Double-Track Decision ratified in December 1979.[21]

Drechsler's essayistic politics intent on making a carefully curated subset of commercially available music matter—i.e., "insider tips" like early Neue Deutsche Welle, post punk, and avant-garde pop—arose at a significant juncture when Marxist hermeneutics began to fatigue and new wave's playful pastiche along with its free-floating signs seemed unstoppable.[22] Looking back on Marxism's legacy for his generation that came of age in the late 1970s, another kindred spirit named Diedrich Diederichsen, the unnamed critic from above, recalled in retrospect his contempt for the lingua franca of the New Left:

> After my youth spent in leftist organizations, a series of dramatic demarcations took place in my life. In 1978, I wanted nothing more to do with them. I hated the German Left. My hatred ignited above all due to the dullness of old-Marxian derivative thinking. I found it untrue. It failed on a daily basis in reality. Yet the counter-model of a radical-popular contemporaneity devoid of any normativity, the whole pop idea, also met its limit after 1982 such that the question arose: what can leftist discussions still achieve?[23]

The breaking point for Drechsler's essayistic approach to good pop music was a postmodern pluralism that, in the wake of the New Left's descent into sectarian K-groups, eventually peaked in West German music circles around the year 1982. Drechsler's sensibility thus stood in many respects as a last-ditch bulwark against the postmodern, a rampart intent on securing with the essay a viable leftist cultural politics (sympathetic to the heroes of the Eastern bloc) that devolved neither into a soundtrack for what she regarded as social democracy's wimpy humanism nor into an anthem for vulgar Marxism's anachronistic call for revolution.[24]

Diederichsen's own answer from the year 1982 to the perennial question "What's left?" was the British new wave band Haircut 100. Writing on the heels of the band's concert at a Hamburg disco in the spring of that year, Diederichsen mused: "Is there anything more beautiful on a day in May than ... amusing oneself at the dance palace 'Trinity'? Add to that the sounds of a band that wants nothing more than to be good. Good sounds. Good looks. Good entertainment. To the point that one's own soul blossoms."[25] Rather than wallowing in the band's sonic "good deed for the spirit, ears [and] soul," the meat of Diederichsen's essay—far from declaring a cultural revolution on par with Mao's—amounts to a defense against naysayers, both British and German proponents of so-called British "rockism" and its allegiance to guitars and all the attendant myths associated with the roar of rock and roll (like authenticity). Rockism's charges of opportunistic appropriation of the subaltern's experience, the rejection of political realism committed to replicating the alleged tristesse of reality, and the absence of any and all subversive strategies attributed to "authentic human beings," all these indictments against Haircut 100, says Diederichsen, fail to acknowledge just how inconsequential the paranoia, pubescent forlornness, and political naiveté really are that fuels these rebukes. "Good art destroys certitudes," he recapitulates, "and nevertheless gives strength, courage and joie de vivre."[26] Far from celebrating feel-good fun, Diederichsen insists, much like the young Friedrich Nietzsche, that along with joy, sadness, too, "has its place among the contradictions, tensions and contrasts that every astute, clear concept of music bestows upon the life of every respective listener."[27] To hear in Haircut 100 a denial of reality is, in other words, to paralyze the dynamic potential of the music, its powerful ability to throw life with all its joy and sorrow into relief. For all their differences over musical taste and good pop music in the year 1982, Drechsler and Diederichsen were, in fact, on the same page insofar as both agreed that music and life were intimately intertwined for the writer. But how can it be that both the tristesse of Joy Division and the joie de vivre of Haircut 100 hold sway over the souls of, at the very least, a couple of West German music aficionados? What, for that matter, is this soul about which they write? Is the soul not an antiquated metaphysical concept to begin with, one that bore both cultural and philosophical relevance an entire century earlier, one that suffered immeasurably with the ascendency of a long string of materialisms, the first, of course, being Marx and Engels' dialectical and historical varieties? Indeed, the German music essay fueled by new wave music channeled the concerns of late nineteenth-century *Lebensphilosophie* in order to recuperate what Marxism had extinguished in the course of the previous decade.

In Defense of the Soul after the New Left

It was the cultural philosopher and cofounder of German sociology Georg Simmel who was the first to articulate in his magisterial *The Philosophy of Money* the political stakes in a modern theory of the soul. In a world shaped by an unparalleled division of labor, on the one hand, and the vast accumulation of objective culture, on the other, the fragmentary existence of individuals begs the question, says Simmel, as to whether and under what conditions our souls are still "master[s] in [their] own house."[28] The soul, he states further, is that life force within our innermost being that "determines our relations to life."[29] For Simmel's student Georg Lukács, the soul is what judges, bestows meaning, and thus schematizes into unified form life's inherently confusing anarchic flow.[30] This metaphysics of forms beyond the reach of historical social reality—a Kantian synthetic *a priori* judgment, or an aesthetics of life—only comes into being through the act of expression. "Art," Lukács exclaims, "offers us souls and destinies."[31] Aesthetic expression is thus the organized form necessary for the articulation of a unique equilibrium between the outer world of things and the inner terrain of "feelings and experiences."[32] Yet, it is neither sculpture nor poetry nor any other of the usual suspects from the pantheon of art on which Lukács sets his sights. As laid out in his *Soul and Form*, the task for the twenty-five-year-old Lukács was instead to "define" the essay as a unique "form of art," a mode of critical writing that orders existing forms–"literature and art" in particular–such that the results speak not only the truth about their "essential nature" but also bestows form upon essayist's own life.[33] Summing up this relationship between the Platonist essayist and the poet, Lukács explains: "the Platonist ... must work through the destinies of others ... so as to penetrate to the most deeply hidden intimacies of his own soul."[34] In so doing, the essayist must himself find "a form spacious enough to contain the conflicting trends" such that "every antithesis, every trend become[s] music and necessity."[35] So when the twenty-five-year-old Diederichsen calls Haircut 100 "organized joie de vivre" to both his defense and that of Haircut 100 he arguably invokes the very same notion of form that for Lukács throws into relief, by virtue of its powers to constrain and contrast, the otherwise formless nature of life itself.[36]

Writing practically at the same time as Diederichsen in 1983, Jürgen Habermas pointed out that in the wake of World War II and the Holocaust Simmel was forgotten for decades in the Federal Republic of Germany and those few, like Lukács in the East, who did recall him, were ideologically predisposed to dismiss him out of hand as an irrationalist precursor to fascism.[37] Whereas the impetus for Simmel's reintroduction to West German discourse was merely on account of an anniversary–the sixtieth of his last volume ever published in German–Diederichsen's coincidental allusions to the young Lukács's project were indubitably strategic. As Judith Butler notes, Lukács gradually jettisoned with his conversion to Bolshevik Marxism in 1918 the romantic keystone of his Kantian theory of form–i.e., the transcendental soul–and in its stead adopted the materialist category of class consciousness, that realm of the mind penetrated by the rational work process.[38] Instilled with a deep-seated hatred for "the dullness of old-Marxian derivative thinking," Diederichsen's concern for matters of the soul backtracks to a pre-Marxian discourse capable of animating the concept of style distinctly from the reigning framework of structural Marxism.[39] (And in so doing, he unmoors the central Marxian concept of contradiction [*Widerspruch*] from revolution.[40]) Lukács asks rhetorically in *Soul and Form* "Is style a matter of a person's *whole* life?" and in this vein Diederichsen's attention to the expansive matters of the soul infers that punk's subcultural style—the last great darling among Marxist critics—rooted in contradiction and refusal had expired on account of its narrow account of life and, by extension, style.[41]

Far from denying Marxist concerns altogether, Diederichsen's invocation of Simmel was accompanied by another paradigm shift hardly taken seriously by West Germany's university intellectuals at the time.[42] Beginning in February 1983, a month after the demise of the music magazine *Sounds*, Diederichsen published with *Spex* the first in a series of nine essays entitled "Krieg und Frieden." Both a declaration of war and the outlines for a possible peace, Diederichsen's screed set its sights specifically on those elder *Spex* editors still wedded to the yardstick that good pop music wears its leftist commitment openly. His inaugural essay—framed by two images, one of Boy George from the new wave band Culture Club and another of Soviet General Secretary Yuri Andropov—the author begins with a quote from the opening of Michel Foucault's own inaugural lecture held at the Collège des France in 1970:

> I wish I could have slipped surreptitiously into this discourse which I must present today, and into the ones I shall have to give here, perhaps for many years to come. ... I should have preferred to become aware that a nameless voice was already speaking long before me, so that I should only have needed to join in, to continue the sentence it had started and lodge myself, without really being noticed, in its interstices...[43]

At the core of Diederichsen's kaleidoscopic essay is the so-called "million dollar question" in the early 1980s, namely "what's your take on politics?" Instead of towing the line of representative democrats and their faith in the public, the politics of consciousness raising, individual agency, and elective power (a position most closely associated older *Spex* editorial board members), Diederichsen employs Foucauldian discourse as the only appropriate weapon in an age when the electorate, the chancellor, news agencies, and mass media are all effects of a ubiquitous system of micropower. When Diederichsen concludes that "everything [is] television" and then instructs his reader to "stop searching for meaning or some underlying idea and setting counter-delirium in motion," he first declares any exclusive taste or style to be entirely dubious, for there is no alterity beyond discourse. And then he celebrates the essay: "Voila! L'amour! Le Look of Love! Le Fantastique Day! ... Les Pommes des Lettres!"[44] The veritable fruits of the fine arts, the essay stands, as it were, at the end of a string that begins with human feeling and then passes through pop songs like "The Look of Love" by ABC and Haircut 100's "Fantastic Day." Boy George was for Diederichsen no different than Yuri Andropov. Both equally stood for a form of political commitment that rejected the rules of engagement with popular culture in western social democracies like the Federal Republic.[45]

1985: The Fall of New Wave and the Rise of Cultural Studies

In his first monograph *Sexbeat* from 1985–the year he became the executive editor of *Spex*–Diederichsen took stock of the recent past with an eye to the future. A cultural history of West German bohemia, *Sexbeat* periodized pop music into three distinct phases. In contradistinction to the rock and roll youth cultures of the 1950s and those linked to rock of the 1960s, what he called "second order hipness," which began around 1973, marked a paradigm shift when the futurist impulse of those earlier cultures expired. Hipness–that sought-after cachet in bohemia's constant battle against mainstream appropriation–had to elevate itself to a higher plane if it was to continue its pursuit of "the further."[46] For a whole generation initially raised on the idea that living the bohemian life guaranteed one's place at the vanguard of modern culture, the reordering of hipness entailed replacing the triumvirate of drugs, politics, and music with a new permissive pluralism. Hipsters replaced "the further" with "the now" and thus turned to recycling older forms. Citationality in music, fashion, and photography quickly advanced as expressions of radical individualism. Androgynous Boy George and his band Culture Club–a wild eclecticism of camp, soul, and pop–came to embody this playful pastiche of this sensibility and its affront to any and all dictates of good pop taste.[47] In October 1982, Culture Club's first album debuted and Diederichsen was convinced in the moment that second-order hipness had solved all problems with bohemia's previous incarnations. Walking through the streets of Hamburg one evening that winter, he noted three young women dressed like Boy George and in a record store eavesdropped on the following conversation between a pimp and his prostitute:

> Pimp: What should I buy?
> Lulu: Try this, Culture Club, she sings like a man, no joke, just like a man, but not so deep. She sounds completely normal like a guy!
> Pimp: Her? But that's a man. That's that crazy guy who was recently on television.
> Lulu: Everyone thinks that's a guy, but that's really a woman. I know it.[48]

Neither mainstream journalism's tastemakers nor pimps could decree definitively what exactly Boy George was or should be for fans. The intensity of the good life–"Life in Bohemia is lived more intensely than anywhere else"–became second-order.[49] The ambivalence inscribed in this second-order hipness allowed for a maximum degree of appropriation, signification, and an irrefutable sense of resoluteness and pride.[50]

By the fall of 1984, Diederichsen grew wary of the high regard for second-order hipness and its play with form and history. Although new wave would remain for many consumers the order of the day, second-order pop music required a savvy grasp of cultural and aesthetic history, something younger generations clearly lacked.[51] In spite of all the recent advances that French theory (e.g., Foucault, Baudrillard, and Lyotard) made possible for German hipster intellectuals in the early 1980s (e.g., the repatriation of both art and the literary avant-garde), French thought fostered an arbitrariness that itself resuscitated bygone hippie values and encouraged a certain cynical anti-intellectualism.[52] At the height of new wave in 1982, sexuality was just another signifier to be mixed and matched promiscuously and as a result relationships were taboo.[53] Above all, pop music began overindulging in its historical references to the point that history, too, the object of the new wave hipster's irreverence, became utterly meaningless. A key moment for Diederichsen's realization was a Gun Club show from late 1984 in Hamburg that left him unnerved:

> Some otherwise utterly quiet, distinguished music connoisseurs were so goaded on, so charged up, their masculinity so aggressively sexed up after the last Gun Club concert in Hamburg that without any provocation they went to every possible bar to instigate fights with fellow human beings far stronger than them.[54]

A potent mix of "horrific lucidity" and "greatest intoxication possible," The Gun Club's music literally drove fans, Diederichsen included, into a hedonistic frenzy. Second-generation bohemia built out of pastiche had failed. Assessing the quandary bohemia had backed itself into, he concluded that everything that second-order referentiality had eliminated—"things and issues" like "the real, the political, the base, material"—suddenly became relevant once again.[55] Bohemia's play with history had reached its own endgame and suddenly the substantive corporeal content (sex, drugs, and rock) of bohemia's previous incarnations (and not its aggrandized forms) came "crawling, smeared with blood, out from its graves."[56]

Sexbeat is as much an insider's account of postmodern culture in West Germany as it is a confirmation that the desire to express the soul through music writing expired after only a couple of years. In the wake of this failure came an about-face before Diederichsen renounced vanguard journalism for academic discourse. In the remaining years before German reunification, Diederichsen began pivoting away from the soul just as Lukács had in 1918, and in its stead he revisited the bygone language of Freud and Marx in order to sketch the third coming stage of bohemia, a moment when the superstructure would be dismantled, a place beyond postmodernism where postculture would emerge. One model from within mass culture for vanquishing culture's ideological authority was the young Madonna, the successor to Boy George's brief reign in bohemia. In contrast to the latter's coquettish play with signs, the former trafficked in a glamorous Catholicism (à la "Like a Prayer") both authentic (like first-order hipster Bruce Springsteen) and pragmatic (à la "Material Girl"). If Boy George's hipness conveyed authentic falsehood, then Madonna's was false inauthenticity, a negativity capable of repudiating culture.[57] Yet, the negative force of Madonna was still not enough. Diederichsen briefly flirted with the idea of a new collective individualism whereby individual and sectarian discourses merged and multiplied such that the entire culture system would collapse. Akin to the later Lukács's call for a "conscious collective will," Diederichsen's new codes of conduct crumbled several years after the publication of *Sexbeat*.[58] In a review of the British neopsychedelic band Spacemen 3, he rejected, for example, both materialist politics and postmodern dandyism as paths for practicing resistance and instead proposed a nihilism whereby fans simply submit themselves to the music.[59] As if to say that writing about music reached a dead end, Diederichsen left his editorial post in 1990 for academic positions at schools of art and design in Germany, the United States, and Austria, and his writing, though still anchored in music, adopted a new, decidedly academic guise full of references to Fredric Jameson and Slavoj Žižek and allegiances with critical race theory and queer studies. It was as if only the language of Cultural Studies could ensconce critique once and for all in a bastion impervious to the wilds of popular culture.

1990s Pop: Life versus Death

Scholarship on German pop literature has made such remarkable inroads in the last decade and a half that the twin subcategories of the "pop writer" and "pop literature" have infiltrated even the most rudimentary accounts of German literary history. A handful of features stands out in the canonization of pop literature. Firstly, many accounts regard the phenomenon as the repetition of an older form of writing that "resurfaced" after reunification and, in this respect, Christian Kracht's 1995 road-trip novel *Faserland* consistently stands out as the trailblazer. Accordingly, histories often trace pop literature's roots backward to precursors that first emerged in the late 1960s and reappeared in the 1980s. Secondly, pop literature is very often cast as a willful commercialization of German literature intent on steeping fiction in the pleasures of falsification and deception. Other historically more encompassing accounts frame it more broadly within the complicated history of postmodern literature and its blurring of distinctions between high and low literature. Still others wax lyrical in order to ward off criticism aimed at pop literature's cynical superficiality by drawing attention to either its mnemonic tendencies or, conversely, its allegiance to the present and its attendant aversion to the past.[60]

Most curious about all the attention to German pop literature is its historical record. In what is arguably the most thorough account of German pop literature's career, Kerstin Gleba and Eckhard Schumacher's comprehensive anthology *Pop seit 1964* brings together a massive cast of contemporary German authors organized around three "historical chapters: 1964-1972, 1982-1989 und 1990-2004."[61] Wholly aware of the lack of conceptual clarity underlying the concept "pop" as well as its intrinsic clash with the province of literature, Gleba and Schumacher's text selection insists on moving beyond pop as "style" or "literary genre" and instead bases its choices according to "a strategy, a stance, an attitude" all of which supposedly disrupt the status quo of the institution of literature.[62] Beyond the unresolved questions of what strategy, stance, and attitude amount to in literature and why style and genre fall miserably short, what Gleba and Schumacher do not account for in any cogent way and what this article argues their history can never resolve is why pop literature surfaces and disappears over time. Why did it fade from view after its initial eight-year foray in the 1960s and 1970s? And why was the rebirth of pop literature in the year 1982 firmly ensconced in music journalism, a driving force neither in pop literature's first phase (1964-1972) nor in its most recent phase (1990-2004)? Was pop literature's "reincarnation" in the 1990s an actual rebirth or something entirely different?

For Gleba and Schumacher, "the new ways of writing, new paradigms, and forms of collaboration" characteristic of early 1980s pop were merely the result of a deep appreciation among "music journalists" like Drechsler and Diederichsen (who back then would have certainly rejected this label outright) for new popular music like post punk and new wave. Gleba and Schumacher's allusion to the influx of French postmodern theory (thanks to efforts by West Berlin's Merve Verlag), the reemergence of figurative painting with the Neue Wilden and the rise of art school fanzines like *Mode und Verzweifelung* creates an expansive network into which they insert both writing about music as well as actual literary works by emergent authors like Rainald Goetz, Joachim Lottmann, and Bodo Morshäuser.[63] Yet, this constellation skirts around what I contend to be the core concern for writing's engagement with music in the early 1980s, namely the life of the soul. Writing about music emerged in the early 1980s not only as an affront to the fatigued Marxian discourse's politicization of consciousness that reigned well after the demise of the student movement and against which the first generation of pop writers from that era (like Peter Handke, Rolf Dieter Brinkmann, and Hubert Fichte) reacted. What the music essay in the early 1980s found in new wave music was a means for harnessing aesthetic form in such a way so as to give expression to that which politics had long squelched: life. The essayist, says Lukács, experiences "his own life through the works of others, and by understanding others he comes closer to his own self."[64] This is precisely what Diederichsen addresses in 1982 when asked what music journalism should be: "free of fear, strong in character, big-mouthed ... not so easily understood," "attentive to details and passionate," "charged up, generous, mood, sassy, and subversive."[65] This cheeky attitude is, in actuality, not a benchmark of good journalistic writing per se, but rather the necessary attitude essayist Diederichsen culls from the encounter of soul and form as facilitated by new wave music.

Questions now emerge that together put the alleged genetic relationship between writing from the 1980s and 1990s into question. Compared to the novels by Kracht and his cohort, is the essay not an entirely different genre? Is the retroactive application of "pop literature" not a misrecognition of the essay's encounter with life through music? Do novels like *Faserland* or Benjamin von Stuckrad-Barre's *Soloalbum* take their motifs from art, as is the case with the essay, or life? For all their attention to pop music—the former drops the names of over a dozen pop bands throughout its story and the latter takes the Britpop band Oasis as its organizing principle—these novels are far less interested in the reality of form than they are in giving the illusion of life's destiny. (Destiny, says Lukács, "is not to be found in the writings of the essayist."[66]) The destiny in these novels could not be any more different than the destiny Lukács says the poet elevates up out of the otherwise undifferentiated flow of life. For Kracht's novel, this destiny ends with the narrator's utter indifference toward life.[67] (It is unclear whether the narrator's friend Rolle commits suicide or accidentally drowns at the story's close.) And for von Stuckrad-Barre's novel about life after love this destiny assumes the form of melancholy—without question *the* productive force, says Lukács, behind essayist Søren Kierkegaard's failed attempts at capturing life. However, melancholy in *Soloabum* never pushes the accidental and arbitrary qualities of life into the realm of the necessary.[68] In the words of one critic: "the author's description-machine runs and runs ... but everything compulsory is missing. The sound of indifference presses itself in the words and the story."[69]

Beyond this structural difference—prose is to life as the essay is to form—it would appear, too, that life has assumed a distinctly new quality in the third and last phase of German pop literary history. The paradox of form for Lukács was that it could not help but arrest the chaos and contingency of life; poetry's form is, in a word, a still life—a *nature morte*—upon which the essayist feasts. Yet the "death drive of form," as Butler aptly calls it, must be held in check by the essayist, for the complete and total arresting of life would naturally lead to the nullification of form.[70] Far removed from the romantic propensity to render death a "necessary feature of the poetic" (and thereby denying it "as a part of life"), pop writers Kracht and von Stuckrad-Barre effectively bracket death altogether.[71] Perhaps the closest Kracht's novel comes to death is the narrator's final pit stop in Zurich where his search for Thomas Mann's grave is unsuccessful and, like everything else, trivial; speaking of the author's headstone, he remarks: "it doesn't really feel like the name of Thomas Mann. What a shame."[72] And the only death von Stuckrad-Barre's narrator knows is either existential ("They bore themselves to death") or spectral ("Lady Di is dead").[73] Death is held at arms length in these works and, as a result, life tends toward the eternal. Whether literary criticism or scholarship concocted the death of pop literature is therefore entirely beside the point, for pop literature was undead from its very inception.[74] In contrast to the music essay's commitment to life in the early 1980s when death in the form of unemployment, nuclear holocaust, and AIDS seemed to pose mortal threats at every turn, pop novels serve up heroes for whom life knows no end and certainly no harm. Life's destiny in the 1990s had very little to do with writing in the early 1980s, for it knew little, if anything, of the soul, let alone its importance for making life "fast, intense, rebellious" in risky times.

The Ends of Cultural Studies

Apart from excavating the distinctions smoothed over by academic discourse on German pop literature, perhaps the more pressing question is the fate of music essayism itself. Throughout the 1990s, Diederichsen published with *Spex* roughly a third of what he had written during his five years at the helm of its editorial offices. While writing would remain for him just as important as it had been in the 1980s, more and more of his work appeared in newsweeklies (e.g., *Die Zeit*), leftist magazines (e.g., *konkret*), art journals (e.g., *Texte zur Kunst* and *Artforum*), museum catalogues, and, above all, academic-like monographs and anthologies. Visual artists like Mike Kelly and Martin Kippenberger, the cinema of Larry Clark and the postdramatic theater of René Pollesch, as well as theoretical ruminations on technology in popular culture, for example, captured more of his attention than ever before, and music, or so it seemed, faded from view. Beginning in 2000, he held *Spex* at arm's length for an entire decade before reconciling his differences with the editorial board that had decided in 2000 to do away with record reviews and therewith the music essay itself.[75] Reflecting on the relatively scant number of music essays penned since his days piloting *Spex*, Diederichsen mused in 2005 whether this dearth was because "the world became more boring, or because he became a Buddhist."[76] Referring to both himself and other veteran music essayists of his generation, he explained: "We have another problem."[77] Echoing Drechsler from two-and-a-half decades earlier, Diederichsen explained that a new writing problem grew out of a new breed of casual pop music journalism in the 1990s and the 2000s fed on one part irony and another part good cheer. Critical standards were out, personal taste and nostalgia were not only in, but featured in every publication imaginable. Instead of reinvigorating the music essay as he had practiced it in the 1980s in order to counter market-driven consumerism, Diederichsen turned to yet another form of writing with an entirely different history.

Writing for the Berlin daily *Tagesspiegel* from September 2000 to May 2004, Diederichsen penned every three weeks one short column dubbed "The Music Room." These "cultural micrologies" were conceived as small vessels in which he accommodated under the heading "music" as many different associations as possible. Exactly how far Diederichsen's little music rooms diverge from the essay as Lukács defined it must remain in closing an open question. Yet, Diederichsen's little music rooms appear at first glance to share much of the very same obsession with time-space compression and expansion in the urban imaginary as well as the sounds and visions within it that were so characteristic of the metropolitan miniatures by modernists like Siegfried Kracauer, Walter Benjamin, and others.[78] Typical of many modernist miniatures was their drive to "capture the fleeting and fragmentary experiences of metropolitan life," but might they not also be equally intent on rendering this fleeting life as form, of raising up the soul out of life?[79] For Diederichsen's music rooms, the answer is a provisional yes. In a final column entitled "For the Soul," Diederichsen writes, "And now the music room is closing." After spinning a web around American postrock, the revival of *musique concrète* and Theolonious Monk, he refers to the deceased French artist and disco-punk musician Lizzy Mercier Descloux: "Let us dedicate to her memory the last installment in this series. We'll shut the door to the music room and put on ... the incomparable 'Long Voodoo Ago' on 'One for the Soul' and think about things that you will never experience."[80] Whereas writing once sought to express the soul through its encounter with music, music in the new millennium seems only to evoke memories of lost souls from another era, memories that elude not only social experience but also the powers of writing.

RICHARD LANGSTON is Professor of German Literature at the University of North Carolina at Chapel Hill. He is the author of *Visions of Violence* (Evanston, 2008), the lead translator of Alexander Kluge and Oskar Negt's *History and Obstinacy* (New York, 2014), and principle editor of the 2015 issue of the *Alexander Kluge-Jahrbuch*. His latest book on Alexander Kluge and Oskar Negt is entitled *Dark Matter: A Guide to Alexander Kluge and Oskar Negt* (London, 2020).

Notes

1. Pascal Jurt, "'So obskur, wie es gerade noch ging': Diedrich Diederichsen im Gespräch über die Zeitschrift *Spex*, Pop und Kultur in Deutschland," *Jungle World*, 28 February 2013; available at http://jungle-world.com/artikel/2013/09/47242.html, accessed 18 September 2016.
2. Diedrich Diederichsen, *Sexbeat* (Cologne, 2002), xxix.
3. For an early position on what German Studies was to accomplish–the initial buzzword was, above all, "interdiscipinarity"–see Paul Michael Lützeler's editorial foreword and Jeffrey M. Peck's introduction to a special issue entitled "*Germanistik* as German Studies: Interdisciplinary Theories and Methods," *German Quarterly* 62, no. 2 (1989): 139-140, 141-143, respectively. For an overview of the aspiration of this emergent reordering of the discipline, see Peter W. Hohendahl, "Interdisciplinary German Studies: Tentative Conclusions" from the same volume (227-234). On overlaps and syntheses, see respectively Russell Berman, "Cultural Criticism and Cultural Studies: Reconsidering the Frankfurt School" in *Cultural Studies of Modern Germany: History, Representation, and Nationhood* (Madison, 1993) 25; and Lutz P. Koepnick, "Negotiating Popular Culture: Wenders, Handke, and the Topographies of Cultural Studies," *German Quarterly* 69, no. 4 (1996): 386.
4. The most prominent of West German music and cultural critics to first establish himself in the eighties is Diedrich Diederichsen, whose 1990s trilogy of pop culture critiques–*Freiheit macht arm: Das Leben nach Rock 'n' Roll, 1990-93* (Cologne, 1993); *Politische Korrekturen* (Cologne, 1996); *Der lange Weg nach Mitte: Der Sound und die Stadt* (Cologne, 1999)–is teeming with theoretical references taken directly out of Cultural Studies' playbook. Diederichsen's works, of concern in this article, could be thought of a culmination of the steady introduction to Cultural Studies offered since 1990 by the music journal *Spex*, of which he was a co-editor. On *Spex*'s systematic introduction to Cultural Studies in Germany, see Richard Gebhardt, "Zur Rezeption der Cultural Studies in *Spex: Magazin für*

Pop-Kultur" in *Die Werkzeugkiste der Cultural Studies: Perspektiven, Anschlüsse und Interventionen*, ed. Udo Göttlich, Lothar Mikos, Rainer Winter (Bielefeld, 2001), 176, 179-182, 192-3. Editorial boards and contributors of intellectually ambitious music magazines like *Spex* took it upon themselves to fill the vacuum left by German universities entirely uncommitted to British Cultural Studies.

5. Diederichsen, *Freiheit macht arm* (see note 4), 264.
6. See Irene Kacandes, "German Cultural Studies: What Is at Stake?" in *A User's Guide to German Cultural Studies*, ed. Scott Denham, Irene Kacandes, and Jonathan Petropoulos (Ann Arbor, 1997), 21.
7. On the "indifference to problems of contemporary culture" at German universities throughout the 1980s, see Gabriele Kreutzner, "On Doing Cultural Studies in West Germany," *Cultural Studies* 3, no. 2 (1989): 242. See also: Ralf Hinz, *Cultural Studies und Pop: Zur Kritik der Urteilskraft wissenschaftlicher und journalistischer Rede über populäre Kultur* (Opladen, 1998), 136-142.
8. An overview of this sort of account of pop literature can be found in: Thomas Ernst, *Popliteratur* (Hamburg, 2001), 66-75.
9. On Kracht's veneration of pop journalist Olaf Dante Marx, see: Tobias Rüther, "Von der Bühne gefallen, aber mitten im Parkett gelandet. Bestenfalls scheintot: Warum die anschwellenden Abgesänge auf die Popliteratur und ihren Journalismus ungerechtfertigt sind," *Süddeutsche Zeitung*, 27 August 2002, 16.
10. On pop literature's affinity to Cultural Studies, see, for example: Thomas Ernst, *Literatur und Subversion: Politisches Schreiben in der Gegenwart* (Bielefeld, 2013), 139; and Margaret McCarthy, Introduction, *German Pop Literature: A Companion* (Berlin, 2015), 10. One early English-language example of how Cultural Studies was brought to bear on pop literature is Richard Langston, "Escape from Germany: Disappearing Bodies and Postmodern Space in Christian Kracht's Prose," *The German Quarterly* 79, no. 1 (2005): 50-70.
11. Diedrich Diederichsen, "Die License zur Nullposition," *die tageszeitung*, 7 August 2000, 13.
12. Diederich Diederichsen, "Dexys Midnight Runners: Die Romantik der Revolution-Manifeste des jungen Souls," *Sounds* 10 (1982): 36
13. Györg Lukács, *Soul and Form*, ed. John T. Sanders and Katie Terezakis, trans. Anna Bostock (New York, 2010), 34.
14. Diederichsen (see note 12), 38.
15. Clara Drechsler, "1 Jahr SPEX," SPEX–*Das Buch: 33 1/3 Jahre Pop*, ed. Max Dax and Anne Waak (Berlin, 2013), 30. Originally published in *Spex* 9/1981.
16. Peter Bömmels, "Joy Division: Ein Stück näher an was?" in Dax and Waak (see note 15), 13. Originally published in *Spex* 1/1980.
17. Ibid., 14-15.
18. On Drechsler's "idiosyncratic" writing, see Hinz (see note 7), 236-246.
19. Gerald Hündgen and Clara Drechsler, "Böse Menschen haben keine Lieder–1982: Musik auf dem Jahrmarkt der Eitelkeiten," in Dax and Waak (see note 15), 44. Originally published in *Spex* 1/1983.
20. Theodor W. Adorno, *Negative Dialectics*, trans. Dennis Redmond (2001), 28; available at http://www.efn.org/~dredmond/nd2.PDF. Of course, Adorno continues by discrediting identity thinking insofar as it "is, even where it claims otherwise, subjectivistic." See Theodor W. Adorno, *Negative Dialektik* (Frankfurt/Main, 1975), 184.
21. Hündgen and Drechsler, (see note 19), 50.
22. Diederichsen (see note 2), 41; see also Hinz (see note 7), 207-208, 240-242.
23. Jurt (see note 1).
24. See Hinz (see note 7), 240.
25. Diedrich Diederichsen, "Haircut 100: Fantastisch!" *Sounds* 6 (1982): 40.
26. Ibid., 42.
27. Ibid., 42.
28. Georg Simmel, *The Philosophy of Money*, trans. Tom Bottomore and David Frisby (London, 2004), 472.

29. Ibid., 233.
30. Ibid. On Lukács's reliance on Simmel, see Frisby's introduction to the translation of *The Philosophy of Money*, 16-24.
31. Lukács, (see note 13), 18.
32. Ibid., 23-4.
33. Ibid., 26. "The hero of the essay was once alive, and so his life must be given form; but this life, too, is as much inside the work as everything is in poetry," 27.
34. Ibid., 42.
35. Ibid., 38-9.
36. Diederichsen, (see note 25), 42 and Lukács (see note 13), 170.
37. Jürgen Habermas, "Simmel als Zeitdianostiker," *Philosophische Kultur*, by Georg Simmel, (Frankfurt/Main, 2008), 17. Habermas's introductory essay originally appeared in 1983. See also Martin Jay, *Marxism and Totality: The Adventures of a Concept from Lukács to Habermas* (Berkeley, 1984), 86, 86n17.
38. Judith Butler, Introduction, *Soul and Form*, by György Lukács, ed. John T. Sanders and Katie Terezakis, trans. Anna Bostock (New York, 2010), 2. See also Georg Lukács, *History and Class Consciousness: Studies in Marxist Dialectics*, trans. Rodney Livingstone (Cambridge, 1997), 88: "With the modern 'psychological' analysis of the work-process (in Taylorism) this rational mechanization extends right into the worker's 'soul.'"
39. Jurt (see note 1).
40. See also Louis Althusser's rumination on the contradiction in Marxist thought in "Contradiction and Overdetermination," *For Marx*, trans. Ben Brewster (London, 2005), 88-116.
41. Unsurprisingly, "contradiction" as Althusser qualifies it, runs to the core of Dick Hebdige's leftist semiotics of punk: "It is here that we encounter the first of punk's endemic contradictions, for the visions of apocalypse superficially fused in punk came from essentially antagonistic sources." Dick Hebdige, *Subculture: The Meaning of Style* (London, 1979), 27. As for punk's expiration, Diederichsen's afterword to the German translation says as much. In the wake of punk, a semiotic catastrophe ensued that witnessed not only the proliferation and plurality of signs but also their "equal possibilities." In effect, both Diederichsen's and Marx's afterwords underscore just how outdated Hebdige's analysis became by 1983. See Diedrich Diederichsen, "Die Auflösung der Welt," in Dick Hebdige, *Schocker: Stile und Moden der Subkultur*, ed. Diedrich Diederichsen and Olaph-Dante Marx (Reinbek bei Hamburg, 1983), 166: "Punk discourse became just as rigid and tough as the skinhead discourse...," 175-176.
42. See Robert Holub, "Michel Foucault among the Germans," *Crossing Borders: Reception Theory, Poststructuralism, Deconstruction* (Madison, 1992), 50.
43. Michel Foucault, "The Order of Discourse," *Untying the Text: A Post-Structuralist Reader*, ed. Robert Young (Boston, 1981), 51. Diederichsen quotes the first German translation already in the February issue of *Spex*. See "Krieg und Frieden," *Spex: Musik zur Zeit* 2 (1983): 35. Diederichsen is most likely quoting from the 1974 German translation, *Die Ordnung des Diskurses: Inauguralvorlesung am Collège de France, 2. Dezember 1970*, trans. Walter Seitter (Munich, 1974).
44. Diederichsen (see note 43), 35.
45. This parallelism between Boy George and Yuri Andropov was symptomatic of what Diederichsen labeled "Bolschevique chic," a short-lived heroism projected onto endearing Soviet leaders who embodied for West German music aficionados the possibility of a counterauthority in aesthetic matters at a time when taste and style were subject to western democracy's "technocratic pluralism." See Diederichsen (see note 2), 122-123.
46. Ibid., 17-24.
47. Ibid., 131.
48. Diederichsen (see note 43), 35.
49. Diederichsen (see note 2), 67.
50. Ibid., 130.
51. Ibid., 102.

52. Ibid., 52-54.
53. Ibid., 108.
54. Diedrich Diederichsen, "Gun Club," *Szene Hamburg* 9 (1984): 45. See also Diederichsen (see note 2), xv.
55. Ibid., 157, xvi.
56. Ibid., 155.
57. Diedrich Diederichsen, "Offene Identität & zynische Untertanen," *Das Madonna-Phänomen*, ed. Diedrich Diederichsen et al. (Hamburg, 1993) 5.
58. Lukács, *History and Class Consciousness* (see note 38), 315-316.
59. Diedrich Diederichsen, "Spacemen 3: Fortgesetzt sündigende Katholiken," *Spex* 3 (1988): 20.
60. Moritz Baßler, *Der deutsche Pop-Roman: Die neuen Archivisten* (Munich, 2002), 21. Eckhard Schumacher, *Gerade Eben Jetzt: Schreibweisen der Gegenwart* (Frankfurt/Main, 2003), 10-11.
61. Kerstin Gleba and Eckhard Schumacher, ed., "Vorwort," *Pop seit 1964* (Cologne, 2007), 11.
62. Ibid., 12.
63. Ibid., 93-95.
64. Lukács (see note 13), 37-38.
65. Diedrich Diederichsen, "Spätsaison: Journaille, Defunkt, Talking Heads," *Sounds* 9 (1982): 44, 45. Compare this with Schumacher's insistence that these are merely the qualities of pop writing. Gleba and Schumacher (see note 61), 92.
66. Lukács (see note 13), 23.
67. See Volker Weidermann, "Gagschreibers Trauergesang," *Frankfurter Allgemeine Zeitung*, 18 November 1998, 42.
68. Lukács (see note 13), 46, 39.
69. Weidermann (see note 67), 42.
70. Butler (see note 38), 12.
71. Ibid., 10.
72. Christian Kracht, *Faserland* (Cologne, 1995), 136.
73. Benjamin von Stuckrad-Barre, *Soloalbum* (Cologne,1998), 110, 187.
74. Eckhard Schumacher, "Das Ende der Popliteratur: Eine Fortsetzungsgeschichte (Teil 2)," *Poetik der Oberfläche: Die deutschsprachige Popliteratur der 1990er Jahre*, ed. Olaf Grabienski, Till Huber, Jan-Noël Thon (Berlin, 2011), 53.
75. Diedrich Diederichsen, "Stirb langsam: Das Magazin *Spex* will in Zukunft keine Platten mehr rezensieren, sondern lieber darüber plaudern. Das kann nicht im Ernst das letzte Wort der Pop-Musik-Kritik sein," *Frankfurter Allgemeine Sonntagszeitung*, 10 January 2010, 23.
76. Diederich Diederichsen, *Musikzimmer: Avantgarde und Alltag* (Cologne, 2005), 11.
77. Ibid., 12.
78. Cf. Andreas Huyssen, *Miniature Modernism: Literature in an Age of Photography and Film* (Cambridge, 2015), 6-7.
79. Ibid., 3.
80. Diederichsen (see note 76), 217.

INDEX

A

Adaptation, 18, 21, 26, 40, 85, 89
Aesthetics, 25-26, 28, 31, 33-34, 37, 39-40, 65, 68, 70, 73-74, 77, 79, 92, 94, 96, 107-111, 118-121, 130, 133-134, 136-137, 139-141, 150, 154, 157, 162
America, 1, 3, 5-10, 12, 14, 22, 50, 53, 56, 58, 77, 84, 87-90, 93-94, 97-101, 104-105, 144-145, 159
Americanization, 99
African-American, 22, 87-90, 93, 98, 100
Analog, 25, 29, 35, 39, 128. *See also* digital
Anti-Semitism, 96, 111, 123
Antifa, 106, 110-111, 113-114, 117, 120
Antifascist, 108, 111, 116
Appropriation, 22-23, 87-88, 92, 145, 149, 153-154
Avant-garde, 1, 26, 34, 40, 96, 106, 118, 120, 148, 154

B

Berlin Wall, 4-5, 7, 9, 59, 64, 67
Borders, 4, 6, 8, 22, 30, 63, 67

C

Capitalism, 17, 26, 41, 50, 53, 65-66, 75, 80-81, 99, 109, 128, 131-132
Censor, 48, 53, 60, 66, 80
Cold War, 4-5, 8, 11, 41, 62-63
Communism, 45, 49, 53, 66, 72, 79, 81, 108, 111
Community, 17, 43, 85, 87, 92, 95, 97, 99, 101, 104, 109-110, 116, 130-131, 139-140
Consumerism, 10, 29, 33-34, 90, 121, 128, 131, 145-147, 154
Cover (album), 8, 29, 40, 47, 55, 58, 65, 67, 70, 76, 83, 89-90, 135, 147
Cover (song), 135
Cultural Studies, vi, 4, 9, 144-147, 153, 155, 158, 160-161

D

Dark wave, dark music, 111, 116, 119, 122
Diederichsen, Diedrich, 1, 149, 160-163
Digital, 13-15, 127-128, 134. *See also* analog
Disco, v, 8, 13, 15-21, 23-24, 149, 160
Drag (drag queen), 8, 21-22, 133, 136-139, 142

E

Ethnicity, 7, 12, 98, 128, 130, 142
Ethnocentrism, 106
Exchange, 10, 99, 128, 138

F

Fanzine, 29-30, 69, 115
Fascism (National Socialism), 12, 107, 110-112, 114, 119, 121-124, 151
Feminism, 1, 18, 96, 127-128, 130-133, 135-136, 140-142
Festival, 12, 46, 116
Film (cinema), 3-4, 6, 9-13, 17, 23-24, 41, 47-48, 58, 60, 68, 84, 87, 92, 94-95, 97-98, 100, 103, 105, 132, 140-142, 159, 163
Flows, 1, 4-10, 40, 63, 87, 96, 99
Folk, 2, 12, 26, 82, 106, 121-122, 124
    Lore, 18, 41
    Music, 26, 82

G

Gender, 8-9, 13, 15, 21-22, 40, 126-127, 130-134, 136-142
Germany, iii, v, 1-14, 16, 20, 23, 25, 29, 33, 37-38, 40-41, 44-46, 49, 53, 55-61, 63-64, 68-70, 73, 79-80, 82-83, 85, 87-89, 92-95, 97-104, 106-107, 109, 111, 113-117, 119, 121, 123, 125, 128, 132, 139, 141-142, 145-146, 151-152, 154-155, 160-161

Index

East Germany (GDR), 6-8, 12, 44-46, 49, 53, 55-56, 59-61, 73, 79-80, 82
West Germany (FRG), 1, 63-66, 99, 151
Globalization, 2, 4, 8-9, 12, 40, 70, 82, 98, 104, 111, 127-128, 130, 131, 133, 139-140

H

Hardcore, 66, 70, 73, 89-91
    Punk, 70, 73
    Rap, 89-90
Heimat, 22, 37-38, 91-94, 102-103
Hip-Hop (rap), v, 1, 7, 9, 12, 59, 84-104
Hipster, 107, 122, 154
Hybridity, 4, 9, 17, 23, 33, 88, 91

I

Identity, v, 2-3, 8-9, 11, 13, 25-27, 29-33, 35, 37, 39-42, 84-88, 90-92, 97-98, 101, 108, 110-111, 123, 126-128, 134, 137, 139, 148, 161
Independent
    Bands, 68
    Music, 75, 79
International, 12, 14, 17, 25, 58, 69-70, 98, 108, 123, 128

J

Journalism, 9, 34-35, 107, 146, 153-154, 156-157, 159
    Music, 71, 89, 126-127, 132, 147, 152

K

Krautrock, 6-8, 11, 26, 34, 36, 59

L

Loops, v, 8, 25, 27, 29-33, 35-37, 39-41, 117
Lyrics, 6, 18, 25, 27, 29, 49, 51-56, 58, 60, 66, 68-72, 77-78, 82, 85, 89, 91-95, 97-101, 106, 108, 111-112, 116-117, 126, 129-130, 132, 136, 142

M

Mass market, 16, 58, 145-146, 159
Marketing, 41, 75, 82, 86, 113, 126
Modern, 3, 21, 97, 105-106, 109-110, 120, 146-147, 150, 153, 160, 16
Modernism, 24, 37, 97, 105, 124, 159, 163

N

National, iii, 1-13, 15, 18, 22, 25-26, 29, 35, 41-43, 85, 90, 93, 97, 100-101, 103, 106-112, 114, 116-118, 120, 123, 128, 130-131, 137, 140
Nationalism, 2, 38, 85, 97, 106, 109, 119-120
Nationality, 3, 89, 98
Neofolk, v, 2, 9, 106-107, 109-115, 117, 119, 121-125
Neoliberalism 8-10, 120, 127-128, 130-134, 139, 140-142
New Wave (Neue Deutsche Welle), vi, 64, 73, 81, 144, 147, 149-150, 152-154, 156-157

O

Opposition, 26, 38, 60, 63, 74, 82, 92, 98-99, 109

P

Performance, 1, 3, 9, 15, 17, 21, 31-32, 47-48, 75-76, 79, 83, 86-87, 112, 126-127, 134, 136-138, 142
Performativity, 22, 32, 85, 137, 141
Politics, 2, 8, 14-15, 18, 22, 25-26, 28, 34, 43-44, 46, 49-51, 53, 55, 57-60, 62-64, 66, 68, 73, 75, 80, 82, 90-91, 93-95, 97, 100, 108-109, 111-115, 118-121, 124, 127-128, 131-137, 140-141, 145-146, 149-150, 154
Politicization, 75, 116, 157
Pop
    Culture, 98, 104, 127-128, 133, 160
    Literature, 9, 141, 145-147, 155-158, 161
    Music, 3, 11, 59, 63-64, 99, 128, 134, 136-137, 140-142, 145-146, 148-150, 152-154, 157, 159
Populism, 9, 118-119
Postmodernism, 11, 24-23, 85, 87-88, 95, 130, 149, 154-156, 161
Postwar, iii, 1-3, 6, 10, 14, 23, 26, 34-35, 42, 109
Production, 4, 8, 26-29, 31, 33-34, 36-37, 40-41, 48, 63, 75-76, 78, 80-83, 90, 98, 121, 136
Producers, 16, 29, 80
Public, 13, 16-17, 19, 26-29, 31-32, 38, 43, 48, 52, 54, 56, 79, 81, 83, 86-87, 89-90, 92, 100-101, 104-105, 114, 126, 132, 136, 147, 152
Publication, iv, 45, 155, 159

Index

Punk, 1, 6, 8-9, 18, 25-28, 31-42, 61, 63-66, 68-71, 73-75, 77, 80-83, 106-109, 111, 120, 122-123, 126, 147-148, 152, 156, 160, 162

Post-punk, 8-9, 33-34, 37, 63-64, 66, 80, 106, 108, 111, 120

R

Race (racism), 9, 12, 15, 22, 98, 116, 131, 134, 136, 138-139, 142-143, 155

Radio, 14, 16-19, 36, 45-47, 55-59, 68, 78-79

Records (vinyl), iv, 10, 34, 36, 41-44, 46, 55, 57-58, 63-69, 71, 73-76, 79-81, 83-84, 86, 97-98, 153, 156, 159

Recording, iv, 29, 35, 48, 55, 57, 65, 68, 73-75, 80, 83, 97, 108

Rock, 1-2, 6-8, 11, 16-18, 21, 26-27, 36, 40-41, 43-47, 49-61, 64-66, 74-77, 82, 86, 89, 91, 100-101, 108, 123, 126, 130, 132, 147, 149, 153-154, 160

S

Sample (music), 33, 37, 90, 94, 102, 117-118

Scene (music), 19, 34, 43, 47, 58-59, 68, 73, 78, 88, 90, 92, 95, 97, 99, 106, 108-109, 111, 113, 116, 119, 122, 128

Schlager, v, 2, 5-6, 8, 13-15, 17-20, 22-24, 98

Sequence (music), 20, 28

Sexuality, 116, 126, 133, 137, 140, 142, 154

Socialism, 25, 29, 35, 41-42, 44-46, 49, 55, 62, 67-68, 70, 73, 75, 79, 81, 106-107, 108-110, 112, 114, 117-118, 120

Spex, 89, 126-127, 132, 141, 147, 152-153, 158-163

Style (fashion), 49, 127, 142, 153

Subculture, 14, 26-27, 40, 85, 87-90, 99, 106, 113, 125, 127, 152, 162

T

Tape (audio), v, 35-38, 40, 42, 65, 68-69, 74, 76-79, 82, 84-88, 96, 99-100, 104

Technology, 16, 25-26, 30-35, 37, 39-40, 42, 138, 142-143, 159

Television, 2, 13-16, 18, 23, 45, 47, 56, 58, 78, 86-87, 97, 102, 105, 152-153

Transatlantic, 4, 9, 11-12, 86-87, 90, 99-100, 145

Transnationalism, iii, 1-12, 70-71, 81, 97-99, 128

U

Underground, 63, 66, 74, 79, 82-83, 85-86, 92, 118, 147

V

Völkisch, 9, 106-107, 110, 121

Volksmusik, 17

Y

Youth, 7, 17, 42, 44-47, 49, 51, 61, 70-74, 85, 98, 108, 122, 149, 153

Z

ZDF, v, 13-15, 18-19, 21, 23, 98

www.ingramcontent.com/pod-product-compliance
Lightning Source LLC
Chambersburg PA
CBHW072157100526
44589CB00015B/2269